More praise for *Überpower: The Imperial Temptation of America*

"An erudite and sympathetic analysis of America's strategic position as überpower in this new century."—Francis Fukuyama, author of *America at the Crossroads: Democracy, Power, and the Neoconservative Legacy*

"A book to ponder and enjoy. The prose is scintillating; the analysis, profound. Written from neither a European nor an American perspective but, with remarkable balance and insight, from both. Americans will understand Europeans better, and Europeans may even find a little of value in America's recent policies after reading Josef Joffe's pages. A remarkable accomplishment."—Kenneth M. Waltz, Columbia University

"As with all of Joffe's work this book is to be warmly welcomed—perhaps even more warmly than ever. He presents an adult outlook with both depth and clarity; his uninhibited grasp of public affairs is both philosophical and, at the same time, readable to a high degree."—Robert Conquest, author of *The Great Terror*

"Joe Joffe is a bold and imaginative writer. From the other side of the Atlantic, this thinker who works on the seam between America and Europe has produced a work at once provocative and grounded in the world. A pleasure to read, a book of great importance, a remarkable interpretation of America's power and its place in the world."—Fouad Ajami, Johns Hopkins University, author of *The Dream Palace of the Arabs*

"Joe Joffe knows the United States better than most Americans know themselves, just as he writes more lucid and amusing prose than most authors who grew up with English as their native tongue. His is the view of a true friend and admirer, who knows what to criticize, and what to shrug off. He is, moreover, a man of considerable intellectual courage, willing to tell fellow Europeans unpleasant truths, about us, and about them. Here is a book which looks at culture and power, at high foreign policy and the deeper significance of MacDonalds and Starbucks."—Eliot A. Cohen, SAIS, Johns Hopkins University

"Europe's anti-Americanism predated and will follow George Bush, based as it is on envy, long-standing fissures in the West, and the post–Cold War preeminence of the United States. But Josef Joffe argues nonetheless that it is the responsibility of Americans to ignore the often flamboyant critics and reach out to our European friends, who, despite their annoyances, are still America's best allies in an increasingly frightening world. *Überpower* is an original global diagnosis by a gifted European who knows America better than most Americans, and is fonder of the United States than any European writing today."—Victor Davis Hanson, Senior Fellow, The Hoover Institution, author of *A War Like No Other*

Überpower

ALSO BY JOSEF JOFFE

The Future of the Great Powers: Predictions

Race and Culture: A World View

The Limited Partnership: Europe, the United States, and the Burden of Alliance

Plotting Hitler's Death: The Story of the German Resistance

The Germanies at 30: All Quiet on the Eastern Front

Alliance as Orders: The United States in Western Europe

The Political Role of Nuclear Weapons: No-First Use and the Stability of the European Order

The Demons of Europe

Überpower

THE IMPERIAL TEMPTATION OF AMERICA

JOSEF JOFFE

W. W. NORTON & COMPANY
NEW YORK • LONDON

Printed in the United States of America
First Edition

For information about permission to reproduce selections from this book, write to Permissions, W. W. Norton & Company, Inc., 500 Fifth Avenue, New York, NY 10110

Manufacturing by Quebecor World Fairfield
Book design by Chris Welch Design
Production manager: Andrew Marasia

Library of Congress Cataloging-in-Publication Data

Joffe, Josef.
Überpower : the imperial temptation of America / Josef Joffe.— 1st ed.
p. cm.
Includes bibliographical references and index.
ISBN-13: 978-0-393-06135-2 (hardcover)
ISBN-10: 0-393-06135-3 (hardcover)
1. United States—Foreign relations—2001– I. Title.
E895.J64 2006
327.73009'0511—dc22

2006003694

W. W. Norton & Company, Inc., 500 Fifth Avenue, New York, N.Y. 10110
www.wwnorton.com

W. W. Norton & Company Ltd., Castle House, 75/76 Wells Street, London W1T 3QT

1 2 3 4 5 6 7 8 9 0

To Jessica and Janina

Contents

1 A World Undone 13

2 A Giant Unbound 30

3 The Rise of Anti-Americanism 67

4 The Rise of Americanism 95

5 A Giant's Grand Strategy: Models from History 127

6 A Giant's Perch 162

7 A Giant's Task 203

Notes 242

Acknowledgments 261

Index 263

Überpower

1

A World Undone

On Christmas Day 1991, death struck the largest empire the world had ever seen. Though a defining moment, the historical significance was hardly understood at the time. The Soviet Union's suicide did not just dispatch one more corpse to the graveyard of empires where so many grandiose dreams had long ago turned to dust—from Rome to Byzantium, from the Habsburg Empire to the Hitlerian Reich. The self-dissolution of the Soviet Union marked one of the rarest events in the evolution of the state system: the transformation of the very *stage* on which world politics unfolds. The consequences, especially for American foreign policy, have been momentous, and they will continue to reverberate all through the twenty-first century.

The departure of the USSR is the starting point for this book, as it tries to illuminate, first, what the revolutionary passage from "bipolarity" to "unipolarity," from dominance à deux to the primacy of one, has wrought: How did the rupture affect the behavior of the United States and the rest of the world? Second, this book will try to limn what America's role on this stage *should* be, now that the simple, but unbending rules of the Cold War have vanished along with the bipolar order that gave rise to them. These rules defined—nay, dictated—American grand strategy for half a century, and no one formulated them as concisely as George F. Kennan, when he wrote, "The main element of any United States policy toward the Soviet

Union must be that of a long-term, patient, but firm and vigilant containment of Russian expansive tendencies."[1]

This single sentence would characterize the core of U.S. foreign policy for the next fifty years. An open-ended contest, the two-nation drama was enacted on a global stage, and the name of the game, in Kennan's immortal words, was either the "break-up" or the "mellowing" of Soviet power. In fact, both came to pass: first the mellowing and then the breakup. That stage is no more; nor is America's one and only mortal rival. The world is now overshadowed by a single überpower. What is the new script, what should it be when history warns that singular power is destined to breed temptation first and invite retribution second? How to use America's power wisely? That is the question the nation faces as it peers into the twenty-first century. And so does the rest of the world as it looks at this restless giant, which, for good or for bad, will command the stage for the next half century.

"Stage" is a metaphor for the term "structure" used by scholars of international politics. "Structure" is but another word for the distribution of power among the actors on the set. Who directs, who follows, who is an extra? The stage of the modern state system came together in the fifteenth century, when out of the ruins of the Roman Empire emerged the forerunners of the contemporary nation-state: France, England, and Spain—states whose borders coincided more or less with language, ethnicity, religion, and culture. For about half a millennium, states rose and fell, consolidated, conquered, and collapsed, but the *structure* of the international system remained the same. Actors strode in and bowed out, but the stage did not change.

The classical structure was defined by several great powers, usually five in changing guises, vying and warring for security, advantage, and aggrandizement. The system was "multipolar," in modern parlance, until the end of World War II, when suddenly only two—the United States and the Soviet Union—towered above the rest. This outcome was dimly foreseen by Alexis de Tocqueville, who mused in 1835, "There are at the present time two great nations in the world, which started from different points, but seem to tend towards the same end. I allude to the Russians and the Americans. . . . Their starting-point is different and their courses are not the same; yet each of them seems marked out by the will of Heaven to sway the destinies of half the globe."[2]

The Death of an Empire

Tocqueville's definition of "bipolarity" is as good as any, and the two superpowers did indeed sway the fate of the globe until Christmas Day 1991. From the end of World War II to the end of the Soviet Union, the stage of world politics was "bipolar," populated by two giants dwarfing first some fifty and then almost two hundred states, ranging from ex- and would-be great to middling and minuscule powers. Yet on December 25, 1991, precisely at 7:32 p.m., the hammer-and-sickle flag of the Soviet Union came down for the last time, and the white-blue-red emblem of Russia rose over the Kremlin. At the time of its dissolution, the Soviet empire, almost twice the size of the United States, was seventy-four years old. It encompassed fifteen republics and myriad races, religions, and nationalities. It extended over eleven time zones, with land borders of 20,000 kilometers and a coastline of 38,000.

How mighty was "mighty" when compared with previous superpowers? The real estate controlled by the Roman Empire was merely the Mediterranean basin (plus outriggers to the British Isles and the Caspian Sea), and though the "sun never set on the Habsburg Empire," the fiefdoms of Charles V and Philip II did not have ten thousand strategic nuclear warheads and four million men under arms. Nor did Queen Victoria's possessions, globe-spanning as they were, command anywhere near the firepower of the Soviet Union's fifty thousand main battle tanks.

And yet this colossus died, so to speak, in its bed, a first in the history of the state system. The Roman Empire was felled by war, revolt, and invasion, though according to Edward Gibbon it took about three hundred years for the sword to undo what the sword had wrought. Force ended the careers of empires all the way into the twentieth century. The Great War, later renamed World War I, was the greatest empire killer of them all, dispatching into history the Wilhelmine, Habsburg, tsarist, and Ottoman empires while mortally wounding the British one, victorious though it had been in 1918.

The Soviet empire was killed softly, and then not by its foes but by its physician, the USSR's last general secretary, Mikhail Gorbachev. As he "tried to heal the nation," wrote *Nezavisimaya Gazeta* on the day after the Soviet Union's self-dissolution, "his choice of cures was commendable—glasnost, democratization, and all—but in the end, even a small dose of these proved fatal to the patient." History owes Gorbachev an eternal debt of gratitude for this instance of mega-malpractice, because he spared the world the conflagration that normally attends the death of an empire. But in contrast to the sudden, thudding collapse of previous giants, the very pacificity of the event helped obscure for about a decade the momentous transformation of the world stage on which the United States and the rest of the world have acted ever since.

As befits a patient who expires in bed, death did not come in one fell swoop. The exchange of the red flag for the Russian tricolor on December 25, 1991, represented but the official certification of the Soviet Union's last, agonal breath, an act that virtually passed without notice. How did the agony unfold? An equally forgotten date is July 16, 1990. In an obscure Caucasus spa called Zheleznovodsk, Mikhail Gorbachev emerged from a two-day meeting with the German chancellor Helmut Kohl and uttered the magic words that had remained unthinkable in half a century of Cold War: "The united Germany, sovereign in every way, will say to which bloc it wants to belong." He added that a "Germany united inside NATO" was just fine with USSR.[3]

These bland words marked the Soviet Union's surrender in the Cold War, for that confrontation—World War III without the rivers of blood unleashed by the two preceding ones—was started in and over Germany. This is where the anti-Hitler compact of the United States and the Soviet Union fell apart in 1946, only one year after the defeat of the Third Reich. The demise of their common enemy would now pit victor against victor. This is where the Berlin Blockade of 1948, the Berlin Ultimatum of 1958, and the Berlin Wall of 1961 dramatized the stylized, and luckily bloodless, contest over who would control the strategically decisive piece of European real estate that was Germany.*

Germany, where the two colossi had drawn their planetary line in the sand, was the fulcrum of the local, European, and global balance of power. It was the arena between the Elbe River and the Rhine where a million armed men plus thousands of nuclear weapons on either side of the Iron Curtain had frozen history, dividing Berlin, Germany, and Europe in a global zero-sum game that allowed for neither retreat nor advance. As George F. Kennan predicted in his "Sources of Soviet Conduct" in 1947, this game of pressure and counterpressure would end either in the "mellowing" or in the "break-up" of Soviet power, and so it did—fittingly in Berlin, the capital of the defunct Reich, where it had all begun amid the rubble of World War II.

*During the Berlin Blockade of 1948–49, the Soviet Union cut all land traffic to West Berlin (governed by the United States, Britain, and France), hoping to starve the Western sectors into submission; they were saved by an Anglo-American airlift that circumvented a military confrontation. With his Berlin Ultimatum, Nikita Khrushchev enacted a more subtle ploy: he would hand over control of the access routes to the Western enclave to his East German satraps, which might have forced the West to submit or to fire the first shots of World War III. (Khrushchev's threat was never executed.) After the Berlin Wall went up, Soviet and American tanks faced each other across the boundary line for weeks, but their guns remained silent.

The date was November 9, 1989, and History crept up softly, as if on cat's feet. It was a mere slip of the tongue by an East German functionary that fractured what was literally cast in concrete: the Berlin Wall. In a meeting with the press around seven o'clock in the evening, the East German Politburo member Günter Schabowski mumbled something about the border being opened for "private trips" to the West. Within the hour, throngs of East Berliners were converging on the Wall, milling across the checkpoints, while the border guards of the "Workers and Peasants State" just stood back in helpless confusion. In the course of the weekend, a million East Germans crossed unhindered into West Berlin, which was suddenly reunited with the Eastern half after twenty-eight years of hermetic closure.

Did any of those present at the destruction expect that an entire international system known as bipolarity would come crashing down along with the Wall? The understatement of the day was uttered by Gennadi Gerasimov, the spokesman of the Soviet Foreign Ministry. "Everybody is surprised by the speed of the changes [in East Germany]."[4] None could have been more surprised than Mikhail Gorbachev, who wanted merely to reform, not to relinquish, the empire. As an Oxford Sovietologist recalls, "He wanted to make [the Soviet] economy more dynamic, introducing some market elements, but without turning it into a fully fledged market system. He wanted more openness and tolerance but did not yet have in mind [a] pluralist democracy."[5] At no point, certainly, did Gorbachev want to yield Moscow's pride of place as the world's second superpower. He was blissfully confident that the risks were tolerable: "There was no reason to fear the collapse or the end of socialism," Gorbachev recalls telling the Romanian leader Nicolae Ceausescu—this three weeks after the Berlin Wall had been breached and three weeks before the dictator was executed by his own people.[6]

Socialism, that is, the Soviet empire, collapsed for the oldest reason in the book: ambition that outpaces resources. When Mikhail

Gorbachev was elevated to the post of general secretary, in 1985, he inherited a country that was inexorably grinding to a halt. Defense expenditures were claiming 15–20 percent of GDP, and rising, while America's stood around 5 percent of a GDP that was several times larger. As the economy stagnated, Siberian oil production, the single-most important "cash crop" of the Soviet Union, began to decline in 1983, and world oil prices, having risen twelvefold in the 1970s, began to plunge in the mid-1980s. In short, the Soviet Union could no longer service its essential national interests: provide a decent standard of living to its population, keep up with the armament juggernaut unleashed under the presidency of Ronald Reagan (1981–89), and subsidize an ever more demanding bunch of indigent clients, ranging from Czechoslovakia to Cuba.

Moscow's last imperial venture, the war in Afghanistan launched during Christmas of 1979, had ground to a halt, too, with Soviet troops pinned down in the cities while the mujahideen, supplied by the United States with deadly Stinger missiles, roamed freely across the countryside. The *Weltpolitik* pursued by Nikita Khrushchev and his heirs had run out of money while the ideology that energized it had run out of steam. The Soviet Union, as the German chancellor Helmut Schmidt liked to quip, was but an "Upper Volta with nuclear weapons."

What Lenin and Stalin had built, what Khrushchev and Brezhnev had transformed into a global power machine that would probe and push wherever opportunity beckoned, Gorbachev lost in a fit of absentmindedness. The last leader of the Leninist empire was a man either benightedly naïve or blind to the fearsome forces he had unleashed. Two years after the fall of the Wall—the symbol and brace of the empire—the Soviet Union itself died with nary a sigh and without benefit of burial or clergy. Three years later still, when the last of Russian soldiers had withdrawn from Central Europe in 1994, the transformation of the international system from bipolarity to unipolarity was complete. Where two superpowers had lorded it over much of the rest, one was suddenly knocked out. At the end of the twentieth century, after two bloody world wars and one stylized one, only a single giant was left standing. The United States was now No. 1, a Gulliver among the Lilliputians, and an unbound one, to boot.*

Bipolarity: The Rules of the Game

It is critical to recall the origins and the defining features of bipolarity in order to appreciate what came next and what will continue to shape world politics for the rest of the twenty-first century.

While Germany and Europe were the central venues of the Cold War (the bloody offshoots took place in Korea and Vietnam), they did not furnish the underlying cause, which was as old as Thucydides' analysis of the outbreak of the first bipolar war between Athens and Sparta. "The real cause," the first theoretician of bipolarity insisted more than two millennia ago, was "the growth of the power of Athens," arguing that "the alarm which this inspired in Lacedaemon made war inevitable." In the Soviet-American case, the verdict should be amended to read "the growth of the power of *both*." Having jointly defeated their common enemy, Nazi Germany, the two victors suddenly found themselves catapulted into positions of unparalleled might. The dark side of this enormous power was mor-

*Inspired by Stanley Hoffmann's *Gulliver's Troubles, or The Setting of American Foreign Policy* (New York: McGraw-Hill, 1968), this metaphor evokes a friendly rather than a fearsome giant, yet one who causes alarm by dint of his sheer size. The name is taken from Jonathan Swift's *Gulliver's Travels* (1726), a satire dressed up as a misadventure story. It revolves around the voyages of Lemuel Gulliver, a ship's surgeon who, in book 1, ends up on the island of Lilliput, where he awakes to find that he has been roped down by Lilliputians, who are only six inches tall. Once untied, he helps them with his enormous strength in war and peace, but runs afoul of local mores and barely escapes renewed enslavement.

tal danger. For each, there was only one existential threat left—the other.

Add to the contest of power the aggravating factor of ideology, which was also present in the murderous rivalry between Athens, a democracy by ancient standards, and Sparta, a dictatorial oligarchy. Liberal-democratic capitalism and one-party communism were not just designs for the here-and-now but teleologies—secular doctrines of salvation. Inimical to the core, these doctrines were destined to redeem mankind and to transcend history. Defeat, on the other hand, would obliterate the very soul of whoever was vanquished. Nikita Khrushchev, general secretary from 1956 to 1964, nicely dramatized the point, when he burst out in 1960, "We shall bury you!" That was not a physical threat; it reflected Soviet Russia's conviction that communism, and not the West, was on the right side of history, which would soon dispatch liberal-democratic capitalism to its foreordained death.

In short, vast power, ideological righteousness, cosmic ambition, and boundless fear were the stuff from which the bipolar order was made. How was the stage set?

The Cold War order was, first of all, defined by the strategic extension of the two superpowers to the farthest corners of the globe. Having divided up Europe, the main strategic arena, between them, the two superpowers engaged in an endless ballet of push and shove, containment and countercontainment. Nothing escaped their attention, and everything mattered. The smallest victory or setback, the slightest tilt in the balance, seemed to forebode a total rout.

Strategy went hand in glove with ideology, as both superpowers defined their security not only in military terms but also in terms of a politically *juste milieu*. It was socialism—one-party rule plus a command economy—wherever the Soviet Union could extend its sway. It was liberal democracy—rule of law, multiparty competition, and free markets—for the United States. Or to recall Stalin's famous dictum: "Whoever occupies a territory also imposes on it his own social system. Everyone imposes his own system as far as his army can reach. It cannot be otherwise."[7] It was an empire by imposition in the Soviet realm, an empire by invitation in the American one. For the American Athens, however, "liberal democracy" was consistently subordinated to coalition building. To have Franco's Spain, Salazar's Portugal, Chiang Kai-shek's Taiwan, Syngman Rhee's South Korea—dictators all—or the kingdom of the Sauds in the American camp was more urgent than blessing them with U.S.-type constitutions.

Second, this order was ultra-stable, if stability is defined by the absence of major, globe-encircling war. There was plenty of peripheral bloodshed—in Korea or Vietnam, where the United States fought enemies sheltered by the Soviet Union and China. There was Afghanistan, where the Soviets tried to quash a foe quietly trained and supplied by the United States. There were two Arab-Israeli wars in the Middle East—in 1967 and 1973—whose protagonists acted as surrogates of the two superpowers. A Soviet client, Cuba, penetrated into the heart of Africa in the mid-1970s. But *never* did the two principals lift their swords against each other. Only once did they threaten to unsheathe them—in the nuclear confrontation over Cuba in 1962 that ended in a barely disguised defeat for Nikita Khrushchev when he was forced to withdraw his nuclear missiles from the Caribbean island.

Yet the United States and the USSR did not go down the same road that led to the ruin of Athens and Sparta. Why not? Two words: nuclear weapons. Or as John F. Kennedy put it in 1963, "A war today or tomorrow, if it led to nuclear war, would not be like any war in history. A full-scale nuclear exchange, lasting less than 60 minutes, with the weapons now in existence, could wipe out more than 300 million Americans, Europeans, and Russians. . . . "[8] The prospect of nuclear annihilation was the single-most important factor that kept the Cold War from degenerating into a remake of the

Peloponnesian War. "Mutual assured destruction" was the sturdiest pillar of stability in the Cold War.

Third, the traditional link between war and politics was broken. In Europe, the central arena of bipolarity, which had seen the bloodiest conflicts of the preceding five hundred years, Mars, the god of war, was dethroned. Force was no longer the natural adjunct of diplomacy. This is why "rollback" remained but a figure of speech, why any political foray ground to a halt, why stalemate was the only fruit of diplomacy. Since war was out, so was change. The reason is obvious. Vast concentrations of peacetime conventional power, buttressed by thousands of nuclear weapons, forever evoked not victory but suicide. To shoot first was to die second. But this very certainty dispelled the risk of deadly miscalculation. The superpowers that buttressed the system were not over-the-horizon presences, but in place, which dramatized their commitment while dousing any lure of adventurism. There was no room for a "Poland," the first victim of Hitler's war, in this contest of two nervous, but well-prepared, Goliaths. Yes, Britain and France had pledged protection to the Poles, but they were neither ready nor nearby, which tempted Hitler to ignore their guarantees. That they *did* declare war was not part of Hitler's plan.

Fourth, bipolarity spelled discipline. The clarity of commitment on the part of the great was fused to the tightest of controls over the small. With their very survival at stake, the United States and the Soviet Union could not for a moment risk "catalytic" war, a classical ploy by which lesser allies had in the past dragged the great powers into unwanted conflicts. Again, Europe furnished the emblematic examples. NATO's forces were integrated under the leadership of an American general, appropriately titled Supreme Allied Commander Europe. Command and control of Warsaw Pact armies was even more direct, with Soviet officers holding the reins at staff levels. In this scheme, war by entrapment was not just unlikely; it was impossible.

Iron-fisted control also suppressed intra-alliance conflict. By dint of its strategic presence in Western Europe, the United States pacified a region that used to be the fountainhead of major war.[9] For the first time since the demise of Rome, there was suddenly a power mightier than all in the system that would guarantee everybody's security against everybody else. When we celebrate the impossibility of war between France and Germany, indeed, in the entire European Union, today, we forget that it was the intrusion of the United States into the "arch-enmity" of Gauls and Germans that subordinated one of the oldest rivalries in Europe. That these two could link hands in community was due to a power greater than either that ensured them against the risks of lowering their guards. Eastern Europe, where many a border had been redrawn by two world wars, also was no foreordained haven of peace. But the heavy hand of Soviet rule squashed all dreams of revisionism—or of entrapping the great into the quarrels of the small.

A fifth, perhaps the most critical, mainstay of the postwar order was the dependence of the lesser powers on the greater. In time, Western Europe's economic dependence on the United States all but disappeared, and so did the need of some regimes, above all the Christian Democratic ones of West Germany and Italy, to secure their tenure by tethering themselves to Washington. In time, the governments of Japan, South Korea, and Taiwan would also loosen the tie that bound their fates to Washington. But as long as the Soviet Union endured, all of America's clients had to rely on the United States as "security lender of the last resort." Strategic dependence was the most powerful glue of bipolarity, the stuff that weathered myriad crises of the Western alliance.

With the Cold War receding into history, we forget that these crises were by no means trivial. By forcing them to withdraw from the Suez Canal in 1956, the United States humiliated its two oldest allies, Britain and France, yet neither of them defected. When the Berlin Wall was built in 1961 without an American response, the

Bonn government felt betrayed—only to huddle even more eagerly under the American umbrella as the Cold War heated up. The scuttling of the nuclearized multilateral force (MLF)* by the Johnson administration left its closest allies in Europe—Germany and Italy—out on a brittle limb; beset by Gaullist foes at home, their pro-American governments ended up not with a finger on the nuclear trigger but with a poke in the eye. They nonetheless submitted to their American protector. The repeat performance came in 1979 when the Carter administration suddenly canceled the deployment of "neutron bombs" in Western Europe, leaving precisely those governments twisting in the wind that had loyally withstood a massive assault from the pacifist left. But to revolt while Leonid Bhreznev's Russia was on an expansionist roll from Africa to Afghanistan? Unthinkable. Though France's Charles de Gaulle, president from 1959 to 1969, cultivated a habit of kicking American shins, bolting from the alliance was not part of the game, as long as *l'empire totalitaire*—the Soviet Union—lurked just three hundred miles beyond the Rhine.

The two "empires"—one formed by imposition, one by invitation—were of course beyond comparison if the rigor of Soviet domination is used as a benchmark. Yet, whatever its source, immutable strategic dependence ruled the relationship between the two Goliaths and their clients. Although America's allies were free to do as they pleased, these consumers of free security Made in U.S.A. could go only so far in defying their patron, even in the economic arena where Western Europe, Japan, and the United States eventually came to meet as equals. Theoretically, clients could have left America's far-flung alliance system, even for the other side. In practice,

*The MLF was to consist of a fleet of surface ships, equipped with U.S.-supplied nuclear missiles and manned by nationals from NATO countries. The idea was to give non-nuclear allies a say over nuclear strategy, but the American proposal was no more than sleight of hand, because any decision to launch remained strictly in American hands.

they would rather bear the yoke of alliance than suffer the angst of neutrality. And the East Europeans were "recentralized" too often by direct or indirect Soviet intervention to dare: East Germany in 1953, Poland and Hungary in 1956, Czechoslovakia in 1968, Poland in 1981. Whether protégés or satrapies, bloc members ran on a short leash embossed with "bipolarity" in large letters.

This order, to recapitulate, was short on options and long on dependence. It chained the weak, but also shackled the strong, precisely because of their overweening military might. Even as fierce an anticommunist as Ronald Reagan wrote in 1976 about "two superpowers [which] face each other with nuclear missiles at the ready—poised to bring Armageddon to the world."[10] Because they could only deter, but not defeat, each other, they were, to recall an overused Cold War metaphor, condemned to the life of two "scorpions in a bottle." There was no exit, only mutual exitus, no advance, only stalemate. Bipolarity was but another name for history frozen in its tracks. Oppressing the strong and the weak, the deadweight of bipolarity was the torturous price of ultra-stability. But the prize was without historical parallel: a world without great-power war—the world of the longest peace that arose in 1945.

Bipolarity was buried on Christmas Day 1991, when the Russian tricolor rose over the crenellated walls of the Kremlin. The death of the Soviet Union marked the birth of a new international system. Let's give it an equally cumbersome name, "unipolarity." This magnetic metaphor is scientific nonsense because alignment in a force field requires at least two poles. But, politically, the metaphor is quite apropos. Though the new distribution of power implies neither empire nor single-country rule, "unipolarity" does suggest a useful image: a bunch of iron filings (two hundred, to be exact) not helplessly sticking to a magnet, but aligned along various gradients of attraction toward a single pole that is the United States.

Is it hegemony? Certainly not, if hegemony is meant to denote direct, ubiquitous, or coercive domination. The United States can subdue tiny states like Grenada and Panama swiftly as well as economically. It can dislodge the Taliban in Afghanistan, and it can slice through Saddam's armies. But among the two hundred "fillings" are rising states like China and India, resurgent nations like Russia, would-be great powers like France, could-be great powers like the European Union, and might-be great powers like Japan. Some of them, like Russia and China, can deter the United States; eventually, Iran and North Korea could be added to the list. And all of them can resist No. 1 in one way or another—even quite economically by just withholding cooperation on matters dear to the United States, be it on war resolutions in the UN Security Council or on trade issues.

Let us, then, resort to a softer definition of hegemony. It rests not on the sweeping ability to compel but on two other capabilities. First, a hegemonic power should be able to repel all challengers, whether they come singly or in combination. Rome could do so only fitfully, and Britain never because it had to fight its global wars (from the Seven Years' War of 1756–63* to World War II) with the help of allies. The same holds true for all other contenders in history. Habsburg and Hitler, Napoleon and Wilhelm II, were eventually vanquished by superior coalitions. The British Empire survived into the mid-twentieth century only courtesy of America's armies, and the Soviet empire collapsed under its own weight. The difference between then and now is America's unprecedented power of survival. There is no way in which any other power, or combination of powers, could defeat the latest claimant to the hegemonial crown—except in the meaningless way of mutual nuclear devastation. Translating into strategic independence, America's singular defensive strength highlights the most critical gap between No. 1 and the rest.

*Known as the French and Indian Wars in the United States, this war—the first global one—was fought in North America, Europe, India, and the high seas around the world.

This is one reason why the post-bipolar order bears an American imprimatur.

That is not enough, however. Any nuclear power with a second-strike capability can deter anybody else, but such reactive power does not elevate its possessor to a hegemonic perch. So a second, "proactive" capability must be in place. A hegemon must command a surplus of usable, not just deterrent, power. Its influence and its interests must extend across the globe. Its sway over contested outcomes—strategic, diplomatic, economic—must exceed the influence of its rivals by a comfortable margin. A hegemon must wield substantial positive, and not just negative, power.

By that token, the United States also is in a class of its own. It spends almost as much on its military as the rest of the world combined, and to dramatize the point, let us recall the *supplemental* defense appropriation granted by the Congress to President Bush in the aftermath of the Twin Tower attack on September 11, 2001. The increment of $48 billion was *twice the annual* total defense spending of Germany or Italy. The critical point, though, is not mere numbers. No other nation even comes close to matching the *usability*, that is, the sophistication and mobility, of America's armed forces. No other nation could project its forces halfway around the world to Afghanistan or Iraq, let alone do so without nearby bases. Such panoply of power rests on an economy that is two and a half times larger than Japan's, which is the next-biggest economy. It rests on research-and-development expenditures that are the world's largest—and on universities that continue to draw the world's best and brightest. America's cultural power—high or low, Harvard or Hollywood—radiates across the globe with an intensity not even seen in the days of the Roman and British empires.

"The United States of America," intoned the French foreign minister Hubert Védrine, "dominates in all arenas: the economic, technological, military, monetary, linguistic or cultural one. There has never been anything like it." In short, the United States is a *hyper-*

puissance, the überpower.[11] The United States, of course, was an überpower throughout the second half of the twentieth century. But it was that only latently as long as the Soviet Union brought the one and only counterweight to bear in the scales of bipolarity. The United States was always Gulliver, but it was Gulliver Bound. With the demise of No. 2, which contained and devalued America's might, the ropes have fallen away. America's liberation from the harsh discipline of bipolarity has not only overturned the stage on which world politics was enacted since 1945. It has also changed the script and the direction for No. 1 as well as for all the other actors, great and small. It is no longer stock theater, but a new drama. The play will continue to intrigue and to infuriate the rest of the world for much of the twenty-first century. And it demands an answer to the question what this giant—no Cyclops,* but the world's oldest democracy—will and should do with its unfettered might.

*In Homer's Odyssey, the giant Cyclopes were rapacious cannibals. Caught in one of their caves, Odysseus escapes death by blinding his and his comrades' captor.

2

A Giant Unbound

IN THE DARK of the desert night, at 2 a.m. on August 2, 1990, the Iraqi army smashed its way into Kuwait; by day's end, Saddam Hussein had hijacked the entire country. His booty sat right next door to the Middle East's biggest prize: Saudi Arabia, the world's largest oil treasure. Two days later, President George H. Bush convened the National Security Council in the White House Cabinet Room. Colin Powell, chairman of the Joint Chiefs, advised him to "draw a line in the sand." At the end of the meeting, Bush the Elder was convinced: "I believe we are ready to go." On the next day, the president and his men huddled again, this time at Camp David, where they laid out the road that would lead to war. This wasn't going to be a mere punitive expedition, cautioned Powell; "this is the Super Bowl," hence "don't count on an easy way."[1]

No easy way was taken. By January 1991, the United States had deployed 540,000 troops to the Persian Gulf, together with British, French, and Arab forces; in all, the coalition encompassed twenty-eight nations and 700,000 soldiers.* Desert Storm, the most intensive aerial bombardment in history, began on January 16, laying waste to Iraq's war-making capacity.[2] America's superiority was not just a matter of raw numbers. By 1991, the U.S. Air Force had

*On D-Day, June 6, 1944, the start of the largest invasion in history, only 156,000 Allied troops were landed in Normandy.

already absorbed precision-guided munitions into its arsenal—World War IV stuff, so to speak—and so its planes were about twenty times more effective than aircraft loaded with conventional ordnance.[3] The air campaign was followed by the "hundred hours' war" on the ground and Baghdad's surrender on the last day of February. Against what on paper was the fourth-largest army in the world, the United States had suffered 146 dead in combat, while the allies had lost a total of 244. How many Iraqis were killed? We still don't know. The estimates run from 70,000 to 120,000. The annihilation of Iraqi equipment affords a more precise tally: almost 4,000 tanks and 3,000 artillery were shredded. America's war machine, unmatched by anything else in the world, had scored an unprecedented triumph.

Whatever the technology, such a feat would have been a wild dream while bipolarity was still intact. The Soviet Union's suicide was still ten months away, but recall that Moscow had already handed in its capitulation in the Cold War (by accepting German reunification) two weeks before Saddam Hussein's Republican Guards lunged across the Kuwaiti border. When Mikhail Gorbachev conceded a "Germany united inside NATO" on July 16, 1990, he gave away the store, signaling that he had neither the will nor the wherewithal to continue the "forty years' war," a.k.a. Cold War, that had split the world down the middle.

With the Soviet Union still in business, the United States would not have dared deploy half a million troops so close to the underbelly of its only mortal rival, certainly not for an attack on a country like Iraq, an all but Soviet ally that had been equipped and trained by Big Brother just to the north. Under the grim rules of bipolarity, that would have been a capital offense. Given these unwritten laws, winning even a proxy war in the Middle East was out of bounds. When Britain and France had gone after Nasser's Egypt, then a Soviet client, during the Suez War of 1956, Moscow threatened both of them with nuclear weapons. The Soviet Union rattled its nuclear saber again in 1973 when Israel, in a spectacular reversal of military fortunes, suddenly found itself on the road to Cairo at the end of the Yom Kippur War. By 1990, though, the Soviet Union would no longer rattle, let alone unsheathe. Nor would the United States have succeeded in extracting a blessing from the UN Security Council while corralling the support of some eighty nations for the war against Iraq. Terrorized by Soviet might, the UN would have coldly ignored Saddam's aggression, telling the elder Bush that negotiation was the better part of valor. Now, however, even countries like Germany and Japan, both first-line Soviet targets during the Cold War, paid double-digit billions into the American war chest.[4]

"We don't have a patron anymore," the Iraqi foreign minister Tariq Aziz lamented while talking to his American counterpart, James Baker, during a meeting in Geneva just one week before the launch of the air campaign. "If we still had the Soviets as our patron, none of this would have happened," he added. "They would have vetoed every U.N. resolution [authorizing the use of force]."[5] Aziz was absolutely correct in his take on Mikhail Gorbachev's foreign policy, and Washington knew it. Trying to put the best face on weakness, the Soviet Union had spent the preceding months in a frantic effort to mediate and moderate in order to stave off its client's destruction and a deadly blow to its own reputation—to no avail.

Unable to stop the Allied air offensive—Saddam simply would not budge—Moscow made a last-minute effort to halt the ground war in order to save at least some face. While the air campaign was grinding away at Saddam's order of battle, Gorbachev politely, even meekly, cabled George Bush that "it might be desirable" to hold off on the ground war until his envoy's talks with Aziz in Baghdad had been completed. "*Desirable*," and then in the subjunctive? This was not how Stalin, Khrushchev, et al. had addressed the United States. The growl had gone out of Moscow's voice, and the soft glove of diplomacy no longer sheathed a mailed fist. Or as a senior administration official put it, "At the end of the day, [Gorbachev] was not ready to put his relationship with the United States on the line. . . ."[6] Two weeks later, the victory against Moscow's protégé was complete, and the United States was now certified as "last remaining superpower."

Though it took a while before the consequences began to sink in, this was one of the rarest moments in the history of world politics. This was not a new act but a new stage—where unipolarity had pushed aside bipolarity. But it did not take the überpower very long to begin to think about the fruits of primacy so suddenly dropped in its lap. It was as if Sparta had folded overnight, leaving pride of place to Athens—or as if Imperial Germany, in 1900, had bowed out of the supremacy race against Britain. What followed from this windfall? The answer was self-evident. A "number 1" above all wants to stay "number 1"; it does not dream of handing back such a glorious prize. And so only one year after victory in Iraq, the Pentagon put together a draft of the Defense Planning Guidance for 1994–99 that stressed some obvious points:[7]

The "victory of the United States" and the "collapse of the Soviet Union" had shaped a "new international environment." Iraq was a "defining event in U.S. global leadership." Therefore, "our first objective is to prevent the re-emergence of a new rival, either on the territory of the former Soviet Union or elsewhere. . . ." Hence, the United States ought to keep "any hostile power" from gaining control over "Western Europe, East Asia, the territory of the former Soviet Union, and Southwest Asia [the Greater Middle East]." Throw in Africa and Australia, and you have the entire world as bailiwick of American power.

Three grand-strategic rules followed, according to the draft guidance. First, shape a "new order" that would protect the "legitimate interests" of potential competitors. In other words, give them a stake in the new enterprise so that they would not have to "aspire to a greater role or pursue a more aggressive posture." Second, the United States ought to take care of the "interests of the advanced industrial nations to discourage them from challenging our leadership." Third, maintain enough military strength to "deter" rivals from reaching for a "larger regional or global role." In the vernacular, the message read, "Don't even go there, because we will outarm each and all of you." In bureaucracy-speak: though the Cold War is over, we must be "prepared to reconstitute additional forces should the need to counter a global threat re-emerge." The first principle was to remain No. 1: "We must maintain our status as a military power of the first magnitude," which will enable us to act "as a balancing force and prevent emergence of a vacuum or a regional hegemon."

Leaked to the press, this February 18, 1992, draft for a one-überpower world, provoked howls of protest around the globe, and so it was duly toned down three months later to excise the provocative language.[8] Yet defusing the phraseology could not possibly overturn the inherent logic of the earlier draft. Unless forced, why would the greatest power in history want to share, let alone yield, its exalted position? In fact, over the coming decade, the United States would act precisely in terms of the logic apparently shelved by the Pentagon planners—at first hesitantly, even reluctantly, then decisively and brutally, as the war in Afghanistan in 2002 and the second war against Saddam Hussein in 2003 would show.

Didn't the February 1992 draft proclaim that the United States would address "those wrongs which threaten not only our interests, but those of our allies or friends, or which could seriously unsettle international relations"? Well, the United States did. In what the Pentagon called "operations other than war," the new Clinton administration intervened in Somalia in 1993, its first year in office. In the following year, 20,000 American troops landed in Haiti. In 1995, with the "Yugoslav war of succession" shaking the Balkans, American planes, along with NATO's, bombed Serbian positions in Bosnia. To uphold the U.S.-sponsored "Peace of Dayton," 16,500 U.S. combat troops (at the height of their engagement) were dispatched to the former Yugoslavia, and another 6,000 support troops went to Croatia, Hungary, and Italy.[9] Next stop, next year: the war over the Kosovo, which would trigger an American-led bombing campaign against Serbia in 1999 lasting ten weeks.

Farther afield, the Clinton administration launched cruise missiles against targets in Afghanistan and Sudan in August 1998—this in reaction to terrorist attacks on the U.S. embassies in Nairobi (Kenya) and Dar es Salaam (Tanzania). As early as 1993, the White House had dispatched cruise missiles against Iraqi intelligence headquarters in Baghdad. In 1996, the targets were military installations. At the end of 1998, President Clinton ordered a four-day bombing assault on Iraq (Operation Desert Fox), citing Baghdad's refusal to cooperate with UN weapons inspectors. When Saddam retaliated by throwing them out of the country, Clinton would surely have escalated heavily had it not been for his domestic troubles—impending impeachment over his dalliance with a White House intern.

In its eight years in office, the Clinton administration used force not early but often—more frequently, at any rate, than had the Reaganites in the 1980s. These had bombed—actually, pinpricked—Libya very briefly and toppled an unfriendly government in Grenada, a small island right in America's backyard. The extensive intervention in the Balkans—by air and ground power—dramatizes the difference between Reagan's world and Clinton's. In a two-superpower world, Ronald Reagan, anticommunist extraordinaire, could merely *amass* military power, which he did aplenty, but he could not use it, except against countries that were neither clients nor protégés of the Soviet Union. Clinton could—even against Serbia, a historic Russian ally abutting on the Warsaw Pact. It no longer mattered that Russia opposed the United States in the UN Security Council; with the United States in the lead, NATO went to war anyway, not bothering to get a resolution. Yet, in a bipolar world, Serbia would have been just as taboo as Iraq. It goes without saying that the Clinton administration would not have dreamed of inducting Poland, Hungary, and Czechia into NATO. In 1998, however, the alliance did take them in, extending America's sway over what once had been Soviet possessions. Through the Partnership for Peace, a host of former Warsaw Pact members and Soviet republics attached themselves to the American alliance in less formal ways—including the Soviet Union itself. That would have been tantamount to France's accepting candidate membership in the British Empire after Napoleon's final defeat in 1815.

The "Indispensable Nation"

Settling into the White House in 1993, Bill Clinton had undeniably inherited a shiny new world. It was more permissive than any other encountered by an American president in the twentieth century. And American power, no longer trammeled by the Soviet Union, stood at its historical apex. No wonder that at least Clinton's military leaders began to look at this world through the lens of the drafted, but never formalized, Defense Planning Guidance of 1992.[10] Though the Clintonites wisely avoided the language of primacy, speaking instead of a five-power world, the chairman of the Joint Chiefs of Staff, John Shalikashvili, did not believe that the United States was merely *unum inter pares*:

> Today . . . , the difference, or the "delta," between the capabilities of our military forces and the military forces of those who would wish us ill is greater than at any time in my 39 years of service. And our challenge for tomorrow will be to maintain that "delta" so that a future Chairman . . . can come before you and say, with the same conviction, that ours are the best Armed Forces in the world, bar none.[11]

That military "delta" instilled in the civilians the heady assurance that anything was possible. Madeleine Albright, the secretary of state, celebrated "America's unique capabilities and unmatched power,"[12] which was but another word for being No. 1. The agenda was not exactly modest, and the United States was always on top. Again in Albright's words: "We must be more than audience, more even than actors, we must be the authors of the history of our age." It is not enough to celebrate the defeat of communism; we must build "a new framework" for the world. In plain English: frozen for forty years, the world is now ours to remake.

What did this framework Made in U.S.A. entail? Boundless ambition. America "must remain a European power." And a "Pacific power," too. And it must make sure that "democratic Russia" becomes a "strong partner." Likewise Ukraine. The United States must also shepherd along NATO's enlargement. In Asia, it "must maintain the strength of our core alliances while successfully managing our multi-faceted relationship with China." In the Middle East, the task was "active diplomatic engagement," that is, playing first fiddle. And so Clinton did—first by forcing Israel's Yitzhak Rabin and Yasir Arafat into their handshake in the White House Rose Garden in 1993, then by sequestering them in Camp David in 2000. There were also proprietary interests in a slew of secondary bailiwicks: Cyprus, Northern Ireland, India and Pakistan, Armenia and Azerbaijan, Central Africa. In each of these areas American leadership was both salutary and necessary.[13]

Bill Clinton put it all in one simple sentence: "We must continue to bear the responsibility for the world's leadership." He continued with a globe-sweeping set of tasks:

> These are the kinds of things that America must continue to do. From Belfast to Jerusalem, American leadership has helped Catholics and Protestants, Jews and Arabs to walk the streets of their cities with less fear of bombs and violence. From Prague to Port-au-Prince, we are working to consolidate the benefits of democracy and market economics. From Kuwait to

> Sarajevo, the brave men and women of our armed forces are working to stand down aggression and stand up for freedom.[14]

"Because we remain the world's indispensable nation," Bill Clinton intoned in 1996, "we must act and we must lead."[15] This was the mantra of a presidency sitting on top of the world. "If the United States does not lead, the job will not be done. . . . [O]ur leadership is essential. . . . American leadership is indispensable. . . . [W]e have to assume the burden of leadership."[16] "We must act and we must lead" betrayed an exhilarating sense of primacy. It was America as überpower, as indispensable and inescapable nation. The Soviet Union had bowed out, allowing Gulliver to shake off the usual strictures of international politics.

This is a new world, and "America's place is at the center of this system," Madeleine Albright liked to declare.[17] Missing from the age-old constraints of world politics was the biggest one of all: the strategic threat that had neutralized so much of America's power in forty years of Cold War. No longer laboring under a deadly risk, the Clintonites bestrode the global stage with a cosmic sense of opportunity. Even better, history was going America's way. According to Deputy Secretary of State Strobe Talbott, it wasn't just strategic but also ideological bipolarity that had died: "The end of the Cold War and the democratic revolution in what used to be the Soviet world have removed the last half century's one anti-democratic ideology with global pretensions."[18] With that enemy gone, history could complete its forward march on the side of America as handmaiden of a secular providence:

> By the 1980s, self-isolating dictatorships from Chile to the Soviet Union had yielded to democratic and free market ideals spread by radio, television, the fax machine, and e-mail. Since then, in addition to undermining the Berlin Wall and shredding the Iron Curtain, the powerful technological forces of the

> Information Age have helped to stitch together the economic, political, and cultural lives of nations, making borders more permeable to the movement of people, products, and ideas.[19]

With history on its predestined path, the sword, which was later so lavishly wielded by the Bush administration in an era darkened by 9/11, could be safely tucked away. But who was the enemy, if any? Bill Clinton gave a prescient answer:

> We are all vulnerable to the reckless acts of rogue states and to an unholy axis of terrorists, drug traffickers, and international criminals. These 21st century predators feed on the very free flow of information and ideas and people we cherish. They abuse the vast power of technology to build black markets for weapons, to compromise law enforcement with huge bribes of illicit cash, to launder money with the keystroke of a computer. *These forces are our enemies.*[20]

What followed? A breathtakingly broad agenda. In Albright's words: "We must fight and win the war against international crime," "stand up to . . . international terror," and "speak out against those who violate human rights." Grand tasks were beckoning. The United States would "fight hunger, control disease, care for refugees and ensure the survival of infants and children." American power would not stop at the borders of other nations. "Appalling abuses are being committed against women, from domestic violence to dowry murders to forcing young girls into prostitution . . . and we each have a responsibility to stop it." To complete this glorious sweep, Albright put it all into a planetary nutshell: "When it comes to the rights of more than half the people on Earth, America should be leading the way "[21]

Blazing a trail for democracy across the world is a purpose now firmly associated with the name of George W. Bush. In fact, the

Clintonites responded to the post-Soviet world in a very similar language. The global triumph of democracy was not just a lofty ideal but a hardheaded national interest because democracy spelled peace, hence safety for the United States. "Democracy is a parent to peace," is how Albright put it. "Free nations make good neighbors. Compared to dictatorships, they are far less likely to commit acts of aggression, support terrorists, spawn international crime or generate waves of refugees."[22] How do we know? Here is the answer of her deputy Strobe Talbott: "The world has now had enough experience with democracy . . . to have established a . . . body of evidence. That record shows that democracies are less likely than non-democracies to go to war with each other, to persecute their citizens . . . or to engage in terrorism. And democracies are more likely to be reliable partners in trade and diplomacy."[23] In short, Immanuel Kant, the best-known author of the "democratic peace" theory, was no longer buried in Königsberg but alive and well on the seventh floor of the State Department.

But what if destiny stumbled on the way, tripped up by "antihistorical forces" like rogue states and terrorists, whose murderous stings the Clinton administration felt throughout its eight years in office?[24] National Security Adviser Samuel Berger was confident that America could master all trials because it was the greatest power of them all: "The bottom line is this: our nation's economic performance is unrivaled, our military might is unmatched, our political influence is unsurpassed. . . . No other nation has the muscle, the diplomatic skill, or the trust to mediate disputes, nudge opposing sides to the negotiation table or . . . help enforce the terms of an agreement."[25]

Such were the thrilling beliefs of the first American administration blessed with the fruits of primacy. It bestrode a world where its power was singular, its risk negligible, and its opportunity unlimited. Yet, unlike George W. Bush, who came to the White House with a similar set of convictions, William Jefferson Clinton seemed to be born under a lucky star. During his eight years in office, his mettle was not tested, and neither was the rhetoric of his administration. Force was deployed frequently because the risks had waned—and modestly because there were no dragons to slay, as there would be in abundance a few months into Bush's first term.

Yes, there was still the unfinished business of Saddam Hussein, but "we have him in a box," as Albright's formulaic assurance went, and so it was like a Punch and Judy show: "Saddam would stick his head up, and we'd whack him."[26] Washington's oratory abounded with all the good things in life—multilateralism, cooperation, and institutionalism—because the new dragons, like Islamist terrorism, still looked more like dwarf alligators. In a world about to transcend history, allies were treated with the deference due to old comrades-in-arms, and former adversaries with the magnanimity that sprouts from victory. Clinton's was a soft triumphalism, and America contained itself, so to speak, because there was no need to throw its weight around.

Yet Gulliver Unbound was not about to bear the chains again, and so the charges of arrogant unilateralism levied against George W. Bush miss the other half of the target. For the roots of Bushist unilateralism reach back to his predecessor's era. The Clintonites signed on to the Kyoto Climate Protocol in 1997, but let the years pass without submitting the treaty to the Senate. The administration did not accede to the Land Mine Ban, on the sound calculation that it needed land mines to protect its far-flung forces around the world, especially along the demilitarized zone between the two Koreas. After lengthy foot-dragging, Clinton signed up for the International Criminal Court in the last days of his administration, but he did not submit the treaty to an unwilling Senate. Prudence was the better part of goodness, given the unpleasant prospect that a country most likely to be embroiled in violence beyond its borders would also be most likely to expose its soldiers to international prosecution. Once he had shed his old ropes, Gulliver was not about to entangle himself in new ones.

Überpower Politics

While still campaigning for the presidency, George W. Bush did not sound like a man who would soon file away Clintonism under "Tried and Found Wanting." Indeed, he seemed downright unassuming when he opined, "If we're an arrogant nation, they'll resent us. If we're a humble nation but strong, they'll welcome us."[27] And he shared the historical optimism of Clintonites when he told the navy's midshipmen in the spring of 2001, "The best days of our nation are yet to come." Then came 9/11, and exuberance changed into fear and fury. At least in terms of U.S. grand strategy, "nothing would ever be the same again," as the phrase of the day had it.

What had changed? "On September the 11th, enemies of freedom committed an act of war against our country," the president intoned. "Americans have known wars—but for the past 136 years, they have been wars on foreign soil, except for one Sunday in 1941. Americans have known the casualties of war—but not at the center of a great city. . . . Americans have known surprise attacks—but never before on thousands of civilians."[28] Henceforth, the shock of 9/11—a vulnerability America had never experienced—would course through the corridors of American power.

One half of Clinton's bright new world was now cast in darkness. America's clout was still unmatched, but the dragons had come back in a different guise. These new demons spoke Arabic and not Russian; they were not a state that could be deterred but a global franchise without a permanent return address. An elusive target, al-Qaeda could not be threatened with "assured destruction," as were the Soviets during the forty years' war, and it could not be defeated in the classic American way—by lots of mass and firepower—as had been done in Nazi Germany and Imperial Japan. Recently unchained, the giant was suddenly engulfed by angst and anger.

So it was back to the hegemonic reflex of the 1992 Defense Planning Guidance and simultaneously forward into a world normally inhabited by nations in relative decline—where those who dread their foe's growing strength strike while the striking is still good. It was all laid out in the *National Security Strategy* (*NSS*) published one year after 9/11. First, the document repeated the überpower motif. The United States "possesses unprecedented—and unequaled—strength and influence in the world," and in spite of 9/11 this was still a magnificent "time of opportunity for America." Second, Mr. Big would stay Mr. Big. "We must build and maintain our defenses beyond challenge" to "dissuade future military competition; deter threats against U.S. interests . . . ; and decisively defeat any adversary if deterrence fails." And again: "Our forces will be strong enough to dissuade potential adversaries from pursuing a military build-up in hopes of surpassing, or equaling, the power of the United States."[29] It was primacy now and forever more.

Then the *NSS* moved onto grounds the country had never trod before. The novelty was "preventive/preemptive war."[30] Not that the United States hadn't attacked first before. The young Republic had launched punitive expeditions against the Barbary pirates in the early 1800s. It had started the foolishly aggressive War of 1812 against Britain, and it had fought campaigns against Mexicans, Indians, and Spaniards, incorporating about as much real estate in one century as Rome had in its entire imperial career. The United States had also intervened routinely in Central America. But never did this continent-sized nation, which in Tocqueville's words was as safe "as if all its frontiers were girt by the ocean,"[31] seek protection in a posture of prevention, that is, in wars against threats that had not yet arisen. Now, the *NSS* vowed, "We must be prepared to stop rogue states and their terrorist clients *before* they are able to threaten or use weapons of mass destruction against the United States and our allies. . . ." The shibboleth was "anticipatory action," but alone, if necessary: "We will respect the values, judgment, and interests of our friends and partners. *Still, we will be prepared to act apart when our interests and unique responsibilities [so] require.*"[32]

Thus was America's new imperial temptation distilled into a thirty-one-page document. The *NSS* marked an extraordinary departure from the rules of bipolarity. These had demanded around-the-clock vigilance while permitting—nay, demanding—unremitting, yet controlled, rivalry on a planetary scale. But these rules had tightly limited America's military opportunities because nuclear Armageddon lurked right around the next bend. Now it was the trio of fear, might, and freedom that guided grand strategy, the most combustible combination in the affairs of nations. As in the Cold War, America faced a deadly foe, but it now had the choice of doing this adversary in, which it did not have while the Soviet Union was still around. And it did choose to do so—twice in the space of thirty months.

The Afghan War. The first target of opportunity was Afghanistan, a state that was less a sponsor of terrorism than sponsored by it. Indeed, al-Qaeda had essentially rented Afghanistan as a base and staging area. This was the first time since the Barbary pirates (who were in the business of abduction and extortion) when terrorism had a reasonably accurate return address. Even better, unlike the Vietcong operating in the protective shadow of North Vietnam, China, and Russia, Terror International had no great-power patron extending shelter and succor from the sidelines. And so, the United States went after the architects of 9/11 with brilliantly executed vengeance.

First, Washington did an exemplary job on the diplomatic front. On September 12, 2001, one day after the collapse of New York's

Twin Towers, Washington extracted from the United Nations an authorization to use force. All major powers, including China and Russia, denounced the attack, and NATO invoked its Article 5 ("an attack on one is an attack on all") for the first time in its history. Formerly Soviet possessions, Uzbekistan, Tajikistan, and Kyrgyzstan offered bases and overflight rights, and so did Pakistan, while Russia gave aid and comfort to the Northern Alliance, an anti-Taliban army of Uzbeks, Tajiks, and Shiites that would soon fight its way into Kabul. Essentially, the United States had the whole world on its side in one way or another.

Second, the United States performed brilliantly on the military level. Within weeks, the United States achieved the kind of victory the Soviet Union had never been able to gain in almost a decade of fighting with about five times as many troops inside the country (100,000). With the help of the Northern Alliance and the British, the United States quickly defeated and dispersed the enemy, an amalgam of Taliban, al-Qaeda, and Arab fighters, in three months. This was the first war fought in totally "un-American ways"—not with mass and firepower, but with speed, precision, and a digitalized battle-management and intelligence system commanded by no other nation.

It was in fact the first "network-centric war" in history, and, miraculously, the intricate choreography worked—some ten thousand miles from home. The network was weaved by B-52 bombers flying round-trip from Diego Garcia, F-14 and F-18 strike aircraft based on carriers offshore, cruise missiles launched from submarines, and special operations forces inside Afghanistan. The system was held together by real-time intelligence from space and from the sky, such as JSTARS, which could detect moving vehicles on the ground and relay this information instantly to the battlefield commanders. By now 90 percent of the ordnance was precision-guided—whereas only around 10 percent had been during the First Iraq War.

In Afghanistan, almost everything was in the right place at the right time. This was also the first "just in time" war that did not require bases or prepositioning—a feat never mastered by a great power before. Supplies were not stocked, but brought forward as needed. Some B-52 bombers simply flew round-trip from Missouri to the Central Asian theater. They did not land for refueling; they simply followed a chain of "gas stations" in the sky stretching from the Midwest to Afghanistan. Allies were nice, but not necessary, which is why Secretary of Defense Donald Rumsfeld ungraciously waved away NATO's offer of help, picking a "coalition of the willing" instead. Initiated on October 7, 2001, the campaign was over on December 7, when the Taliban surrendered. This was a far cry from the slogging matches, involving millions of men, that brought the United States to Berlin and Tokyo in World War II, and a farther cry still from the stalemate in Korea and the barely disguised defeat in Vietnam. Gulliver was not only unbound but also ecstatic as he tasted the fruits of his unprecedented prowess.

The Second Iraq War. The Afghan War was sheer serendipity when compared with the Second Iraq War, in 2003. The military campaign against Saddam Hussein unfolded as brilliantly and swiftly as had the First Iraq War (1991) and the Afghan War—even more brilliantly when compared with the nastier odds.

In Afghanistan, the United States had fought the ragtag army of an isolated regime oppressing one of the world's most backward nations, and it had taken three months to bludgeon the Taliban into surrender. This time, the task looked more daunting. On paper, Saddam commanded one million men under arms, who in spite of a long-standing embargo were still well equipped. The enemy also enjoyed a sudden windfall when Turkey turned against its American ally, denying it a second axis of attack from the north. Unable to engineer a two-front war, the United States and the United Kingdom were reduced to a single avenue of advance in the south, thrusting upward from Kuwait to Baghdad. And yet, U.S. troops were in control of Baghdad only two weeks after the ground attack had begun on March 19, 2003. "Major combat operations," as the president put it, ended on May 1. Some 90,000 U.S. ground forces supported by 26,000 Britons had sliced through Saddam's divisions like a hot knife through butter. Again, speed, training, and technological wizardry (including the debut of the F-117 "stealth" bomber) had carried the day—and faster than in Afghanistan and Iraq I. It was a victory with a minimum of blood and tears. American losses amounted to 139 dead, with 109 killed in action.[33]

Once more America's singular military apparatus had triumphed with economy and dispatch. Were there any limits to what the überpower could do? The politics went awry from the very moment President Bush targeted Iraq, Iran, and North Korea as "axis of evil" and as "grave and growing danger."[34] A few months later, temptation knew no bounds, when Bush declared "the Cold War doctrines of deterrence and containment"—anchors of the bipolar status quo—to be unfit, even pernicious, guidelines for the twenty-first century.[35] For "if we wait for threats to fully materialize, we will have waited too long."[36]

And so, "inaction is not an option."[37] What will replace inaction? "We will send diplomats where they are needed, and we will send you, our soldiers, where you're needed," the president told the graduating class at West Point.[38] Against whom? In the summer of 2002, references to Saddam Hussein were still vague, but it was clear whom George W. Bush had in mind: "We cannot put our faith in the word of tyrants, who solemnly sign non-proliferation treaties, and then systemically break them."[39] Barely three months later, Vice President Cheney had fingered the tyrant and outlined the purpose: "*Regime change in Iraq* would bring about a number of benefits to the region. When the gravest of threats are eliminated, the freedom-loving peoples of the region will have a chance to promote the values that can bring lasting peace."[40] It was back to the oldest tradition in American foreign policy: remaking the world in its own liberal-democratic image. The status quo was out; revolution was in.

This is where the wondrous new world of the unshackled superpower began to fall apart, and the not so happy consequences are still with us. The single-most critical difference between the Afghan War and Iraq II consists of one word: "legitimacy." Looking back at the Afghan campaign, Bush could rightfully assert in 2002, "Our cause is just."[41] It did not take a bevy of international lawyers to make his case. The devastation of the Twin Towers was a heinous act in any culture and under any legal system: the murder of the innocents. Retaliation shifting into regime change, though a revolutionary notion, was legitimate for many reasons. Washington had given the Taliban an option short of war: hand over the al-Qaeda leadership. It had the blessings of the great powers assembled in the UN Security Council. And ridding the world of a universally despised regime that was the twin of terrorism was accepted, though more sullenly than enthusiastically, by the majority of nations.

None of these conditions prevailed in the Second Iraq War. Had Saddam committed aggression against the United States or any other country? No. Did he harbor terrorists as proxies? No, the "Baghdad connection" could never be established. Was he stockpiling, or about to produce, nuclear weapons and other paraphernalia of mass destruction? That assumption was dubious to begin with, given the destructive efficiency of the UN inspectors in the aftermath of the First Iraq War, and it proved utterly false once the second was over. Did he defy the UN sleuths during the run-up? In a passive-aggressive way, he did, but not systematically enough to be nabbed for obstructing justice.

On this slender evidence, no jury would have convicted, let alone voted for capital punishment. Yet the real issue was not the fine points of international law, a most pliant code nations have always bent to their purposes, but America unchained. True, "objectively speaking," as the Soviets used to say, Russia, China, France, Germany, et al. were lining up behind the most murderous despot since Pol Pot, Stalin, and Hitler. It was also true that "regime change" was less a revolution in American foreign policy than the revival of its oldest tradition, ranging from the founding fathers via Wilson's "making the world safe for democracy" to the Clintonian faith in making the world safe *through* democracy. As early as 1791, Thomas Paine had asked, "Why are not Republics plunged into war?" He answered, "Because the nature of their Government does not admit of an interest distinct from that of the Nation" and because "the republican principles" stand for "peace and domestic prosperity."[42] George W. Bush did not invent this tradition, but he did reinfuse it with muscular Wilsonianism when he stressed that "the defense of freedom requires the advance of freedom."[43]

What really rattled the naysayers was a very different revolution: the liberation of American power from the age-old checks and balances of international politics. Ridding the world of Saddam may have been good, but reining in Uncle Sam was better—for three reasons. First, letting America have its war of choice would signal consent to a single-überpower world under the Stars and Stripes—to the certification of U.S. supremacy. Second, it would imply acquiescence in preemptive and/or preventive war, with the United States as prosecutor, judge, and Globocop rolled into one. Nos. 2, 3, 4, et al. naturally were not cheered by this prospect. Third, victory in Iraq would confirm the United States as overlord of the Middle East, the world's most critical strategic turf, oil and all. America's triumph would grant yet more power to the one and only superpower—and this on a stage where it had already reduced France and Russia, the EU and the UN, to bit players.

Why did the president and his cohorts go after Saddam? By thrusting all the way into Baghdad, did he want to show his father that he was the man the elder Bush allegedly never was? Short of putting Bush *fils* on the couch, we will never know. But let us resist reducing affairs of state to compulsions of the psyche. Oedipus killed his father and slept with his mother, but he did not go to war, which is a more complex social activity than patricide. Psychiatry deals with individuals, not with institutions, and so it is a treacherous guide to the behavior of states, especially of a democratic one that is beholden to many centers of power. After all, it took a Homeric imagination to transfigure the Trojan War, an imperial gambit if ever there was one, into the product of a foolish love affair.

Did Bush want to make the Middle East safe for Bechtel, the giant construction company? Reducing a nation's strategy to the profit motive of a single corporation makes for a compelling op-ed piece. But for the indictment to stick, the prosecution would have to show how Bechtel, even though close to Vice President Cheney, could bamboozle an entire country. The same logic militates against the notion of a "Jewish conspiracy" allegedly bent on making the Middle East safe for Israel. While the Pentagon's most articulate advocates of the Iraq War, Paul Wolfowitz, Douglas Feith, and Richard Perle, were Jews, the president and his vice president, the national security adviser and the secretary of defense, let alone the Joint Chiefs of Staff, were not exactly members of the tribe. Nor were they secret devotees of the faith, like Spain's Marranos, who pretended to live as Christians after their more stiff-necked brethren were expelled from the country in 1492. Did Bush want to trade "blood for oil"? It would have been safer and cheaper to cozy up to Saddam by lifting the oil embargo.

The best explanation is power, opportunity, and devotion to the democratic dogma, the oldest in America's secular religion. Above all, it was the exuberance that comes from singular strength and minimal risk. If it can be done, it will be done, especially when the prize—a Middle East stripped of its political pathologies—was so enticing. America's imperial temptation was precisely the casus belli that riled the souls of those who would rather see the giant safely bound. Even as the centuries-old Westphalian system* of absolute sovereignty was being riddled from Haiti to Serbia, even as "humanitarian intervention" was creeping into international law, the lesser powers would not stand for a giant that was arrogating unto itself the role of jury and executioner. "We, the jury," was the rest of the world under the would-be leadership of Russia and China, France and Germany, and it demanded a veto right over the conduct of the last remaining superpower. In the summer of 2002, just a decade into America's still fresh primacy, the containment of Goliath had begun in earnest.

Balancing against Mr. Big

"Now, the United States is alone in the world," mused the dean of the realist school of international politics, Kenneth N. Waltz, in 2000, and realist "theory predicts that balances disrupted will one day be restored." Why so? "As nature abhors a vacuum, so international politics abhors unbalanced power." Hence, "some states try to increase their own strength or they ally with others to bring the international distribution of power into balance."[44] Such are the age-old dynamics of the state system. The question is not why it happened, but why it took so long for power to beget power—why the international system began to kick in against the United States only a decade after the suicide of the Soviet Union.

History provides one answer to the puzzle: balances take time to ripen. Sometimes it happens very quickly; by 1792, much of Europe

*In the making since the Augsburg Peace of 1555, the "Westphalian system," named after the Westphalian Peace that ended the Thirty Years' War (1618–48), denotes a body of treaty law granting rulers absolute sway over their subjects. What he did inside his bailiwick was to be of no concern to surrounding powers. Only his behavior outside could serve as a legitimate cause for war. Intervention for religious or political reasons was out of bounds.

had taken up arms against the three-year-old French Revolution, and by 1815, Europe's would-be emperor Napoleon was crushed. In the case of Stalin's Russia, an anti-Soviet alliance began to crystallize within a year of Nazi Germany's defeat in 1945; three years later, the United States had recruited into NATO Canada and ten European nations, all of which had been in a state of war against Nazi Germany, hence on the side of the Soviet Union. The *renversement des alliances** was complete when America's previous arch-enemy, Germany,† was invited into NATO in 1955. But other "reaction formations" took much longer.

In the case of the Third Reich, the rise of Hitler in 1933 and his rush to rearmament triggered not an anti-German alliance but appeasement—for six long years. Only in 1939 did Britain and France, underequipped and unprepared, declare war, which is the most drastic method of balancing. Stalin actually collaborated with Hitler, and the United States, under the sway of isolationist fervor, dallied until the end of 1941, entering the war against Germany only after the Japanese assault on Pearl Harbor (with Hitler declaring war first). Bismarck's Germany enjoyed a much longer break. After its unification in 1871, Germany was undoubtedly the preeminent power on the Continent. But only at the beginning of the twentieth century would it confront formalized opposition, when France, Russia, and Britain coalesced in the entente of 1907. Antihegemonial war, that is, World War I, did not break out until 1914, forty-three years after the Second Reich's rise to Continental primacy.

The second reason for the hiatus was self-containment. The balance kicks in most swiftly against rapacious powers, and so the Third

*This term, the "reversal of alliances," dates back to the Seven Years' War (1756–63), when France and the Habsburg Empire, arch-enemies for the preceding two centuries, made common cause against Frederick the Great's Prussia.

†More accurately, it was two-thirds of it, the Federal Republic of Germany. The other third of the Third Reich, the German Democratic Republic, was incorporated into the Warsaw Pact by the Soviets.

Reich, granted a free ride for six years, had a war on its hands the moment the Wehrmacht forged into Poland on September 1, 1939. The Cold War broke out in 1946 when Stalin extended a covetous hand toward Western Europe and toward the Balkans as well as Turkey. Why didn't the world gang up on the United States when it invaded Iraq in 1991? That war and the one against Afghanistan in 2001 were seen as defensive and/or retaliatory, hence legitimate, while their objectives were tightly circumscribed. The elder Bush stopped his army in 1991, although the gates to Baghdad had swung wide open, and the younger Bush withdrew the bulk of his forces from Afghanistan as quickly as they had entered it. In between, the America of Bill Clinton hardly behaved like a bloodthirsty *Tyrannosaurus rex* and more like a placid bull that would only swing its tail to lash out at some irksome horseflies like Saddam and al-Qaeda.

Clinton did mount a sustained bombing campaign against Serbia in 1999, but given years of hesitation, nobody could accuse Clinton of aggrandizement masquerading as humanitarian duty. There were no prizes to be had in the Balkans. Above all, the three wars shared a reassuring feature. They were prosecuted with the consent of many nations, large and small, and sanctioned either by the UN or by NATO. America was Gulliver sans ropes, but acted most of the time as if still bound by them—even while dispatching half a million troops to the Middle East during the First Iraq War.

The third reason for the delay was systemic—the very disparity of power that balancing is supposed to set right. How to thwart a behemoth that can deter and defeat them all, whether they come singly or in combination?* Every would-be hegemon in the modern world—from Charles V to Louis XIV, from Napoleon to Hitler—was eventually laid low or exhausted by superior military coalitions. Yet alliance and war, the two sharpest arrows in the quiver of balance-of-power politics, are not an option against the twenty-first-

*This theme will be explored in greater depth in chapter 6.

century No. 1. What kind of coalition could triumph over the United States, and what would victory look like after a thermonuclear exchange? How to defeat and drive into surrender a nation that spends almost as much on defense as the rest of the world combined?

Without a practicable military option, balancing against the überpower cannot really resort to the *ultima ratio*, but there is much more to containing and constraining than brandishing the sword. Ganging up and going to war are but the extreme end of a broad spectrum.[45] On a scale ranging from indirect and implicit to direct and explicit, the mildest variant is *conceptual balancing*—how the lagging powers talk about the world as it should be. This was a discourse favored by Russia, China, France, and Germany, and it was suffused with locutions such as "effective multilateralism" and "multipolarity"—shibboleths implying the dilution and devaluation of American power.

Next on the scale comes *symbolic balancing*, such as the "strategic partnership" (called "friendship treaty" in earlier days) routinely celebrated by Moscow and Beijing and vaguely directed against you-know-whom—a show of opposition with little substance. A somewhat harsher version is *institutional balancing*—the attempt to defang American power in international bodies, where it is "one nation, one vote," or, even better, "one nation, one veto," as in the UN Security Council. Here China, Britain, France, and Russia can sink whatever the United States floats. Closely related is *balancing by denial*, as practiced by those who withheld their votes for a war resolution or refused to commit troops to America's assault on Saddam. Closest to the "explicit/direct" end of the scale is *organized balancing*—the diplomatic equivalent of a genuine alliance. Set up by France and Germany in the run-up to Iraq II, the goal was to recruit a worldwide coalition that would bar America's road to war.

The last gambit was the harshest of them all, moving from rhetoric to revolt in what was arguably yet another "reversal of alliances" in modern times. Old allies of the United States were suddenly linking hands with old adversaries like Russia and China. While this was not exactly an act of kindness—France and Germany could have sat out the war without assembling a diplomatic *fronde* against the United States—it is important to recall what triggered it all. There is no better, though unwitting, reminder than the one provided by Charles Krauthammer, the most articulate spokesman of the neoconservative faith, which enjoyed a longish ascendancy in the inner sanctum of American power:

> In place of realism or liberal internationalism, the last four-and-a-half years have seen an unashamed assertion and deployment of American power, a resort to unilateralism when necessary, and a willingness to preempt threats before they emerge. Most importantly, the second Bush administration has explicitly declared the spread of freedom to be the central principle of American policy. . . . [T]he President offered its most succinct formulation: "The defense of freedom requires the advance of freedom."[46]

This mind-set marked the passage from a placid to a charging bull, from a conservative to a revolutionary power—a mutation that does not reassure the weaker denizens of the barnyard. Their motto is: let him be strong as long as he is in harness, be it self-chosen or imposed. Frightened by Terror International and freed from its Soviet yoke, the United States was going to remake the world, and no matter how lofty the purpose, the smaller nations were not amused, because raging bulls threaten the tranquillity—or at least the familiarity—of the status quo. Nor do they relish a world where raw strength suddenly matters most and so devalues their civilian assets like trade and aid, which fetch a much nicer return in a peaceable setting. Worse, if the strong prevail, they will be stronger still, hence more tempted to throw their weight around tomorrow. War dramatizes the hierarchy of the international system while Nos. 2, 3,

4, and all the rest crave equality. Unable to dethrone No. 1, the world was at least going to defy and discipline it, and so the reaction formation of the state system ran the whole gamut short of forging a military counterweight: from balancing by discourse to hardball diplomacy. A decade into unipolarity, the überpower began to feel the slings and arrows of misfortune that have always been the price of primacy.

Balancing by Locution. "Any community with only one dominant power is always a dangerous one, and provokes reactions," lectured the French president Jacques Chirac whenever given a chance. "That's why I favor a multipolar world, in which Europe obviously has its place. . . . And anyway; the world will not be unipolar." Presaging France's strenuous tackling during America's end run into the Second Iraq War, he wrote, "I am totally against unilateralism in the modern world. . . . If a military action is to be undertaken, it must be the responsibility of the international community, via a decision of the Security Council."[47] The message, *tout court*, was: the strong must submit to the veto of the weak.

His German "axis" partner, Chancellor Gerhard Schröder, warned darkly, "Though America is the sole superpower in this world, the administration does know that it needs friends and allies. Nobody can act on his own."[48] Decoded, the message read, "Don't rush into war, because we will abandon and even defy you." One year later, in the midst of the Second Iraq War, Schröder was ready to call a spade a spade. "Our conception of world order is not a unipolar but a multipolar one. This means that the settlement of conflicts must respect state sovereignty and international law, and it must proceed under the aegis of the United Nations. And that's it."[49] Neither Germany nor the United States had respected "state sovereignty," when NATO bombed Serbia in 1999 to chasten or topple Slobodan Milosevic, nor did that intervention receive the blessing of the UN. But Germany had a say in NATO, and no longer in Washington, and that was precisely the point of their demarches: the one and only strong must bend to the will of the many weak, lest its inordinate power become even more so. Schröder's foreign minister, Joseph Fischer, couched the same message in more intricate language. Only the UN "disposes of the asset of global legitimacy."[50] After the Second Iraq War, he invoked this principle: "The United States can live up to its leadership responsibilities only by developing an effective multilateralism."[51] Bind yourself or be bound, this obiter dictum read in translation.

His French colleague Dominique de Villepin, who would become prime minister in 2005, obliquely threatened a worldwide coalition against the United States: if "a country [relies] solely on its own power," it "will draw together all the forces of opposition, frustration and resentment."[52] Indeed, the United States was out of step with the rest of the world, a retrograde among the reformed: "International legitimacy is central. We can see today that America's military agenda is not in synch with the calendar of the international community."[53] France, de Villepin meant to imply, was the guardian of the global consensus—and the United States was the sole remaining rogue power: Our "conception of world order is being shared by a very large part of the international community. . . . The temptation to resort to force in a unipolar world cannot produce stability. No nation must arrogate unto itself the right to solve all conflicts on its own."[54] These were the tutorials in proper conduct offered by France and others to chasten the restless Behemoth.

Balancing by Institution. In a world shorn of the ultimate—that is, military—response to the United States, international regimes occupy the middle ground between balancing by word and balancing by deed. The purpose is to deny the overlord the fruits of his excessive power, hence to limit his freedom to use it by swaddling him in governance by committee. It is the many against the one, a regime of rules against the reign of No.1. Institutional balancing against the United States had already begun while Bill Clinton was still in charge. In the late 1990s, Washington found itself regularly alone and on the other side of such issues as the Antiballistic Missile Treaty, the Comprehensive Nuclear Test Ban Treaty, the Land Mine Convention, the Kyoto Climate Protocol, or the International Criminal Court.

Up front, all these duels were about principle; *au fond*, about power. Take Europe's, Russia's, and China's hostility to America's national missile defense, which would unhinge a thirty-year-old-regime under which the United States and the Soviet Union had forgone the deployment of a shield against rocket attacks. Their message to the United States was the power of tradition, a classic status quo argument: longevity is legitimacy, and so you must respect time-honored arms control institutions. Yet the real purpose, perfectly logical from the perspective of the less advanced, was to suppress a quantum leap in what was already a surfeit of American power.

Assume a functioning missile shield in the sky. Such an umbrella threatens three grim consequences for those who are not so blessed. First, it would devalue their missile forces; they could have them, but not use them, because their nuclear weapons would not get through. Second, they could engage in an arms race against the United States, piling up offensive weapons that might overwhelm the defense—not a winning strategy when the United States is good for close to one-half of the world's total military outlays. Third, and worse, a reliable defense would add to America's *offensive* options. If the United States could really protect itself against intercontinental missiles, it need not fear retribution when hitting out at the malfeasant du jour. It could fend off a Chinese attack on Taiwan or intervene against any "rogue state" with little risk to itself. Shields, in short, make it easier to unsheathe the sword. Yet usable, as opposed to merely deterrent, power does not make the rest of the world feel any safer. Ignoring all protests, George W. Bush served notice on Russia in the final days of 2001 that he was abrogating the ABM Treaty.[55]

Take the Land Mine Convention or the Comprehensive Nuclear Test Ban Treaty, to which the United States refused to adhere despite wide international disapproval. The moral argument was beyond challenge. Land mines kill the innocents long after the armies that flung them across the battlefield have departed, and low-yield nuclear weapons, refined through underground testing, gnaw away at the nuclear taboo. Yet moral revulsion dovetailed smoothly with hardheaded interest, and so the gainsayers could not have ignored the balance-of-power side of the coin. Antipersonnel mines deliver a shield for power projection abroad, and the better the United States can protect its forces, the less hesitant it might be to send them into action.* A less than complete test ban would also expand America's military opportunities by allowing for the development of smaller nuclear weapons like subkiloton "bunker busters." Eroding the firewall between conventional war and nuclear war, such devices might increase the temptation to use them. That, too, irked those who worried about unbridled American power so recently liberated from the cruel discipline of bipolarity. Naturally, Europe et al. insisted on adherence to the Comprehensive Test Ban Treaty, while the United States balked at accepting new chains.

Take America's refusal to submit to climate conventions. Though the Europeans framed the issue in terms of global good citizenship, the underlying contest was over American power. Would the giant defer to the many or defy them? Unless it accepted limits on its carbon dioxide output, the world's largest consumer of fossil energy would continue to take liberally from the global commons and

*The negotiations foundered on the U.S. insistence on keeping its land mines along the thirty-eighth parallel between the two Koreas in order to protect its troops against a North Korean invasion.

improve its economic position vis-à-vis Europe. (At that point in the story, China, polluter extraordinaire, had not yet swept into the international energy market, and so it was exempted from carbon dioxide limits.) Once more, the politics of goodness went hand in glove with the politics of balance, for instance during the negotiations on the implementation of the Kyoto Climate Protocol at The Hague in November 2000. When the talks ended in a storm of bitter recrimination against the United States, the *Economist* noted, "Some European ministers made it clear that they wanted Americans to feel some economic pain more than they wanted a workable agreement."[56]

And so with the International Criminal Court (ICC). In the end, even before George W. Bush dismissed the ICC with a peremptory wave of the hand, the Clinton team correctly understood the unspoken balancing strategy enshrined in the ICC, dumping the treaty into the lap of the incoming administration. For both America and Europe, the underlying issue was U.S. power. Having shed its old Cold War chains, the überpower was not going to bear new ones. It was not in the giant's interest to have an international court scrutinize its interventions by way of prosecuting members of its military ex post facto. But this was precisely the tacit interest of Europe and the rest of the world. Though the ICC was to go after the likes of Slobodan Milosevic and Saddam Hussein, it might also establish a handy precedent against Uncle Sam, who had been known to take the law into his own hands. Granted the right of review, the court might deter and thus constrain America's forays abroad.

What is the common moral of this tale of global regimes? Not to put too fine a point on it, hegemonists hate international institutions they do not control, and they share their sovereignty with lesser players only as long as these do not question its precedence. These nations treasure international institutions precisely because they strengthen the many against the one—just as the Lilliputians liked their ropes on Gulliver once he went off on his own. Naturally, the United States honored the UN all the way into the 1960s, as long as multilateralist virtue was rewarded by guaranteed majorities in America's favor. Naturally, Washington turned against the UN in the 1970s when the General Assembly began to churn out anti-American votes in the manner of an assembly line. The United States happily deferred to the UN over Iraq I and blithely circumvented it over Iraq II. The difference was a yes to war in the first case, and an impending no in the second. In a world where the many cannot fell the Behemoth, they must try to tame him. And so, international regimes have become the functional equivalent of traditional hard-core balancing by alliance and arms.

Balancing by Coalition. The contest turned from jujitsu to tackling in summer of 2002—once the Bush administration began to prepare the world for a second round against Saddam Hussein. The first clarion call was Gerhard Schröder's indictment of American adventurism. "Playing with war and military intervention," he warned, "will have to be done without us. . . . We are not available for adventures."[57] It was followed by a categorical refusal to join the American effort—not even under a UN mandate. In January 2003, the chancellor went one worse, threatening to vote against a war resolution in the Security Council.[58] In February, France and Germany, with Belgium in tow, practiced the pure politics of denial by vetoing an American request to NATO to begin planning for the defense of Turkey in case of war against Iraq.

Was it all domestic politics? To argue that Schröder tapped into German pacifism and anti-Americanism during the election year of 2002 in order to save his sinking campaign—the gambit worked by a few thousand votes—misses the deeper point. No German chancellor, right or left, would have dared play politics with the American connection while Soviet armies were poised to lunge through the Fulda Gap. Better to lose the elections than to lose the Americans.[59] That Schröder chose to save himself was the most vivid proof of bipolarity lost and dependence shed. He did so again during the electoral campaign of 2005. Trailing the Christian Democrats by a dozen points, he played the pacifist, anti-Bush card by telling the president (who had refused to rule out force against Iran's nuclear program), "Take the military options off the table. . . . [U]nder my leadership, the government would not participate [in a military action]."[60]

The point goes deeper still. The demise of bipolarity abroad had translated immediately into its collapse at home. For fifty years, there was always an "American party" in the system—the Christian Democratic and Liberal right—and a victorious one, to boot. This was also true for Italy's Democrazia Cristiana as well as for the rest of Western Europe's center-right parties, which would never refuse a call from Washington. This time, in the run-up to the Second Iraq War, Germany's Christian Democrats did not rush to the defense of the United States; unlike their Cold War chancellors from Konrad Adenauer (1949–63) through Helmut Kohl (1982–98), they squirmed and waffled. And so again in 2005, when the conservatives carefully maintained their distance from the United States. It may be true that all politics is local, but it helps to have a permissive international setting on your side when playing a strictly local game.

"It's the system, stupid," Bill Clinton might have said. Jacques Chirac did not face an election in 2002, yet he, too, took to balancing against *la hyper-puissance* with a vengeance. During the Cuban Missile Crisis of 1962, his predecessor Charles de Gaulle had assured John F. Kennedy of his unflinching support against *l'empire totalitaire.* That was history; now the strategic threat was gone, and the United States was on a roll. Liberated, just like the United States, from Cold War discipline, France and Germany coalesced into an anti-American bloc. France and Germany are "entirely coordinated and in permanent contact every day," affirmed Chirac.[61] Schröder named "France, Russia, China, and many other states" that opposed the war, emphasizing that the "decision monopoly on the use of force must remain with the Security Council."[62]

Given a defrocked superpower in Moscow, they sought to extend their twosome to Russia in a latter-day Triple Entente*—with Germany as architect and the United States as target. On the eve of the war, the Franco-German duo had recruited Moscow into their game. "We will not let a [U.S.-proposed] resolution pass that would authorize the use of force," the trio proclaimed. In the same declaration, France and Russia threatened use of their veto: "As permanent members of the Security Council," they would "assume all their responsibilities on this point."[63] But this was not enough. With the United States pressuring the council for precisely such a resolution, Paris and Berlin went out of their way to harness a *global* coalition of refuseniks. Their emissaries fanned out to work on the council's ten rotating members to forestall a majority for the United States, rendering a veto by any of the permanent members unnecessary. The French and the Germans cajoled, threatened, and bribed, and in the end the United States conceded the game by going to war without the blessing of the world's would-be government.

Chirac and Schröder could savor a triumph of sorts; having organized an "antihegemonic" alliance, with Russia and China as subsidiary members, they had won on the principle that "military action could be decided only by the Security Council."[64] But in a class of its own, the United States did have the last word. And why not, given that America's might was no longer stalemated by the sole counterweight that mattered, the Soviet Union? As a popular English ditty of the late nineteenth century put it, "We've got the ships / We've got the men / And got the money too."[65] The world richest and strongest nation, the United States had it all.

So what was the rest of the world going to do to Mr. Big?

Balancing by Terror. The most economical and efficient attack came from totally unexpected quarters. Call it "sub-rosa" or "illicit"

*This was the pre–World War I alliance against Germany, joining Britain, France, and Russia.

balancing through "asymmetric warfare," a.k.a. "international terrorism." The actors were—and are—not states, as in the classic game, but private entities ranging from the freelance bombardier Osama bin Laden, via a global franchise by the name of al-Qaeda, to the assorted jihadis who launched "Iraq War II—The Sequel" against the United States in November of 2003. The opening shot was the assassination attempt on Paul Wolfowitz, the deputy secretary of defense, during his trip to Baghdad. It has been escalation ever since. What is the objective?

The ends of jihadism are total, ranging from the expulsion of the "crusaders" (America and Israel) from the realm of Islam to the rout of a decadent and unbelieving West. The means are heinous under any moral code—the mass murder of civilians. In coldly strategic terms, however, Terror International (TI) has discovered the most efficient method to hurt, perhaps even demoralize, the überpower. Balancing by terror was born on April 18, 1983, when an Arab suicide bomber drove a truck full of explosives into the U.S. embassy in Beirut, leaving seventeen Americans dead. Two years after the "end of major hostilities" in Iraq, Terror International—al-Qaeda, foreign jihadis, and Sunni locals—had killed fifteen hundred Americans in Iraq, more than three times the number of dead suffered in all of America's Middle Eastern wars since 9/11.

The enemy is not a state but a loose network, whose address is unknown. By definition, suicide bombers cannot be deterred, and a reliable defense is impossible on a battlefield where a minimally vulnerable aggressor meets with a maximally vulnerable victim. TI has found and exploited the weakest point in Western society: a flow economy that demands around-the-clock mobility and concentrates large numbers of "soft targets" in confined spaces like office towers, airports, buses, trains, and subways. While the weapons of terrorism are substrategic—a truck or just a backpack filled with explosives—the consequences are more than just tactical.

Merely take, for example, the costs of securing airports and of waiting in line for passenger inspection. Worldwide, there are about two billion passengers per year. Assume that each arrives at the airport one hour early to make it through security, and assign opportunity costs of $10 per hour. That adds up to a global tax of $20 billion per year. Consider a budget of $6 billion for the U.S. Transport Security Administration (TSA). Add the wages of tens of thousands of security personnel hired around the world. Then put a price on the delays suffered by the hauling and shipping industries, which must submit their cargoes to inspection. Tally the cost of successive investments in security technology for surveillance and eavesdropping after each fresh attack in a major Western city. A global terrorism levy of $100 billion per annum is not an unreasonable estimate. And how do we assess the invisible costs of liberties curtailed and social trust denied?

Direct costs for the United States in 2005 were $81.9 billion in supplemental appropriations for the war on terror on top of $25 billion already allocated for fiscal year 2005.[66] Terror International's war against the United States is not only total in its ends and global in its scope but also extremely cost-effective in its means—considering that a few thousand jihadis could tie down over a hundred thousand American troops in Iraq while imposing a terrible tax on the United States and the West as a whole. An old rule of counterinsurgency warfare warns: the government loses as long as it does not win; the insurgents win as long as they don't lose. The überpower cannot lose this war in a strategic sense, for even a primitive nuclear device—a "dirty bomb"—delivered onto its soil will not force the United States into surrender in the way Nazi Germany and Japan were so compelled in 1945.

Yet Terror International has found a dreadfully effective way to sap the strength of Gulliver Unbound. Its strategy of asymmetric warfare is more "productive" than were the frustrated attempts of

France, Germany, Russia, et al. TI will compel the United States either to leave Iraq and then Afghanistan or to station troops (and suffer casualties) sine die—not to speak of the monetary toll, which runs to triple-digit billions per year. The greatest irony of the twenty-first century is the vulnerability of the mightiest power on earth to the most minuscule of foes. Terror International's army numbers but thousands; its weapons are trucks and TNT, assault rifles, and IEDs.* And it feeds on the "cultural balancing," also known as anti-Americanism, analyzed in the two following chapters.

*Improvised explosive devices.

3

The Rise of Anti-Americanism

Anti-Americanism Redivivus

When General Motors announced plans to cut twelve thousand jobs in Germany, *Stern* magazine, with a circulation of one million and a readership four times larger, appeared with a cover replete with some classic symbols of anti-Americanism. It featured a huge cowboy boot with "GM" branded on the sole. The boot, stitched with red, white, and blue colors on its side, was poised to crush hundreds of little people arrayed underneath in the shape of the emblem of Opel, GM's subsidiary in Germany. The cover title read "Ways of the Wild West."[1]

Even with its semiotic wave to George W. Bush and the favorite footwear of Texas, this image contained a whole slew of anti-American motifs as old as the Republic itself. On the most general level, the cover depicted the United States as a profound threat, recalling the oft-quoted diatribe of the French novelist Henry de Montherlant (1896–1972): "I accuse the United States of being in a permanent state of crime against mankind."[2] Another familiar theme is the depiction of the United States as an overwhelming, arrogant power, a victimizer of all these small, and soon to be jobless, people. A third one evokes the ruthless intrusion of the "Other," the outsider, who is about to trample a hallowed way of the good life. A fourth motif is crudeness or violence, as symbolized by the cowboy boot with its fierce-looking spurs; it evokes the quintessential American, who is boorish, brutal, and uncultured. Or to recall a famous quip about America by Talleyrand, "thirty-two religions and only one dish to eat." The whole ensemble sets forth one of the oldest indictments of America: Americans will do anything for a buck; profit is their God, to whom they will sacrifice decency and social justice. As early as 1794, a French visitor to the United States summed up the views of his compatriots as follows: the Americans are "vain, greedy, grasping, and engaged in cheating in all of their business dealings."[3]

If these are the symbols, what are the real facts? At the end of 2004, earnings revealed that GM was slightly ahead in the Americas and the Middle East while turning a $100 million profit in Asia. Its losses in Europe, though, had vaulted from $152 million to $236 million. In the preceding three years, GM had bled $3 billion there. Its straits in Germany, the mainstay of GM production in Europe, were particularly dire. The president of GM Europe pointed out, "If Opel used French workers instead of Germans, and left other costs the same, it would save 500 to 700 million euros a year in wage costs."[4] So expenditures had to be cut. In other words, the objective economics of the planned layoffs did not quite measure up to the conspiracy suggested by the stomping Texas boot.

Here was an archetype of the long-running story of anti-Americanism. The circumstances were brand-new, but the "reaction-formation" was as old as Heinrich Heine's denunciation of the United States in the early nineteenth century. Though this icon of German literature was as liberal and democratic as any intellectual of his age, he fumed, "Worldly gain is the true religion [of the Americans], and money is their Mammon, their one and only almighty God."[5] The not-so-hidden hand of the market was transmuted into moral degeneracy revolving around inbred greed and false gods. Misery, the image insinuated, was not homemade (Germany's wages are among the highest in the world, and its work rules among the most rigid), but a conspiracy by the "Other," who was previously known as scapegoat.

There was no one to blame but the mighty, ruthless stranger. Thus was complexity reduced to demonology, which is a defining feature of anti-Americanism, anti-Semitism, or, indeed, any "anti-ism."

Why is this anti-Americanism, as distinct from "anti-Bushism" or anger against a real object like General Motors? Pure and up-front anti-Americanism today is rare. Montherlant's diatribe against America as such is anti-American, and so was the utterance of the Canadian parliamentarian Carolyn Parrish, when she burst out, "Damn Americans, I hate the bastards."[6] In 1999, two years before the Bush administration took office, the Greek composer Mikis Theodorakis offered another such glimpse: "I hate Americans and everything American."[7] Another example is Peter Zadek, the dean of Germany's stage directors, when he allowed a flash of honesty to illuminate his loathing. "I was never there [but] America deeply disgusts me." And no, he did not mind being called "anti-American," he told a German news magazine. In fact, it was "cowardly that so many today distinguish between the American people and the current American administration, [which] was more or less democratically elected. . . . Hence, you can be against the Americans, just as most of the world was against the Germans in the Second World War. In this sense, I am anti-American."[8] Nonetheless, Germany's most famous theater director was not completely candid. The most monstrous charge was transported by this not-so-subliminal syllogism: Hitler was Germany, Bush is America, and so the Americans of today are like the Nazis of yesterday. "Nazi" is the universal symbol of unprecedented evil; to apply such comparison to contemporary America is to inflict maximal moral damage on it.

Anti-Americanism Defined

What is anti-Americanism?

Here are some misleading answers culled from a *Newsweek* poll:

"A plurality or majority in five of the six countries polled agreed that a strong American military presence around the world increases the chance of war. The fear of American military power was greatest in Mexico. . . ." Only one country, Brazil, "approved—and by a bare 31 to 29 percent margin—of U.S. government policy. . . . By large margins [respondents] agreed that American influence on the world is growing." There was "heighten[ed] skepticism about American power and intentions." And there was too much cultural influence. "By majorities ranging from 55 percent (in Japan) to 83 percent (in Mexico), those polled for *Newsweek* found a 'great deal' of American influence on television, movies and pop music in their countries, exceeding the perceived American impact [on] science and even business."[9]

According to the director of the Pew Research Center, these *Newsweek* numbers painted a "tarnished global image" of America.[10] Yet these data were collected by *Newsweek* not during the reign of Bush II but in 1983! So the dislike of America is hardly new. It precedes George W. Bush; it is an enduring fixture of the global consciousness. But it is "getting worse," the man from Pew wrote on the cusp of 2004. How so? The answer runs as follows (all emphases added):

> In 2002, in a survey of 38,000 people in 44 countries, the Pew Research Center found that the U.S. global image had slipped. But when we went back this spring [2003] after the war in Iraq . . . it was clear that *favorable opinions* of the U.S. had plummeted . . . [and] how *anti-Americanism* has spread. It is not just limited to Western Europe or the Muslim world. In Brazil, 52% expressed a favorable opinion of the U.S. in 2002; this year, that number dropped to 34%. And in Russia, there has been a 25-point decline in positive opinions of the U.S. over the past year. . . .
>
> To pinpoint the *causes of anti-Americanism*, we asked people . . . the reasons for their hostility. Is it President Bush or Amer-

> ica generally? *Not surprisingly, solid majorities in most countries blamed the president, not America.* Yet these results do not tell the whole story. Undoubtedly, Bush has become the lightning rod for anti-American feelings, but the problem is bigger than Bush. *American policies and power* fuel resentment for the U.S. throughout the world. The administration brought those resentments to the surface and intensified *unhappiness with the U.S.*
>
> Global publics believe the *United States does too little to solve world problems and backs policies that increase the yawning global gap between rich and poor.* Again, these sentiments were evident well before the war in Iraq.
>
> Similarly, opposition to strong American support for Israel long predates the Bush administration. . . .
>
> But *resentment of American power*, as much as *its policies or leadership*, also drives anti-American sentiments.[11]

Is this anti-Americanism? The Pew Research Center has launched a thousand polls on the world's views of the United States. The strength of these surveys is that they gauge variation (and constancy) over time. The problem with them is that they use the term "anti-Americanism" very loosely and hence may not measure what they purport to unearth. To dislike an American president or to oppose American policies is *not* anti-American. Nor is the complaint that "the United States does too little to solve world problems." Nor does one have to be anti-American to "resent American power," for that feeling has a solid rational core. America's power is indeed "unrivaled." In 2005, Pew plumbed another "source of resentment": only about one-fifth of the respondents in France, Canada, Holland, Spain, and Russia believed that the United States "pays . . . attention to the interests of other nations."[12] This may even be true, but it is not anti-Americanism.

What Pew has measured is not anti-Americanism but hostility to

American policies, which ought to be distinguished from the real thing. Another much quoted report, which raises similar problems, is *Worldviews 2002,* sponsored by the German Marshall Fund of the United States and the Chicago Council on Foreign Relations. It measures European reactions to six foreign policies of the Bush administration.[13] The verdict "poor" is distributed as follows among the six items:

International terrorism:	17%
Global warming:	50%
Arab-Israeli conflict	33%
War in Afghanistan	23%
Situation in Iraq	32%
Relations with Europe	9%

Apart from the fact that the Pew Center and the German Marshall Fund have different agendas—the former being more critical of the U.S. government and the latter more supportive of good Euro-American relations—these figures, too, fail to penetrate to the core of anti-Americanism. Like the Pew surveys, they plumb opposition to particular U.S. policies and personalities, and the feelings are mixed. The German Marshall Fund numbers reach the highest hostility level, with 50 percent "poor," on "global warming," which stands for the U.S. refusal to join the Kyoto Climate Protocol. Sizable European pluralities dislike American policy on the Middle East and on Iraq, with only one-fifth handing out a grade of "excellent or good." More revealing are these data: a clear majority believes that U.S. policy is at least partly to blame for 9/11. And only 14 percent believe that the United States "should remain the only superpower."

A more recent poll by the German Marshall Fund (2005) underscores this point by measuring the difference between anti-Bushism and a more general aversion to America as such. The difference is 13 percent, so to speak. Some 72 percent of Europeans dislike Bush's foreign policies, while 59 percent dislike the very idea of American leadership, that is, American power.[14] Figures such as these attach themselves not to policies or persons, but to concepts such as blame, conspiracy, and omnipotence, which come closer to the mark, as will be argued below.

Policy Anti-Americanism versus the Real Thing

Basically, these frequently invoked polls, as well as the Pew follow-up of 2005,[15] measure hostility to American policies, not anti-Americanism. How does one distinguish "policy anti-Americanism" from the real thing? What is the difference between anti-ism and criticism, between the rabid and the reasonable? There are two quick tests. One is *language*; the other is *selectivity*. As to language, take the familiar argument that the Bush administration defied international law in the 2003 war against Iraq, followed by similar indictments in 2004 and 2005, which targeted detention practices in Guantánamo (the American base in Cuba) and prisoner abuse in Abu Ghraib (Iraq). Accusations of illegality may be true or false; they are not anti-American. But to attribute American behavior to inbred imperialism ("look what they did to the Indians"), to American capitalism ("blood for oil"), or to religious bigotry ("they claim divine guidance") transcends policy criticism. Classics in the repertoire of anti-Americanism, such statements equate the *pars* with the *toto*, condemning the country and the culture. They denounce not the policy but the polity. As such, they deliver good prima facie evidence for what more generally might be called anti-ism.

The second test plumbs for selectivity. We may suspect an unconscious or hidden agenda when censure singles out the United States but ignores, say, Islamic terrorism, Russia's war in Chechnya, China's deadly oppression of Tibet, the genocide of non-Arabs in Sudan (and Arabs, as well), or state-organized terror against white farmers in Zimbabwe. To take note of selectivity is not to claim that one wrong detracts from another, but it does highlight a double standard that smells of anti-ism. Selective condemnation—pointing reflexively to the same culprit—is a convenient way to hide bigotry from oneself and from others.

Another flag is the selective demonization of American leaders, as happened during the worldwide demonstrations against George W. Bush in 2002 and again in 2003. The telling aspect was the absence of Saddam Hussein from these manifestations of disgust, let alone of lesser targets like Vladimir Putin (for oppressing Chechnya) or Ayatollah Khamenei (for suppressing dissent in Iran) or Yasir Arafat (for manipulating terror against Israeli civilians). It was George W. Bush who was compared to Hitler and condemned for setting the world aflame. A bit farther down the line, it was Israeli prime minister Ariel Sharon, who stood accused of similar crimes against humanity.

Yet another flag is selective representation. In the European media as well as on the public stage, prizes and publicity go overwhelmingly to Americans who serve as witnesses against their own government and nation. The author Gore Vidal and the linguist Noam Chomsky have been lead players in this role; more recently the filmmaker Michael Moore and the literary critic Susan Sontag have stepped forward (Sontag received the prestigious Peace Prize of the German Publishers' Association in 2003 and died in 2004). Their critique may range from the moderate to the malicious, but their main function is to render legitimate what the audience (rightly) fears is not, given the taboo encasing all forms of explicit anti-ism. The defense mechanism is simple enough: "After all, *they* are saying this, too; so how can we be accused of anti-Americanism?" A similar phenomenon attaches itself to Israel, where "post-" or anti-Zionist spokesmen are given top billing in the European media.

Language and selectivity serve as better gauges of the real thing, as opposed to "policy anti-Americanism," because in polite Western society it is usually infra dig to say, "Yes, I hate the Americans." But it is a thousand times more likely to hear, "I hate this American president." At this juncture, Professor Freud would begin to muse about "displacement," about the human habit of clobbering one object or person, but actually targeting another that is protected by fearsome power, be it a taboo or real clout. Lashing out at specific American policies and leaders doesn't risk the raised eyebrows that demonizing the country as such would do. In a postracist age, collectives usually are protected; individuals are not.

Freud might also invoke another standby of his craft: the patient who is in denial. "Thou shalt not be bigoted" is the first commandment of the postmodern consciousness, and though that injunction is more often honored vis-à-vis formerly colonialized peoples than Westerners, the injunction against hostile stereotyping affords some shelter to America as such, too. The denial mechanism offers a clue why opinion surveys, though they deliver much harder evidence than voyages through the unconscious, tell only part of the story. A classic Jewish joke of post-Holocaust vintage makes the point quite nicely. It is about a Jew, suitcase in hand, accosting various passengers in Vienna's central train station: "Excuse me, are you anti-Semitic?" One after the other fumes, "How dare you! Of course, I am not!" Finally, one fires back, "Yes, I am. I can't stand the Jews!" Exclaims the Jewish traveler, "At last, an honest man! Would you please watch my suitcase for a few minutes?"

Denial, displacement, and taboo are not amenable to survey research, let alone to covariance or factor analysis. But such concepts at least get a suggestive grip on anti-Americanism (and the related phenomenon of anti-Semitism), where social-scientific tools slip because manifest realities do not necessarily reveal hidden ones. They may be hidden even to a carrier of anti-ism, who claims, "I just hate Bush; I love America, and some of my best friends are Americans." How, then, to define the distinctive features of anti-ism?

Anti-ism consists—at all times and in all places—of five elements.[16] One is hostile *stereotypization*, a set of general statements attributing certain negative qualities to the target group. Closely related is *denigration*, the ascription of moral inferiority all the way to an irreducibly evil nature; hence the application of the Nazi comparison to America (and Israel). *Demonization* is the third step, moving from what the target group *is* to what it *does* or *intends* to do. The key theme is conspiracy. If the Jews (or African Americans, in the racist imagination) wanted to soil racial purity, America wants to trade "blood for oil," impose winner-take-all capitalism everywhere, subvert sacred traditions, or destroy social justice. Above all, the United States seeks domination over the rest of the world (which is also the theme of the anti-Jewish *Protocols of the Elders of Zion*, recently revived throughout the Arab world, as well as in Japan, among other countries).

A fourth critical feature is *obsession*[17]—the idée fixe that America (or *x*) is omnipresent and omnicausal, hence the invisible force that explains all misery, whether it is Third World poverty, Islamist terror, or even the attack on the World Trade Center in 2001.[18] As in all cases of obsession, the belief is both compulsive and consuming; that is, it springs to mind reflexively and expands relentlessly to leave no room for alternative explanations, let alone falsification. (This is why all debates on anti-ism degenerate into an endless ballet across shifting grounds.) The final step is *elimination*, be it by exclusion or by extrusion. This is where anti-ism assumes a quasi-religious quality, as in the "Great Satan" motif of the Iranian regime. Satan is not only the symbol of supreme evil; he must also be exorcized. Get rid of those who torment us, and salvation will be ours. Or as al-Qaeda's Ayman al-Zawahiri has put it, the task is "*purifying* our country from the aggressors and resisting anyone who attacks us, violates our holy places, or steals our resources."[19]

Anti-Americanism, to belabor the point once more, is not criticism of American policies, not even dislike of particular American leaders or features of American life, such as gas-guzzling SUVs or five hundred TV channels. It is the obsessive stereotypization, denigration, and demonization of the country and the culture. The most vicious, sustained, and direct expressions of this state of mind are found in the Arab and Islamic world.

Anti-Americanism in the Islamic World

Here is a particularly vivid example by the Saudi princess Reem al-Faisal, a granddaughter of the late King Faisal.

> The Americans insist that most criticism directed toward their policies stems from a deep-seated anti-Americanism which the entire world has been suffering from since the founding of the U.S. In fact, I find that the world has been more than forgiving toward the Americans from the very beginning.
>
> If you take a quick look at American history, you will realize instantly that the atrocities committed by the Americans . . . might be one of the worst in human history, and that's saying much—one, because humanity has reached levels of evil that no other creature on earth can compete with, and two, because the very short history of the American nation makes its crimes even more shocking when compared with other, more ancient lands.
>
> The Americans are responsible for one of the most thorough and extreme genocides in history, that of the Native

> Americans. . . . [A]nd the few of them who are left still suffer from discrimination to this day. . . .
>
> How dare America look the rest of the world in the face, when it refuses even to admit or ask forgiveness from just these people it has so wronged. . . .
>
> It is time for the American nation to acknowledge its crimes and apologize and ask forgiveness from the many people it has harmed. Beginning with the Native Americans, followed by the Africans and South Americans, right through to the Japanese, who have suffered such horror by being the only race to know the true meaning of weapons of mass destruction.
>
> The U.S. should leave Iraq after apologizing for over a million dead after an unlawful embargo and a colonial war which at best is a farce and at worst a crime.[20]

America, under this dispensation, is unregenerate evil—an unending conspiracy against the rest of the world. Whatever the country does today is not contingent but foreordained; it is the malign outgrowth of its national character. Next to Saudi Arabia, there is Egypt, also an American ally, which offers one of the richest troves of anti-Americanism. For example, a columnist of the opposition weekly *Al-Usbu*, depicted the United States as "founded by the deported and criminals of Europe on the blood and flesh of an entire people [Native Americans]." In the same issue, a colleague deploys a favorite Arab theme of America as Jew, invoking the image of "the American Shylock cut[ting] its knife into the flesh [of Egypt] to feed it to the wild wolves of its avaricious aspirations in the region."[21]

Cartoons, because they trade in images and not words, are one of the best conduits into the unconscious. A favorite image in three hundred cartoons surveyed is cannibalism. *Al-Watan* (Qatar, February 13, 2003) depicts Uncle Sam with a mouthful of shark's teeth. *Al-Dustur* (Jordan, October 16, 2002) shows George W. Bush boiling the globe in a huge cannibal's pot, a theme repeated in *Al-Ittihad* (UAE, January 25, 2003), where Uncle Sam, his mouth watering, roasts the world on a spit. *Al-Quds Al-Arabi* (London, February 20, 2001) displays a blood-spattered Uncle Sam, about to ingest an Arab speared on his fork—this long before 9/11 and the unleashing of American power in Afghanistan and Iraq. *Al-Ahrar* (Egypt, March 5, 2003) joins, as is frequently the case, the anti-American to the anti-Semitic motif by showing an American and a Jewish figure sticking their eating utensils into two bodies on their plates labeled "Iraq" and "Palestine."

Next to sheer evil, global conspiracy is the second theme. A favorite image is America as kraken, gripping the globe in its tentacles (e.g., *Al-Ahrar,* March 7, 2003). *Al-Hayat* (London, October 9, 2002) shows Bush riding a Trojan horse, a classic symbol of treachery, into Arab oil fields. Another oil field motif joins American capitalism to mass murder: against a background of oil derricks, George W. Bush is surrounded by piles of skulls, dressed in a Superman costume with a large dollar sign emblazoned on his chest (*Al-Watan,* March 21, 2003). America is rendered not as slayer of despots but as murderer in *Al-Ahram* (April 24, 2003), the semiofficial organ of the Egyptian government. Taking a cue from the toppling of the Saddam statue in Baghdad, the cartoonist draws a Saddam-like figure standing on an oil barrel; an execution hood in American colors covers his head while a hangman's rope around his neck is about to strangle him. While most cartoons employ white figures as objects of demonization, a few go after black targets like Colin Powell, the secretary of state from 2001 to 2005, and Condoleezza Rice, the national security adviser of the first George W. Bush administration and the secretary of state of the second. One example (*Okaz,* Saudi Arabia, August 19, 2002) shows Rice with the starkly negroid features of the racist imagination—a quashed, gorilla-like nose and enormous lips. To add to the overload of loathing, she wears Stars of David as ear clips.[22] At best, all of these themes are only remotely related to what American policy does; the message of these images is maximal denigration and demonization—indeed, pure hatred.

Anti-Americanism in Europe

Such gruesome tropes will not be found in the European discourse on the United States. But present are all the essential features of anti-Americanism: stereotypization, denigration, demonization, obsession, and elimination. On the level of stereotypization and denigration, three basic themes obey a single common denominator: Yahoo America vs. Superior Europe.

One: America Is Morally Deficient. It executes its own people, which Europe does not, and it likes to bomb others, which Europe does only when dragged along by the United States "On the Old Continent," notes a pillar of the French establishment, "we invoke the moral superiority conferred on Europeans by the abolition of capital punishment."[23] The Italian president Carlo Ciampi has stressed Europe's gaping moral distance from the United States by defining opposition to capital punishment as a "most eloquent signal affirming a European identity."[24]

America is the land of intolerant, fundamentalist religion, "with screaming TV evangelists calling homosexuals Satan's semen-drenched acolytes,"[25] while Europe is charting a path toward enlightened secularism. The point here is not to note the growing "faith gap" between the United States and Europe—indeed, the progressive "de-Christianization" of Europe, which is a stark (and, until recently, underanalyzed) fact.[26] The purpose of such denigrations is to assert Europe's moral superiority, as in the oft-heard comparison of Iran and the United States as the only two nations ruled by fundamentalist regimes. It is obscurantism versus enlightenment, blind faith versus rational politics. The fact that George W. Bush prays in the White House has been routinely interpreted as proof of insufferable self-righteousness or of a delusional personality, as if he were a latter-day Joan of Arc listening to voices in his head.[27]

Jean Baudrillard, the French opinionator who is also billed as philosopher, generalizes the point: "There is this dialogue between God and America." Even during the Cold War, "the Americans saw themselves as accomplices of God, even then, they were the Good Guys, and Evil was on the other side." Then his loathing overwhelms all logic. Though engaged in "this dialogue" with God, America is simultaneously a victim of autism, as manifested in the "self-pity" it exuded after 9/11. "There only is what is American," he continued, and it is "locked into its traumatism." There is no conception of the outside world, according to Baudrillard, only a "totalitarian consensus." It is God, autism, and totalitarianism—all in the space of a few paragraphs.[28]

The United States also is a nation that will not submit to the dictates of global goodness; hence it will not respect climate conventions, or ratify the International Criminal Court, the Comprehensive Nuclear Test Ban, or the Land Mine Convention. Internationally, it is "Dirty Harry" and "Globocop" rolled into one—an irresponsible and arrogant citizen of the global community. America, in short, is "the world's biggest rogue state."[29] Invariably, the bill of indictments reaches its climax with the Nazi-American comparison, which long preceded the wars in Afghanistan and Iraq.

Here is a report from a pro-Serbia demonstration in Vienna in the spring of 1999, four years before the Second Iraq War: "The posters grew increasingly threatening: 'USA = Nazi,' . . . '1939 = Hitler, 1999 = Bill Clinton, Jews = Then, Serbia = Now'. . . . Replicas of the United States Flag were all over the rally, many with a swastika covering the blue and white corner. . . . It was clear this was more than a political statement; it was a war against our country's mentality."[30] Or, as the German essayist and poet Hans Magnus Enzensberger recalls, "The turbulent crowd of '68 lost no time in denouncing their former object of desire. 'USA—SA—SS,' they shouted. 'Imperialism' was their rallying call, the CIA took the place of the Devil, and at the end of the day a few desperadoes on the left went so far as to throw bombs at the very US bases which had protected us from the Soviets."[31]

Question: **In this list of words, which ones fit the United States best?**

All Frenchmen	***Survey of French-Americain Foundation / TNS Sofres September 2002***		***June 2004***	
	%	Rank	%	Rank
- Power	73	1	65	1
- Inequality	47	3	42	2
- Prosperity	42	4	41	3
- Violence	53	2	40	4
- Imperialism	33	6	33	5
- Freedom	20	8	28	6
- Dynamism	31	7	27	7
- Racism	39	5	25	8
- Naïveté	10	9	19	9
- Youth	6	10	17	10
- Generosity	5	11	10	11
- No Opinion	2		0	

Percentages add up to more than 100 because multiple responses could be given.

How do these personal reports compare with the verdicts of public opinion surveys? In a French poll, below, the three most highly ranked responses in 2002 were "power," "violence," and "inequality"—concepts charged with strongly negative connotations. In 2004, "power" and "inequality" were still ranked in first and second place, while "violence," had dropped to third place, and "imperialism" had moved up one notch. "Good" moral qualities like "freedom" and "generosity" remained at the bottom of the field.[32]

Two: America Is Socially Retrograde. It is the land of "predatory capitalism" (*Raubtierkapitalismus*) in the words of the former German chancellor Helmut Schmidt, a country that denies critical social services, like welfare and health insurance, to those who need it most. Coming from behind in the German electoral campaign of 2002, Chancellor Schröder resorted (successfully, in the end) to carefully coded anti-Americanisms. In a campaign speech in Hanover, he damned America's ways by praising the superiority of the "German way" (*deutsche Weg*). "The days are now truly over when America and others were to serve as an example to us. The plundering of little people in the United States, who must now worry about their old-age pensions, while top managers carry home millions and billions after a company bankruptcy, that is not the German way we want for ourselves."[33] Nonetheless, Schröder's "Agenda 2010" provided for precisely the kind of welfare cuts mandated by Bill Clinton's 1996 "workfare" legislation, which would cause seven million people—one-half of all recipients—to leave the welfare rolls and start working.[34] Apart from the fact that U.S. executives do not make "billions," the point of this tale is the functionality of anti-Americanism in the domestic political contest. The chancellor denounced the United States while emulating it, setting up the country as a convenient scapegoat (and smoke screen) for the harsh policies enacted by him. Freud would clap his hands over such a vivid instance of projection.

When the British author A. N. Wilson unleashed his hatred of the Bush administration, he used language redolent with classic clichés about *America*: "They are the most merciless exponents of world capitalism, with the determination to have a McDonald's and a Starbucks . . . in every country on earth."[35] The standard lore continues along these lines: instead of bettering the lot of the poor and unskilled, the United States shunts millions of them, mainly dark-skinned minorities, off into prison. Europe, on the other hand, metes out rehabilitation, not retribution. America accepts—nay, admires—gross income inequalities, whereas Europe cherishes redistribution in the name of social justice. The United States lets its state school system rot, not to speak of the public infrastructure—a fact that was underscored in the European press after Hurricane Katrina, when many newspapers seemed giddy with glee at the American government's incompetence in responding after levees broke in New Orleans in August of 2005.

A French poll (2002) puts numbers on these projections. The United States scores well on only two counts. One is "developing new technologies," where three-quarters of the respondents believe "the U.S. functions better" than France. The second is "higher education," where one-half of the French sample thinks U.S. universities trump their own. On other items of social worth—the battle against crime, racial coexistence, integration of immigrants, unemployment—France is ranked superior to the United States by margins ranging from two-to-one to three-to-one.

The most interesting aspect of these polls is the projection mechanism they reveal. Ironically, where France does objectively worse, failure is projected onto the United States. For instance, 42 percent of Frenchmen think that their country does better in the "battle against unemployment" than the United States (while only 25 percent think the United States does so). The reality was, in fact, the reverse. While France at the time faced, and keeps facing, a 10 percent unemployment rate, the U.S. numbers were half that high. By a margin of 50 percent to 17 percent, Frenchmen believe that their nation is better at dealing with the "integration of immigrants." Looking at the realities of the *banlieues* and the crime rates of North African immigrants, one wonders about the 30 percent share of Asian students gracing the best American universities. Or about the lengthening roster of Hispanic, African American, and Asian names in the

Congress and in the state houses. Or about New York City's burgeoning African-American middle class, whose growth has brought about a large decline in New York's overall crime and murder rates.

Three: America Is Culturally Retrograde. With the exception of John F. Kennedy, America elects only mentally or morally deficient men to the presidency. Roosevelt ("Rosenfeld") was a Jew in the right-wing and Nazi imagination of the 1930s and 1940s. Truman, who built a towering edifice of international institutions like UN and NATO, was a haberdasher, and Eisenhower, who had commanded millions of men in World War II, was a dolt in uniform. Johnson was a Texan brute and Nixon a thug (even before the 1972 Watergate break-in); both were war criminals. Jimmy Carter, the nuclear engineer, was a "peanut farmer," and Reagan, who had cut his teeth in politics as president of the powerful Screen Actors' Guild and sharpened them as two-term governor of California, remained until his last day in office a "second-rate actor" of B-movie fame.

From Portugal to Poland, George W. Bush, a Yale graduate, has been depicted as cretin, cowboy, and illiterate—as "a political leader who at times can barely string a sentence together."[36] The defamatory reflex at work here was nicely illustrated by words attributed to Bush that have sped around the world: "The French have no word for 'entrepreneur.'" Google lists 1,650 entries for this statement (December 2004), but none is sourced. The closest these stories come to sourcing is the phrase "according to unconfirmed reports in the London *Observer*." The most cautious lead-in is something like "*There's a story told about* a conversation between George Bush and Tony Blair at the last G7 economic summit. Tony asks George W: 'Tell me, George, why is it we can never do a deal with the French?' To which George replies: 'I'll tell ya, Tony, it's because the French don't have a word for 'entrepreneur'!" This projection of presidential stupidity has become the gospel truth, as has another global myth: that only 80 out of 535 U.S. congressmen carry a passport.

"It is impossible to make a Norwegian say that Americans are intelligent," notes a Norwegian author of a book on anti-Americanism in an interview. Asked whether it didn't mean "anything that 70% of the Nobel Prize winners in history have been Americans?," he responds, "No, it does not help. Even if all Americans were professors, we would call them stupid." Why? "Because by speaking negatively about them, we elevate ourselves. It confirms that we are the opposite. We Europeans have refinement, culture, and intellectual life. To think this way, raises our image of ourselves."[37]

The litany continues. America gorges itself on fatty fast food, wallows in tawdry mass entertainment, starves the arts, and prays only to one God, who is Mammon. Instead of subsidizing what is serious and high-minded, as do the Europeans, the United States ruthlessly sacrifices the best of culture to pap and pop—never mind the Metropolitan Opera, MoMA, and the world's most highly touted research universities. Although these schools are much admired, the compliment is routinely followed by "But they are for the rich and well-connected, only." Like all such anti-Americanisms, the myth is promulgated in blissful (or willful) ignorance of the fact that Harvard, Stanford, et al. subsidize 60 percent of their college students with loans and grants, while Ph.D. students normally have both tuition and living expenses paid for by the university. Even though this complaint is routine lore in Germany, German data show that, in spite of open admission and no tuition, 85 percent of all students are middle-class and higher. America's high schools, so another standby goes, breed vast illiteracy and ignorance of the world. Here, too, the facts are more complex. In various comparative studies, as in PISA 2000 and 2003, U.S. high schoolers end up in midfield along with France, but ahead of their contemporaries in Belgium, Spain, Germany, Switzerland, and Italy.[38]

The common theme of these stereotypes is the denigration of America and the elevation of Europe. The motifs are summed up nicely in a piece in *Le Monde* right after the terror attacks of 9/11: "cretinism, Puritanism, barbarian arrogance, unbridled capitalism."[39] America is morally, culturally, and socially inferior to Europe. "The United States," as the British philosopher Bertrand Russell put it as early as 1967, "is a force for suffering, reaction and counter-revolution the world over."[40] It is a society where Europe's finest values—solidarity and community, taste and manners—are ground down by rampant individualism and capitalism. America is Yahoo, whereas Europe is civilization. Europe, in short, is the "Un-America."[41]

So much for stereotypization and denigration.[42] Now to those items that are even more emotionally charged: obsession, demonization, and conspiracy. "Anti-Americanism," the Stanford historian Russell Berman has argued,

> functions like a prejudice, magnifying the power and presence of its presumed opponent, turning it into a ubiquitous threat. The empirical superiority of American military power, for example is transformed by the anti-Americanist imagination into a fantasy of infinite omnipotence: there is no evil in the world that cannot be blamed on American action. . . . Anti-Semites, similarly, have always been able to imagine an ineluctable network of Jewish power. As a paranoid fantasy, anti-Americanism is cut from the same cloth. Instead of facing up to the detailed complexity of reality, it can only see Washington's hands controlling every conflict. . . . Anti-Americanism is not a reasoned response to American policies; it is a hysterical surplus that goes beyond reason. That difference is evident in the constant recycling of anti-American images that have a history that long antedates current policy.[43]

Obsessions are compulsively repeated thoughts and images that allow no room for falsification or alternative explanations. This is why debates on anti-Americanism or any anti-ism turn into spirals without resolution or escape. An archetypal discussion follows this pattern:

X: Americans have no culture.
Y: But what about the Met and MoMA?
X: That's just New York, and New York is the most European city in America.
Y: What about the Cleveland Symphony and the Chicago Art Institute?
X: (shifting ground): The state does not support high culture, as it does in Europe.
Y: Americans privately give $80 billion a year to charities like museums and universities, and more people go to museums than to football games.
Y: (shifting ground again): That just proves that American culture is run by and for the rich.
X: Even granting that, doesn't private support of the arts make for greater diversity, hence creative competition?
Y: Sure, for musicals and other forms of low-class entertainment; just look at their TV.
X: And we don't have reality TV, soaps, and afternoon talk shows that deal with sexual perversions?
Y: These are all American imports, which they are inflicting on us.
X: *Who Wants to Be a Millionaire* is a British and *Big Brother* a Dutch invention.
Y: (escaping into circularity): This just goes to show how much American vulgarity has seeped into European sensibilities.
X: What about the inundation of European TV with hard-core porn movies and telephone-sex ads, which are strictly homemade?
Y (shifting ground again): Americans are too Puritan to confront sex honestly.[44]

Obsessions are not about facts, but about filters. They grant passage only to those facts (or fabrications) that confirm the prejudice. As the Latinate word implies, the judgment comes *before* the evidence, and thus it accepts only what fits, while turning every part into the whole. A telling illustration is the bill of indictment Europeans have leveled a thousand times at the first administration of George W. Bush: the cancellation of the ABM Treaty as well as the refusal to sign on to the Kyoto Climate Protocol, the Land Mine Convention, the Biological Weapons Convention, the Comprehensive Nuclear Test Ban, and the International Criminal Court. Now, all of these choices were open to reasoned attack, and they were so attacked in the United States, as well. What turned the objections into obsessions was the compulsive reiteration at every twist and turn; this is what sprang to mind "on cue." These items were listed not as illustrations of unwanted or misguided policies but as self-evident proofs of maliciousness that required no further examination. Just uttering the indictment was proof of perfidy. Nor was right versus wrong the real issue; the psychological function of this argumentative rosary was to demonstrate the moral superiority of Europe vis-à-vis the Yahoo nation of America.

Another feature of obsession is the tendency to accuse an opponent of one thing and of its opposite. Like the Jews who were simultaneously denounced as capitalist blood suckers and communist subversives, America gets it coming and going. In matters sexual, Americans are both prurient and prudish, a far cry from the wiser ways of Europe. America is both puritanical and self-indulgent, philistine and elitist, sanctimonious and crassly materialist. It is morally derelict when it does not use its awesome force, as against Serbia in the early phase of the Balkan wars, and arrogantly imperialistic when it does, as in the bombing campaign of 1999, let alone during the Afghan and Iraqi campaigns.

Obsessions tend to spread, as Freud reminds us in his "Little Hans" case study, where a little boy first fears a certain horse, then all horses, then large animals like giraffes. An amusing instance comes from Germany, where a Hamburg high school student wrote this letter to a local paper:

> A pleasant place in the woods. Brown squirrels are happily jumping from branch to branch. But suddenly a black squirrel darts in and begins to hunt down the brown members of his species. The first black squirrels were slipped in here from America. Ever since, their number has ballooned. . . . Now, they are almost as numerous as European squirrels. They are displacing our beloved Browns—*Americanization in the animal kingdom.* (emphasis added)[45]

As a quick trip through German parks and forests will disclose, the squirrels are still reddish-brown, while in the United States the typical bushy-tailed rodent is gray rather than black. This example reveals less about comparative zoology than about obsession and projection. Accordingly, a single black squirrel is interpreted as evidence of a vast and growing threat that engulfs even the animal realm—the black squirrel as symbol of the aggressive "Other" that is America. The absence of detailed knowledge about America seems to correlate very nicely with the strength of negative opinions. In a study of teenagers across twelve countries, America was most readily associated with "sexual immorality," "domineering," "warmongering," and "materialism." Yet fewer than 12 percent of those young people had ever traveled to the United States.[46]

Closely related to obsession is conspiracy and demonization. We have already noted the spate of books that portrayed the Twin Tower attack as an American (or Israeli) plot.[47] The best visual dramatization of these themes was enacted during the 2003 World Economic Forum in Davos. A demonstrator wearing the mask of Donald Rumsfeld and an outsized yellow Star of David (with "Sheriff" inscribed) was driven forward by a cudgel-wielding likeness of Ariel

Sharon, both being followed by a huge rendition of the Golden Calf.[48] The message nicely combines an old and a new conspiracy, the Jewish and the American. The culprits now are Jews/Israelis and Americans who act as acolytes of Mammon and as avant-garde of pernicious global capitalism. It is Israel as the *Über*-Jew, America as its slave, and both now rule the world.[49]

Lest this be trivialized as a prank of the usual young suspects who gather at meetings such as the World Economic Forum, let us examine how an establishment organ like *Le Monde diplomatique* views the United States. Under the title "The Axis of Evil," one of its regular commentators outlines America's global conspiracy. Its "clandestine" tools are the International Monetary Fund, the World Bank, and the World Trade Organization, which are all in thrall to the United States. The purpose is to impose on the world the "dictatorship of the market." A second front of the conspiracy is made up of U.S. institutions ranging from the universities via the American Enterprise Institute to the *Wall Street Journal*—a "veritable industry of persuasion put in place to persuade the planet that liberal globalization will finally bring about universal happiness . . . with the passive complicity of those it dominates."[50] (To explain the triumph of any conspiracy, its theorists always resort to the false consciousness of the victims.) The French prime minister Lionel Jospin made the same point in more sober language. Speaking before French officials, he reminded them that their task was the "affirmation of [the power] of the states against the unbridled laws of the market."[51]

Once the conspiracy/demonization theme is sounded, the Nazi-America comparison won't be far behind. In another issue of *Le Monde diplomatique*, the same author opines that the U.S. doctrine of "preventive war" is precisely what "Hitler invoked against the Soviet Union in 1941, and Japan at Pearl Harbor."[52] The Mexican writer Carlos Fuentes outdid him: "Neither Hitler nor Stalin had the military power Bush has. Next to Bush, Hitler and Stalin were but petty officers."[53] During the German demonstrations against the impending Iraq war in February 2003, one poster proclaimed, "USA-Third Reich, Both Alike" (*USA-Drittes Reich, Ihr seid so gleich).* Yet another stated, "One Hitler Is Enough," the unspoken message being "Bush equals Hitler." To top them all, a placard made the Nazi-U.S. equation explicit in the most hateful way: "Remember Nuremberg, Mr. Bush: Death by Hanging."

Finally, there is the eliminationist theme. Let us again quote Jean Baudrillard and claim that his views, bizarre as they may sound to those untutored in the language of deconstructionism, represent more than just one individual's mind-set (especially since they were given wide play in the European media). Writing about the attack on the Twin Towers, he exclaimed, "How we have dreamt of this event, how the whole world has dreamt of it because nobody could fail to dream of the destruction of any power that has become hegemonic." He continued, "It is they [the terrorists] who did it, but we all wanted it to happen . . . the growth of power sharpens the will to destroy it." The immoral deed "is the reaction to a globalization that is itself immoral." And so the terrorists could count on the "profound complicity" of the rest of the world. The theme sounded here is the bottommost layer of any anti-ism: destroy what (allegedly) destroys you, and you shall be delivered from the evils of this world.[54] America the Omnipotent thus joins a long list of Satanic malefactors, ranging from "Popists" to Jews, from Freemasons to Communists, who must all be unmasked and undone in order for deliverance to begin.

A milder version of the eliminationist theme is a French best seller, *Après l'empire: Essai sur la décomposition du système américain*, by Emmanuel Todd, translated as *After the Empire: The Breakdown of the American Order*.[55] Whereas Baudrillard dreams of an America laid low by its enraged enemies, Todd ruthlessly selects facts to predict that the United States will do itself in. Painting America as a "predatory" but doomed empire, he argues that its "theatrical micro-militarism" against miserable Third World countries merely masks an accelerating decline. Its economy hollowed out by wrongheaded free-trade policies, its men emasculated by the "castrating" feminism of American women, America is but a parasite of the world economy, generating ever larger deficits, but producing nothing of value. And so, this would-be hegemon will soon fall under its own weight. In this breathless indictment, facts count only insofar as they nourish a fantasy of (self-) elimination. America, the universal intruder, will extrude itself from the game of nations, letting genuine powers like Europe, Japan, and Russia assume their rightful places at the top.

This chapter began by recounting that anti-Americanism is as old as the American Republic itself. As Philippe Roger recalls in his excellent *The American Enemy*, both Benjamin Franklin, who arrived as the first American ambassador in Paris in 1776, and his successor Thomas Jefferson, who came in 1785, fought patiently, and to little avail, against the "universally negative image of America now firmly anchored in cultivated people's minds."[56] A bit later, it was Talleyrand who complained (in very modern terms) about America's ultra-religiosity and lack of culinary culture ("thirty-two religions and only one dish to eat"), while the reactionary thinker Joseph de Maistre harped on America's democracy as a breeding ground of "weakness and decay." In the nineteenth century, it was Baudelaire who foreshadowed another contemporary horror vision: the "Americanization" of the world. Stendhal, reacting like De Maistre against the cataclysm of the French Revolution, railed against the "mindless tyranny" of public opinion in America.

In Germany, it was the three H's of the nineteenth century (Hegel, Herder, and Heine, followed in the twentieth by two more, Heidegger and Habermas) who declared America to be the embodiment of degeneration, stupidity, greed, vulgarity, perfidy, or injustice. America was a temple of either too many gods (Talleyrand) or the wrong ones (Heine). It was on a collision course with everything Europe held dear: culture, wisdom, refinement, community, and justice, and the attacks transcended all ideological boundaries. Anti-Americanism traveled as easily from right to left as did anti-Semitism. "By the end of the nineteenth century," notes the historian Simon Schama, "the stereotype of the ugly American—voracious, preachy, mercenary, and bombastically chauvinist—was firmly in place in Europe."[57]

If these are the tropes, what are the triggers? The richly documented continuity of anti-Americanism is a significant historical fact, hence a useful reminder that anti-Americanism, like anti-Semitism, is an ineradicable feature of the global consciousness. But to affirm constancy is hardly the end of the story. Nor does it crack the puzzle that lurks beyond "there is nothing new under the sun." After all, poverty and greed, neurosis and superstition, floods, wars, and recessions are also ineradicable fixtures of life. As with all recurrent phenomena, the more interesting questions on the cusp of the twenty-first century are about the why and the when. Why do sleeping dogs begin to bark, why now the "hysterical surplus" and the "constant recycling of anti-American images that . . . long antedate current policy"?[58] When do ever-present viruses suddenly overwhelm the immune system? Whence, in short, the epidemic of anti-Americanism that gripped the world at the turn of the new century? The next chapter, on the "Rise of Americanism," will offer four answers.

4

The Rise of Americanism

STUDENTS OF CONTEMPORARY anti-Americanism stress its longevity and continuity. It is as old as the American Republic itself, and it shares many features with anti-Semitism, which is much older. If anti-Semitism has been a historical constant for two thousand years, anti-Americanism is a fixture of modernity—a mind-set that arose with the crumbling of the feudal order under the onslaught of industrialization, capitalism, and liberalism. A classic response to the unending assault was the transfiguration of feudalism and the "Dark Ages" into a heartwarming memory of order, community, and simplicity. Modernity, as unleashed by the steam engine, came to be associated with inexorable, brutal change—as described in these famous lines from the *Communist Manifesto*:

> The bourgeoisie . . . has put an end to all feudal, patriarchal, idyllic relations. It has pitilessly torn asunder the motley feudal ties that bound man to his "natural superiors," and has left no other nexus between man and man than naked self-interest, than callous "cash payment." . . . Constant revolutionizing of production, uninterrupted disturbance of all social conditions, everlasting uncertainty and agitation distinguish the bourgeois epoch from all earlier ones. . . . All that is solid melts into the

> air, all that is holy is profaned. . . . All old-established national industries are daily being destroyed. . . . In place of the old local and national seclusion and self-sufficiency, we have intercourse in every direction, universal interdependence of nations.

Written more than 150 years ago, these lines still offer the best shorthand description of modernity—and globalization. They also help to explain why America as the very steamroller of modernity has always been identified as its agent, for good and for bad. Founded in revolt against feudalism and sworn to permanent self-reinvention, America was the first modern nation. Deliberately abandoning the mainstream of European history in the seventeenth century, the United States, though the "daughter of Europe," as Charles de Gaulle put it, has stuck to its own course ever since. No feudalism, no socialism; no established church, no religious war; no absolutism, no statism—that is the gist of the American story, which also explains why in the United States market and modernity keep trumping the providential state embedded between Iberia and Siberia.[1] Conversely, none of the deadly ideologies of the twentieth century—communism, fascism, Nazism—that promised a happy fusion between modernity and community sank roots in America. And so the country was spared the nightmare that oppressed Europe in the first half of the twentieth century.

Like the Jews, America remained the "Other," but unlike the imagined omnipotence of the Jews, America's power was real—and soaring, to boot. To taint the agent as culprit demands little effort. And so it is easy to blame America for the miseries of modernity, for a relentless revolution in the way we live, produce, and consume. America embodies the "constant revolutionizing" that Marx and Engels cheered and reviled in the *Communist Manifesto.* Here is a more recent lament by the distinguished South African writer Breyten Breytenbrach that reiterates many of the frozen clichés of anti-modernism throughout the ages:

> A chicken on almost every plate, and we are stuffed with hormones and antibiotics. We are turning rich and fat through a myriad of designer-bred pigs and can no longer drink the water of our earth. We consume voraciously and are suffocated by mountains of garbage. We are destroying the planet in an orgy of pollution. Even the poor can afford hamburgers and fries, growing overweight. . . . All of this reveals the Golden Thread of globalization, which is but a code word for globalized capitalist exploitation. . . . [T]he poor are getting poorer.[2]

"Global capitalist exploitation" is an instantly understood code word for "America." A large part of anti-Americanism is indeed anti-modernism. But noting this connection does not resolve the more interesting issues: Why and when does anti-Americanism change from latency to virulence, from mind-set to manifestation, as it has at the turn of the twenty-first century? Here is a very rough measure of the surge that is only suggestive and in no way systematic. In 2005, Google showed 280,000 entries for the keyword "anti-Americanism," without a year attached. When "anti-Americanism" followed by a particular year was entered, there were 180,000 entries for 2004. In 2003, there were 150,000; in 2000–03, an average of 100,000. This was in dramatic contrast to an annual average of 40,000 throughout the 1990s. The 1980s, when searched year by year, yielded an average of 18,000. For the 1970s, the average was 12,000, as it was for the 1960s and in the year 1950.

These numbers are only suggestive, but they do underscore the original question: Why the sudden surge? What has driven deeply embedded constructs (and obsessions) about America to the surface? The best shorthand answer is: "The Rise of Americanism." This catch-all, in turn, breaks down into "Ubiquity," "Seduction," "Modernity," and "Überpower."

America the Ubiquitous

"America is everywhere" is a statement attributed to the Italian novelist Ignazio Silone (1900–1978). Today, the dictum should be expanded with "and even more so by the day." When this author grew up in postwar West Berlin, America was *not* everywhere. At that time, America was military bases, but usually well isolated from the rest of West Germany. America was the Berlin Airlift (1948–49), which saved the Western half of the former *Reich* capital from Soviet encirclement; it was the M-48 tanks that faced down Soviet T-55s across the Berlin Wall in the fall of 1961. America was Westerns and Grace Kelly movies at the local cinema, interspersed with lots of German, Italian, French, and English films. And it was just a single station, the American Forces Network (AFN), which twice daily played forbidden rock 'n' roll during programs like *Frolic at Five* or *Bouncing in Bavaria* on AM radio.

The only true American piece of apparel was a pair of Levi's, prized all the more for being the real thing as opposed to the cheap German knockoffs. U.S. TV fare was rationed—mainly because there were only three public channels in Germany until the mid-1980s, when private networks were legalized, as they were throughout Europe. Vacations were spent in the Alps or at the North Sea, not in Yosemite or on Cape Cod. A phone call to America was so expensive that it was placed only once a year, at Christmas or for an important birthday. Neither *USA Today* nor CNN was in Europe, and the Paris editions of the *New York Times* and *Herald Tribune* were read only by American tourists. Mickey Mouse comics, which arrived in Germany in 1951, were too costly for the average child (one week's worth of pocket money). In school, it was the occasional Steinbeck or Hemingway work in translation, and a lot of Goethe, Schiller, and Shakespeare. Food was strictly of the local kind: sausages, seasonal vegetables, pork, herring, cabbage, dark bread, potatoes. So was drink. When ordered in 1960 at the Berlin

Hilton, a Coke consumed 60 percent of a teenager's weekly allowance.

Above all, any European could spot an American from fifty feet away. Telltale signs were the short-cropped hair, the "flood leg" pants, the white socks, the mighty horn-rimmed glasses, the loafers or the bulky wingtips, and the bluish coiffure of the older women. Save for the tourists and soldiers, America was not a reality but a distant myth, as portrayed in soft brushstrokes on TV by series like *Lassie* and *Father Knows Best.* No more. Today, the entire world watches, wears, drinks, eats, listens, and dances American—even in Iran, where it is done in the secrecy of one's home.

Today, it is impossible to distinguish a young American from a young European (or Chinese, Japanese, Russian, Arab) by his or her clothes. The international look consists of jeans, loafers, button-downs, Nikes, baseball caps, T-shirts, backpacks, iPods—all either made or invented in the United States. Though H&M and Zara have established beachheads in American department stores, there is nary a European city without its Gap, Hilfiger, DKNY, and Ralph Lauren store—not to mention Shanghai, Tokyo, and Tel Aviv. Among the even younger set, the bulky pants of street surfboarders became de rigueur almost instantly, as did Oakley sunglasses (which were preceded and succeeded by Ray-Bans). Hip-hop and rap have radiated outward with an intensity that is reflected in local-language knockoffs throughout Europe and the rest of the world.

Suddenly, Halloween, complete with the American paraphernalia, has become an institution in Germany and even in France, a country that prides itself for defying all things American.[3] Valentine's Day, arguably an invention of the American greeting card industry has been etched into the European calendar. Suddenly, the German *Weihnachtsmann* looks a lot like the American Santa Claus, and the garish Christmas decorations that festoon middle-class American suburbs in December have sprouted up all over Europe, complete with the (electrified) reindeer that had previously never been a feature of Continental Yuletide. Thanksgiving, this most American of feasts, complete with turkey and cranberries, is making its debut in the more cosmopolitan homes of Germany. Even the lowly bagel is spreading across Europe as an ironic testimony to America's gastronomic clout. Originally, the bagel (from the German word *beugel*, meaning "that which is bent") was parboiled and baked in the southwest of Germany, whence it emigrated with German Jews to eastern Europe and then traveled across the Atlantic to New York's Lower East Side. Unseen circa 1990, muffins can now be ordered in any bakery. Pizza, though invented in Naples, has changed citizenship and swept the world, courtesy of the U.S.-based chains.

Why would Starbucks open up in Rome and Vienna, the two historical capitals of coffee? By 2003, Starbucks had established its 1,000th coffee shop in the Asia-Pacific region, bringing the total outside the United States to 6,500.[4] In the meantime, this global chain has spawned many imitators. The Hamburg version is called Balzac Coffee, complete with Starbucks-type interiors, and it advertises its wares (in English) with "Coffee to Go." Walk through a Continental shopping street, and you'll see the stores abound with "SALE" signs and names in English like "Labels for Less." Even American punning habits have infiltrated store signs, as a barbershop in Munich demonstrated. Its moniker was *Hairgott*, a bilingual pun on *Herrgott*, "Our Lord." A German television chain's slogan (in English) is "We Love to Entertain You."

The obsession with American (or American-sounding) mottos sometimes leads to amusing consequences. A German cosmetics chain with branches elsewhere in Europe, recently plastered its storefronts with "Come In and Find Out." Literally translated into German, this meant to those less familiar with English basics "Come In and Find Your Way Out Again," which did not sound very enticing. Indeed, English—or, more accurately, "Bad English"—is the world's fastest-growing language, with an American accent, of course. Or a bowdlerized version of American English, as reflected in such *Deul-*

ish words as *downloaden* or *downsizen*. Lufthansa advertises itself (in a *German* ad) with "There Is No Better Way to Fly," and Volvo with "Move Forward." Siemens praises its cell phone as "Designed for Life," while Skoda, a VW subsidiary, adorns its logo with "Simply Clever."[5]

Not only is American English the world's lingua franca, American culture became the world's *cultura franca* in the last fifth of the twentieth century. Assemble a few kids from, say, Sweden, Germany, Russia, Argentina, Japan, Israel, and Lebanon in one room. They would all be wearing jeans and baseball caps. How would they communicate? In more or less comprehensible English, with an American flavor. And what would they talk about? About the latest U.S.-made video game, American hits on the top-ten chart, the TV series *South Park*, or the most recent Hollywood blockbuster. Or they would debate the relative merits of Windows and Apple operating systems. No, they would not talk about Philip Roth or Herman Melville, but neither would they dissect Thomas Mann or Dante. The point is that they would talk about icons and images Made in U.S.A. If there is a global civilization, it is American—which it was not twenty or thirty years ago.

Nor is it just a matter of low culture. It is McDonald's *and* Microsoft, Madonna *and* MoMA, Hollywood *and* Harvard. If two-thirds of the movie marquees carry an American title in Europe (even in France), the American ratio is even greater when it comes to translated books, with traffic across the Atlantic overwhelmingly going one-way. The ratio for Germany in 2003 was 419 versus 3,732; that is, for every German book translated into English, nine English-language books were translated into German.[6] A hundred years ago, Berlin's Humboldt University was the model for the rest of the world. Tokyo, Johns Hopkins, Stanford, and Chicago were founded in conscious imitation of the German university and its novel fusion of teaching and research. So was Harvard's Graduate School of Arts and Sciences. Stanford's motto is taken from the

German Renaissance scholar and soldier Ulrich von Hutten (1488–1523): *Die Luft der Freiheit weht*—the winds of freedom blow.

Today, Europe's universities have lost their luster, and as they talk reform, they talk American. Ancient degrees are being changed to the B.A. and M.A., and they have to be completed in a set time in contrast to the open-ended studies of yore. With America's top universities in mind, their European counterparts are speaking more about "excellence" and less about "equality." They are rethinking free tuition and open admission while eying a rigorous separation between undergraduate and graduate education in the American way. Read through mountains of debate on university reform, and the two words you will find most often are "Harvard" and "Stanford." An amusing instance of this trend was a conversation this author had with a left-wing German parliamentarian. Delivering himself of the usual bill of indictments against the United States, he suddenly stopped: "You went to Harvard, didn't you? How could I get my daughter in?"

America is one huge global "demonstration effect," as the sociologists call it when they want to avoid a normative term like "model." America's cultural sway at the beginning of the twenty-first century surpasses that of Rome or any other empire in history. For Rome's or Habsburg's cultural penetration of foreign lands stopped exactly at their military borders, and the Soviet Union's cultural presence in Prague, Budapest, or Warsaw vanished into thin air the moment the last Russian soldier was withdrawn from Central Europe. American culture, however, needs no gun to travel. It is everywhere, even in countries where it is denounced as "Great Satan." In his *Second Treatise concerning Civil Government*, John Locke wrote that "in the beginning all the world was America."[7] Today, he might muse, "All the world is *becoming* America." If so, all the world does not necessarily like it.

Joseph S. Nye, the Harvard political scientist, has coined a term for this phenomenon: "soft power." That power does not come out of the barrel of a gun. It is "less coercive and less tangible." It derives from "attraction" and "ideology."[8] The distinction between "soft power" and "hard power" is an important one, especially in an age where bombs and bullets, no matter how "smart," do not translate easily into political power—that is, the capacity to make others do what they would otherwise not do. A perfect example is America's swift military victory against Iraq, which was not followed so swiftly by either peace or democracy. Still, "soft power" does not deal very well with contemporary anti-Americanism. Indeed, the relationship between "soft power" and "hard influence," that is, America's ability to get its way in the world, may be nonexistent or, worse, pernicious.

In the first instance, there may be no relationship whatsoever between America's ubiquity and its influence (or ability to capture hearts and minds). Hundreds of millions of people around the world wear, listen, eat, drink, watch, and dance American, but they do not identify these accoutrements of their daily lives with America. A baseball cap with the Yankees logo is the very epitome of things American, but it hardly signifies knowledge of, let alone affection for, the team from New York or America as such. It is just an item of apparel with a pleasing art nouveau logo, though cool enough to wear—either straight or sideways, which is another U.S. import. The same is true for American films, foods, or songs. The film *Titanic*, released in 1997, has grossed $1.8 billion worldwide in box office sales alone. It is still the all-time best seller. With two exceptions, the next 257 films in the revenue ranking are American as well.[9] But this pervasive cultural presence does not seem to generate "soft power." These American products define images rather than mentalities, let alone sympathies. There appears to be little, if any, relationship between artifact and affection.

If the relationship is not neutral, it is one of repellence rather than attraction—that is the dark side of the "soft power" coin. The European student movement of the late 1960s took its cue from the

Berkeley free speech movement of 1964, the inspiration for all post-1964 Western student revolts. But it quickly turned anti-American; America was reviled while it was copied. A telling anecdote is a march on Frankfurt's Amerikahaus during the heyday of the German student movement. The enraged students wore jeans and American army apparel. They even played a distorted Jimmy Hendrix version of the American national anthem. But they threw rocks against the U.S. cultural center nonetheless. Though they wore and listened American, they targeted precisely the embodiment of America's cultural presence in Europe.[10]

Now shift forward to the Cannes Film Festival of 2004, where hundreds of protesters were denouncing America's intervention in Iraq until the police dispersed them. The makers of the movie *Shrek 2* had deposited large bags of green Shrek ears along the Croisette, the main drag along the ocean. As the demonstrators scattered, many of them put on free Shrek ears. "They were attracted," noted an observer, "by the ears' goofiness and sheer recognizability."[11] And so the enormous pull of American imagery went hand in hand with the country's condemnation.

Between Vietnam and Iraq, America's cultural presence has expanded into ubiquity, and so has the resentment of America's "soft power." Or as Richard Kuisel puts it: "In France, Germany, Great Britain, and Italy, but especially in France, majorities say the spread of something vaguely called 'American ideas and customs' is 'bad.'"[12] As early as 1997, the French foreign minister Hubert Védrine couched the resentment in diplomatic language: "The United States has assets not yet at the disposal of any other power: political influence, the supremacy of the dollar, control of the communications networks, 'dream factories,' new technology. Add these up—the Pentagon, Boeing, Coca-Cola, Microsoft, Hollywood, CNN, the Internet, the English language—the situation is virtually unprecedented."[13]

Ubiquity breeds unease, unease breeds resentment, and resentment breeds denigration as well as visions of omnipotence and conspiracy, as evoked by Védrine's carefully chosen words. In some cases, as in the French one, these feelings harden into governmental policy. And so the French have passed the Toubon law, which prohibits on pain of penalty the use of English words. A car wash must be a *lavage voiture,* and perhaps the day is not far when another such edict decrees that the *disque-tourneur* (DJ) must call the hit parade *parade de frappe.* In 1993, the French coaxed the European Union into adding a "cultural exception" clause to its commercial treaties exempting cultural products, high or low, from normal free-trade rules. Other European nations impose informal quotas on American TV fare. America the Ubiquitous has become America the Excessive.

Even America's high culture is not immune to the impulse of denigration nourished by fantasies of conspiracy. A fine example is how the art critics of two distinguished German newspapers, *Süddeutsche Zeitung* (leftish) and *Frankfurter Allgemeine Zeitung* (centrist), dealt with an exhibit of two hundred pieces from the New York Museum of Modern Art (MoMA) in Berlin in 2004. More than a million visitors had stood in line from February to September, many for up to nine hours, to view the *objets* from across the Atlantic. Yet the fervor of the hoi polloi mattered little to their betters whose comments ran the gamut from contempt to conspiracy.

The opening shots were fired by the *Süddeutsche Zeitung* of Munich. Without having seen the collection, its critic aimed his volley straight against imperial America. Regurgitating a standard piece of European *Kulturkritik*, the author insinuated that what America has in the way of culture is not *haute*, and what is *haute* is not American. Or as Adolf Hitler famously proclaimed, "A single Beethoven symphony contains more culture than all that America has ever created." After World War II, the critic contended, America had wrested "artistic hegemony" from Europe in two sleazy ways. One culprit was "a new abstract school of painting [Abstract Expressionism] that had hyped itself into high heaven." The other was American mammon: "Everything still available in old Europe was bought up." And this "stolen idea of modern art will now be presented in Berlin." Thus was pilferage and grand theft added to the oldest of indictments: America's cultural inferiority.

The critic of the *Frankfurter Allgemeine* went further. If his colleague had claimed that America's art was either hyped or heisted, the man from Frankfurt thundered that MoMA's Berlin show was a mendacious ploy, indeed, an imperialist conspiracy. It was done by "concealment" and "censorship" in a game full of "marked cards," and its name was not only to blank out Europe's greats but also to suppress their magnificent contribution to American art in the second half of the twentieth century. This was an instance of the selective perception that suffuses any anti-ism. For in truth, the exhibit happened to contain an impressive number of European works: Matisse, Picasso, Manet, Rousseau, Brancusi, and Mondrian, plus assorted Expressionists and Surrealists.

That did not count. What about contemporary Germans like Beuys, Baselitz, and Kiefer? the critic huffed. The untutored million, who had spent a total of 446 years waiting in line, according to a local newspaper, might have thought that bringing such artists to Berlin was like carrying coals to Newcastle. But even here, MoMA had done its universalist duty, capping the progression with Gerhard Richter's "18 October 1977" cycle, which depicts dead members of the Baader-Meinhof terrorist gang. That MoMA would display these German works enraged the *feuilletoniste* from Frankfurt even more. That particular choice, he fumed, was the final proof of American perfidy. The terrorist motif was insidiously selected to finger Europe as a "creepy" place, as a messenger of "bad news." With that, anti-ism came full circle. First it was denigration ("the U.S. has no culture of its own"), then it was demonization ("it steals or obliterates Europe's grand tradition"), and finally projection ("Europe is the victim of American malevolence").[14]

There is a moral in this tale of two critics (which could easily be retold throughout Europe). It is the *curse* of "soft power." In the affairs of nations, too much hard power ends up breeding not submission but counterpower, be it by armament or by alliance. Likewise, great "soft power" does not bend hearts but twists minds in resentment and rage. Yet how does one balance against "soft power"? No coalition of European universities could dethrone Harvard and Stanford. Neither can all the subsidies fielded by European governments crack the hegemony of Hollywood. To breach the bastions of American "soft power," the Europeans will first have to imitate, then to improve on, the American model—just as the Japanese bested the American automotive industry after two decades of copycatting (and the Americans, having dispatched their engineers for study in Britain, overtook the British locomotive industry in the nineteenth century). Imitation and leapfrogging is the oldest game in the history of nations, and in the civilian aircraft market, Europe's Airbus is already a worthy competitor of Boeing. But competition has barely begun to drive the cultural contest where Europe, mourning the loss of its centuries-old supremacy, either resorts to insulation (by quotas and "cultural exception clauses") or seeks solace in the defamation of American culture as vulgar, inauthentic, or stolen. If we could consult Dr. Freud again, he would take a deep drag on his cigar and pontificate about inferiority feelings being compensated by hauteur and disparagement.

America the Beguiling

As the tale of MoMA in Berlin illustrates, America's ubiquity goes hand in glove with seduction—why else would more than a million visitors have crowded into the exhibit, a few hundred thousand more than at any other time in Berlin's museum history? Europe—indeed, most of the world—also wants what America has. Nobody has ever used a gun to drive Frenchmen into one of their eight hundred

McDonald's, and we have the French foreign minister Hubert Védrine to make the point when he attributed to America "this certain psychological power . . . this ability to shape the dreams and desires of others."[15] No force need be applied to make Europeans buy clothes or watch films Made in U.S.A. Germans take to *Denglish* as if it were their native tongue. So might the French to *Franglais* if their authorities did not impose fines on such linguistic defection. Contemporary Western dictionaries do not even contain words such as "anti-Frenchism" or "anti-Russism" or "anti-Japanism." Japan's cars and electronics have conquered the world, but very few people want to dance like the Japanese. Nor does the rest of the world want to dress like the Russians or (outside India) watch movies made in "Bollywood," though India produces more movies than all Western nations put together. Nobody risks death on the high seas to get into China, and the number of those who want to go for an M.B.A. in Moscow is still rather small.[16]

America's "hard power" is based on its nuclear carrier fleets and its "stealth bombers," as well as on its twelve-trillion-dollar economy. But its allure rests on pull, not on push, and it has done so since Columbus set out to tap the riches of India, but instead ended up in America. Why? One need not resort to such sonorous terms as "freedom," the "New Jerusalem," or John Winthrop's "cittie upon a hill with the eies of all people upon them"—concepts that evoke religious transcendence and salvation. America's magnetism has very tangible roots.

If it is transcendence, it is of a very secular type—a society where a peddler's son can still move from Manhattan's Lower East Side (now heavily Chinese, and no longer Jewish) to the tranquil suburbs of Westchester in the span of one generation, never mind his uncouth accent. Hence, the best and the brightest still keep coming, even if there is no Metternich, Hitler, or Stalin to drive them out. Nor is citizenship bequeathed by bloodline. People can *become* Americans; they need not have it bestowed on them by their progenitors. They do not have to invoke *Deutschtum* or *italianità* to acquire citizenship; they merely have to prove five years of legal residence, swear allegiance, and sign on, symbolically speaking, to documents like the Declaration of Independence and the Constitution. American-ness is credal, not biological. Nor do the newcomers have to profess fealty to a particular faith, because America never had an established, let alone state, religion. And the newcomers' ethnic origins matter less in a society where everybody, at one time or another, came from somewhere else. A degree from a top engineering school, whether from Bombay or Shanghai, will trump a birth certificate anytime.

These factors explain the two million legal and illegal immigrants who push into the United States year after year. But they do not explain the seductive force exerted by things and ways American on those who remain at home. The best explanation is the universality not only of American citizenship but also of American culture. Though the "American dream," as Samuel Huntington has argued, may be an Anglo-Protestant project,[17] it is a "work in progress," and it has recruited an endless string of collaborators: not just WASPs, but Irish, Germans, Scandinavians, Jews, Africans, Italians, Poles, Russians, Vietnamese, Chinese, Indians—the whole world. Every new group has contributed its own ingredient to the melting pot (or "salad bowl," as the more correct parlance has it).

In fact, it was Russian Jews with (refurbished) names like Goldwyn, Mayer, and Warner who first interpreted the "American dream" for a worldwide audience on celluloid. It was the descendants of African slaves who created an American musical tradition, ranging from gospel via jazz to hip-hop, that has conquered the world. It was Italian Americans who turned the lowly Neapolitan pizza into a global dish. The most "American" cuisine is not catfish or chitlins but "fusion"—a blend of Asian, Italian, and French.

It was a Bavarian Jew by the name of Levi Strauss whose jeans swept the planet. Frenchmen transformed Napa Valley into a household word for wine. Scandinavians implanted a social-democratic tradition into the politics of the Midwest, while Irish built the great political machines of Boston and New York. Hispanics set the architectural tone of California and New Mexico. And the "work in progress" continues. At the end of the twentieth century, 60 percent of the American-based authors of the most-cited papers in the physical sciences were foreign-born, as were nearly 30 percent of the authors of the most-cited life science papers. Almost one-quarter of the leaders of biotech companies that went public in the early 1990s came from abroad.[18] In a seminar that this author taught at Stanford in 2004, three out of five straight-A papers were written by students named Zhou, Kim, and Surraj Patel (and the course was not about computer science but about American foreign policy).

And so, America has become the first "universal nation." A universal nation, one surmises, creates artifacts, images, and narratives that appeal to a universal audience. Take Disneyland near Paris. Condemned as American imperialism by France's guardians of culture, it contains a plethora of ur-European motifs taken from the German brothers Grimm, but expressed in a universally comprehensible language. Whereas French and German films (which each wrote chapters of the canon in the first half of the twentieth century) have come to rely on parochial, sociocritical, or torturously introspective plots, Hollywood's output replicates myths imbedded in the human consciousness: good versus bad, evil overcome, trials mastered, dangers vanquished, love requited, friendship triumphant, loyalty rewarded. It is boy meets girl, the eternal plot since Adam and Eve, and boy gets girl, either after a dramatic or funny battle of the sexes. In literature, Ole Rölvaag (*Giants in the Earth*) and Henry Roth (*Call It Sleep*) could not appeal only to Norwegian or East European immigrants; they had to make themselves understood to an American audience that was itself multiethnic. Philip Roth can be understood everywhere; the *nouveau roman* takes some cross-cultural effort. And so it continues into the twenty-first century, for instance, with Jeffrey Eugenides (*Middlesex*). The book starts out with a Greek American love story and then builds up to a real-life incarnation of the hermaphroditic myth whose roots reach back to the beginnings of mankind.

If it is not universal myth, it is universal convenience. This is America's most powerful export, as evidenced by a never-ending imitation effect radiating outward. Power windows and air-conditioning in cars; the cash machine that saves a trip to the bank; the side-by-side, no-frost refrigerator that requires neither deicing nor crouching; the self-service supermarket that allows for endless choice in countless aisles without an intermediary behind the counter; the cafeteria that eliminates menus, waiters, and waiting time; the motel that demands only a few feet of luggage hauling; the iPod that stores hundreds of CDs. Convenience is modernity, and modernity is America—one huge "demonstration effect."

Imitation even extends to the import of American mores. Suddenly, in Europe, it is no longer the gruff voice of a receptionist on the telephone. It is: "This is [company name]. My name is . . . What can I do for you?" Suddenly, bidding somebody good-bye is transformed into "Havaniceday" in the local language, while "Hi" or "Hello" is turning into a universal greeting. "Smileys"—emoticons—are everywhere, on Post-its as well as in e-mails. Why? Modernity is the experience of anonymity in an ever-expanding circle of daily contacts—a far cry from traditional interaction, where roles and identities were fixed, few, and familiar. To avert collisions or misunderstandings, people seek to signal benevolence with friendly overtures; to reduce anonymity, they identify themselves quickly. As the first modern—that is, both geographically and vertically mobile—society, America developed these rituals early on. As other nations follow America into the service economy with its plethora of nameless encounters, they adopt them because such etiquette fits the new realities of interaction better than do the traditional ways.

Demonstration, seduction, imitation—this is the progression

that feeds into "America the beguiling." So why doesn't irresistible imitation generate affection and soft power? The answer is simple: seduction creates its own repulsion. We hate the seducer for seducing us, and we hate ourselves for yielding to temptation. A fine illustration is offered by a cartoon on the Jordanian website www.mahjoob.com (April 29, 2002, since removed) that transcends its Arab origins. It shows a jeep-like SUV, a pack of cigarettes with a Marlboro design, a can of Coca-Cola, and a hamburger—all enticing objects of desire, but dripping with blood. These products Made in U.S.A., the cartoon insinuates, are the weapons that drive America's global domination. They are meant to seduce, and yet they drip with blood that symbolizes heinous imposition. Yield to the seduction, and the price will be the loss of your own culture, dignity, and power.

Why has McDonald's become a universal target of resentment, if not hatred? Because it globally epitomizes the fast-food outlet. And whence this universal seduction? It is a hot meal that requires no eating utensils, not even a table—it can be eaten on the run. And so, it fits smoothly into modern modes of work that leave ever less time for a proper sit-down meal. Finally, a fast-food burger spells not only convenience but also freedom. Freedom? From what?

Etched into this author's mind is an exchange with a Hamburg judge of the 1968 generation, a scion of the local *haute bourgeoisie* and a father of three. He started out with a profession of disgust for McDonald's that triggered the following dialogue:

"Why do you hate McDonald's?"

"Because you never know what kind of dreck its hamburgers contain."

"That's the least of McDonald's problems. We know exactly how they're made—with buns, beef, ketchup, mustard, and pickles. What we really don't know is what goes into a German sausage, nor do we want to know."

"True, but I still hate McDonald's."

"Why?"

(Bursting out) "I hate it because my children don't come home for dinner any more. They just go to the burger joint whenever they feel like it."

"So the real reason for your disgust is that you hate your kids' freedom to choose between mother's and McDonald's. You resent the fact that they are no longer tied to the family table, that you have lost power over them."

"Yes, they no longer respect order and family tradition."

In the mind of this irate father, a mere meat patty had become a tool of subversion wielded by America, and he was right. We all remember the anxiety that attended our first unaccompanied trip to a regular restaurant. We did not know how to order, tip, and behave. But today a twelve-year-old need not conquer such fears. Ordering is done by picture, and tipping, as well as the proper use of utensils, is unnecessary. The kid can just saunter in, pay, and eat—while his parents rightly bemoan the loss of yet another tradition (and source of family power) that is the price of modernity.

The Steamroller of Modernity

A key battle cry in the German electoral campaign of 2002, which continues to reverberate through the country's political discourse, was "no *amerikanische Verhältnisse*"—"American ways." In 2005, the enemy was yet another American intruder—private equity and hedge funds, or "locusts," that were accused of gobbling up German companies and destroying jobs for the sake of a quick profit.[19] "I don't want *amerikanische Verhältnisse*," said Chancellor Gerhard Schröder as early as 2001.[20] *Amerikanische Verhältnisse* were flogged not only by the chancellor, a Social Democrat, but also by his rival Edmund Stoiber, a conservative, who lectured, "Of course, you could quickly produce more growth with maximally flexible labor markets. But we have a completely different history and mentality. For us, solidarity and social protection play a completely different role, as compared with America."[21] "American ways," a seemingly neutral term, was in fact a fighting word with the same import as the French prime minister Lionel Jospin's diatribe against "the unbridled laws of the market."[22]

"American ways" were pernicious to the better ways of Europe, or as Schröder put it, "We have no reason to hide the German, the European social model from the Americans. I have enough self-confidence to say that it is superior."[23] *Amerikanische Verhältnisse* were the foes of social justice, predictability, protection, and redistribution. The slogan was a battering ram pointed at high wages, employment security, and the munificent state—against the social-democratic dispensation that is the core of Europe's unwritten social contract from Lisbon to Leipzig, from Narvik to Naples, no matter what the government's ideological coloration. That social contract could be reduced to two articles: first, no change; second, if change is unavoidable, losers must be compensated.

But why raise this flag on the threshold of the twenty-first century? Because the "European way," which had brought both private and public prosperity, could no longer be sustained. The state that had typically taken around half of the gross domestic product and disbursed about one-third of GDP as transfer payments like social supports and subsidies—almost twice as much as in midcentury—depended on sustained growth. With steady growth, the expanding welfare state could give to Peter without taking from Paul, thus nipping society's conflicts in the bud. Yet growth began to falter and then to stagnate in the mid-1990s.

And so, the blissful arrangement of the postwar period began to groan under its own weight. Full employment gave way to stubborn joblessness of around 10 percent (closer to 12 percent if retraining and subsidized jobs were counted). As tax revenues declined, social expenditures soared. Enter globalization or, more accurately, "Europeanization," that is, the admittance of ten low-wage East European states to the EU. "China" was suddenly right next door. Economic decline and EU enlargement began to gnaw away at the very foundation of the welfare state, which presupposes a closed economy. "Closed" does not mean "no trade," for Europe's economies have a much higher trade component than do America's and Japan's (a typical EU country exports about 30 percent of its GDP, while the U.S. share is about 10 percent). Rather, "closed" means a high degree of state control over the economy plus a "social contract" that favors producers (including workers and farmers) over consumers, domestic suppliers over foreign ones, and consensus over competition.

The assault on the fortress of the European welfare state has been proceeding on three axes. Let's call one "China," which stands for the export offensive of low-wage and ever higher-tech economies in Asia with their undervalued currencies. Let's label the second axis "Czechia," which symbolizes the low-wage and high-productivity nations east of the former Iron Curtain. And let's use "Brussels" as metaphor for the least dramatized and most momentous force of them all: the relentless razing of national economic borders by the European Commission.

Those "Eurocrats" have done more to break down the walls of separation, which allowed protection to flourish, than either China or Czechia. Berlin wants to subsidize Volkswagen? The EU's competition commissioner says *nein!* France wants to stop foreign takeovers? Brussels says *non!* Governments want to procure nationally? *No, nein, and non*—everybody must have access to the public trough. One edict after another has opened up markets not only for goods but also for capital and financial services, like banks and insurance. If a Danish dentist can say "Open your mouth" in Spanish, French, or German, he could set up his drill in these countries. Telecoms and transportation, once the jealously guarded preserves of national regulators, have been liberated, and so national favorites like Siemens, Sabena, and Alcatel, either had to compete or perish.

The EU has been turning twenty-five countries into a single market of 450 million people, and technology, which keeps shrinking the costs of transportation and communication, is doing the rest. To dispatch a multimegabyte program file via the Internet costs exactly nothing. Europe's "China" is not ten thousand miles away but inside—in Poland, Czechia, Hungary. These investment magnets need only be mentioned by management, and the unions will start talking cost cutting. So when Europeans bemoan "globalization" as a code word for "Americanization," they should actually target "Europeanization." That they began doing in 2005, when the German government, along with the French one, demanded a halt to EU efforts to liberalize all services, that is, to create a free market for labor, on the grounds that it would trigger a "race to the bottom."[24] The battle cry was "social dumping" or "tax dumping," and the targets were those ten new members to the east that had been admitted to the EU in 2004.

Sacred dispensations are crumbling, and so are jealously guarded privileges. The thirty-five-hour week has turned into a distant dream, and Europeans must work more for less. Big-box stores, with their lower prices, are crowding city outskirts, driving out not only mom-and-pop shops but also downtown department stores. Municipal hospitals must outsource or sell part of their operations to private investors. Cozy patronage is yielding to the privatization of utilities, airlines, and arms manufacturers, and firings are becoming easier to navigate past or through the labor courts. Social security, pay-as-you go schemes throughout the West, will have to be flanked by private insurance. Copayments to doctors by clients of national health services are increasing, and such wonderful privileges as six-week cures have gone the way of the thirty-five-hour week.

In short, the market has been rearing its mighty head, and just as Jewish capitalists (or communists) were blamed for what the "invisible hand" had wrought in the first third of the twentieth century, America has been designated as culprit in the beginning of the twenty-first. When Germans attack *amerikanische Verhältnisse,* or when a French prime minister castigates the "unbridled laws of the market," they are responding not to America but to the travails of societies that can no longer hold back pent-up change. And so, such statements are mendacious at heart, because all Continental leaders have been in the business of transformation since the late 1990s. They have all been trying their hand at the reform game by chiseling away at labor market rigidities, constraints on competition, and lavish welfare payments. And all of them, especially those of France and Germany, were punished in and at the polls. So scapegoating America offers a number of advantages, *all of them domestic,* for governments that are conservative at heart, no matter whether they carry a leftish or a rightish label.

To assail *amerikanische Verhältnisse* is to delegitimize those rivals for political power who praise America's flexible labor markets as a "model," as the German Federation of Industry has done. Summing up a survey of German business leaders, the monthly *Capital*[25] reports, "Eighty percent say that the future belongs to the American system." This is a dramatic testimony to the enormous demonstration effect that is America, especially during the boom years of the 1990s, when U.S. unemployment was half that of Europe's (as it has remained in this decade). And the implicit prescription is "Make us like America." This does not sit well with chancellors and prime ministers who can change course by only a few degrees because their clientele, junkies of the welfare state, are wedded to maximal social protection.

But change they must, and so *amerikanische Verhältnisse* serve as a nice distraction from the necessary evil that must be done. As the bitter medicine is dispensed in small doses, the soothing message is "We will never be like America." Another part of the sugarcoating is "We are better than America—and so we *need* not become like them."[26] Hence the tone of superiority and deprecation that runs through the European discourse. The mendacious subtext is that

America, the "home of ultracapitalism," is to blame for the ailments that Europe must overcome. America is a nice shorthand for the Europeanization and globalization that is eroding group privileges while killing jobs and driving down wages. This is the oldest theme in the history of anti-ism: turn the abstract into the political, and the political into the personal—into the "Other." And presto, misery is explained and exorcized in the way of the biblical scapegoat that was loaded with all the sins of Israel and then dispatched into the desert.

On the most general level, anti-Americanism is both a conservative utopia and an ersatz European nationalism. The weightiest example, and by no means an idiosyncratic one, is an appeal, "Our Renewal," authored by a German, Jürgen Habermas, and cosigned by Jacques Derrida, a Frenchman, two writers categorized as philosophers in Europe.[27] The buzzwords are "a model-like European welfare system," "taming of capitalism," "pacification of class conflicts," "skepticism about markets," "trust in the steering capacities of the state," "limited optimism about technological progress," "preference for the protective guarantees of the welfare state and solidaristic solutions," low "tolerance for force." All these European virtues ought to feed into a "common [European] identity." And against whom might this identity be established? Against those who stand for an "individualistic ethos that accepts flagrant social inequalities" and who have refused to imbibe the moral lessons learned by postimperial Europe: no more war and, instead, the "mutual limitation of sovereignty." The message is that Europe has risen to a higher moral plane, while America is still mired in its pre-postmodern state.

The French foreign minister Hubert Védrine lists the indictments in more concise language. The ideological enemies of France are an "ultraliberal market economy," the "mistrust of the state," "nonrepublican individualism," the "reflexive pursuit of the universal and 'indispensable' role of the USA," flanked by "common law, the English language, [and] Protestant rather than Catholic values."[28] So anti-Americanism feeds not on what America does but on what America is—or, more accurately, on what Europe (and the rest of the world) does not want to be, but cannot fully avoid.

Nor is this a new phenomenon. In Europe's ideological history, there are at least two such waves of ressentiment translating into an anti-Western nationalism that fed on the assertion of moral-cultural superiority. The first reaction against modernity, a.k.a. Enlightenment, was spearheaded by German Romantics like Fichte and Herder (who, like Hegel, had started out as a liberal thinker). *Volk*, faith, and myth were held up as superior to the Enlightenment's cult of reason and secularism carried forward by Napoleon's armies. Overwhelmed by the power of ideas and bayonets, societies in crisis smoothly turned toward philosophers serving as handmaidens of anti-Western (then anti-French) nationalism.

The second wave was represented in Germany by the sociologist Werner Sombart, in France by Charles Maurras and Maurice Barrès, in Italy by Gabriele D'Annunzio. It was the predictable reaction to modernity's second great assault—the first "globalization" of the late nineteenth century, marching in lockstep with the by now usual suspects of modernization: urbanization, secularization, industrialization, and democratization. Werner Sombart's influential *Händler und Helden* (*Traders and Heroes*), published in 1915,[29] provides the most apropos instance of revulsion. His targets are capitalism, as then embodied by Britain, and the spirit of trading and profit-seeking that he opposes to the superior ways of the Germans as heroes who are willing to sacrifice their lives for the sake of "higher values." From there, it is but a small step to conflating capitalism not only with Britain but also with the Jews and with America. Though Britain is the main enemy, America is also depicted as avatar of capitalism and killer of *Kultur*. Naturally, the United States is a "Jewish land."[30]

What Sombart foresaw only dimly in 1915 is a full-blown reality today. Having inherited Britain's imperial mantle, the United States is modernity's mightiest engine—the agenda setter that inflicts adaptation—indeed, engenders emulation from the rest of the world (with China and India jostling forward on the no longer so distant horizon). No wonder that Europe, clinging to its formerly winning ways, resents the intruder that it is forced to mimic. Is envy the motor of resentment, as so many commentators have surmised[31]—with America embodying the might and the glory Europe no longer has and therefore pretends to disdain? Perhaps, but it is more plausible to point to the seductive demonstration effect that is America, coupled with the angst that Europe must (at least partly) become what America already is. That does not sit well with societies that have been weaned on a very different dispensation in the aftermath of the twentieth century's cataclysms. Fair Europe, attractive and dynamic in so many ways, a magnet for many nations pushing into the EU's "empire by application," has been in a state of social and economic crisis and paralysis since the mid-1990s. The crisis is measured by low growth, high unemployment, massive aging, and demographic decline. The problem extends from Madrid to Moscow. It is further exacerbated by Europe's limited ability to integrate another "Other" into its cultures, the "Other" being immigrants of different color and faith who are thronging into the *banlieues* of Paris and Rome, and into the inner cities of Berlin and Amsterdam. Societies in crisis, as illustrated by the torturous encounters with modernity between 1789 and 1945, tend to succumb to anti-ism, whether of the American or the Jewish kind. No wonder that Arab society, which has to battle many more dysfunctionalities than Europe, harbors the most virulent anti-Americanism and anti-Semitism of them all.*

*See the preceeding chapter.

America the Überpower

Anti-ism flows from what the target is, and not from what it does. It is revulsion and contempt that needs no evidence, or will find any "proof" that justifies the prejudice. As a general diagnosis, this interpretation is valid enough. Hence, visions of omnipotence and conspiracy dancing in the anti-ist's head are mere figments of an imagination that pines for a quick reprieve from crisis and complexity. The problem with America, though, is more intricate. Unlike African Americans, Jews, and Freemasons, America *is* powerful—indeed, the mightiest nation in history. And being easily leads to doing, or to fears of what America *might* do. This is part of the story of anti-Americanism redivivus. Latency began segueing into virulence in the late 1990s, the decade that followed the United States' coronation as last remaining superpower, and it reached a hysterical climax in the run-up to the Second Iraq War in 2002 and 2003.

As early as 1997, France's foreign minister Hubert Védrine began to muse about the temptations of "unilateralism" afflicting the United States and about the "risk of hegemony" it posed. Though George W. Bush had not yet flashed his Texas cowboy boots on the world stage (Bill Clinton was still in the White House), it was time for Paris to shape "a multipolar world of the future."[32] In 1998, France "could not accept a politically unipolar world or the unilateralism of a single hyperpower."[33] By then, the United States was the "indispensable nation," as Bill Clinton and his secretary of state Madeleine Albright liked to put it. It was a power that, in 1999, would unleash its cruise missiles to bludgeon Serbia's Slobodan Milosevic into the surrender at Dayton. By 2002 and 2003, it was sheer hysteria in the streets and squares not only of Europe but of the rest of the world—complete with the most vicious anti-American epithets like "Nazi" and "global terrorist."

Singular power, especially power liberally used, transformed a festering resentment into an epidemic, and so the anti-American obsession that swept the world contained an at least semirational nucleus—the fear of a giant no longer trammeled by another superpower. No, the United States would not unleash its smart bombs against France, Germany, Brazil, or Malaysia as it had done, or was about to do, against Milosevic and Hussein. But anti-ism is not about rational expectations, for power breeds its own angst. It is the fear of the unknown, of what *might* happen when ropes that once bound the colossus have fallen away.

There had been plenty such safeguards in the era of bipolarity—another giant that would contain and constrain No. 1. Moreover, America had contained itself, so to speak, by harnessing its enormous strength to a host of international institutions, from NATO to UN. Now, it had become a raw power, which intimated as of 2002 that it would go to war against Iraq with or without a Security Council resolution. This tempted the German chancellor into the carefully coded anti-Americanisms of his 2002 campaign: "Playing with war and military intervention—I cannot but warn against this. They won't drag us into this, ladies and gentlemen."[34] Angst of power unbound also led to the perverse spectacle of millions demonstrating against the United States and thus, "objectively speaking," seeking to protect Saddam Hussein, one of the most evil tyrants in history. Deep down in the subconscious of the protesters, raging fear was transformed and a fear arose that they must stop America, lest they be the next victims of its unbridled power.

Any anti-ism harbors fantasies about its target's omnipotence; hence the paranoid frenzy of 2002–03, which, interestingly, subsided when American weakness in pacifying Iraq was demonstrated in the aftermath of military triumph. It was part schadenfreude, part relief that the giant's feet of clay were finally being revealed. At any rate, the fearsome power differential between the United States and the rest of the world seemed to have shrunk a bit. Less clout, less loathing—four words that explain hysteria's decline. What prescription might follow from this diagnosis?

Reducing its might to reduce hatred is not an option for the last remaining superpower. Nor can America seek to please the world by becoming more like it—less modern or more postmodern, less capitalist or less religious, more parochial and less intrusive. The United States is unalterably enmeshed in the world by interest and necessity, and it will not cease to defend its dominance against all comers. Great powers do not want to become lesser ones, nor can they flatten themselves as a target. There is no opt-out for No. 1, unless forced to do so by a more potent player, and there is no change in persona for a nation whose exceptionalist self-definition is so different from that of the rest of the West.

The United States *is* different from the rest, in particular from the postmodern states of Europe stretching from Italy via Germany and Austria to the Benelux and Scandinavian countries. The European Union is fitfully undoing national sovereignty while failing to provide its citizens with a common sense of identity or collective nationhood. Europe is a matter of practicality, not of pride. As a work in progress, it lacks the underpinning of emotion and "irrational" attachment. Europeans might become all wound up when their national soccer teams win or lose, but the classical nationalism that drove millions into the trenches of the twentieth century is a fire that seems to have burned out. If there is a common identity, it defines itself in opposition to the United States—to both its culture and its clout.

Europe, with the partial exception of Britain, France, and some of the eastern newcomers like Poland, takes pride in overcoming the strictures of nationhood and the "atavism" of war. Its ideology reflects (and protects) actuality. The fountainhead of all major conflict in the past millennium, Europe suddenly, after 1945, enjoyed a surfeit of gratis security, courtesy of American power. As strategic dependence on the United States has trickled away, new strategic threats have not emerged. And substrategic threats like Islamist terrorism are not potent or pervasive enough to change a creed that proclaims, "Military violence never solves political problems." Of course, massive violence did solve Europe's existential problems twice in the preceding century, but that memory takes second place to the horrors of two world wars or to Europe's refusal to sacrifice a bit of butter for lots more guns. But why should Europe make that sacrifice? Its actuality is peace, which has made for a far happier way of life than did the global ambitions of centuries past.

Europe's empire is no longer abroad. Its name is European Union, and it is an "empire by application," not by imposition (see also chapter 6). Its allure is a vast market and a social model given to protection, predictability, and the ample provision of social goods. Its teleology is one of transcendence—of borders, strife, and nationalism. Its ethos is pacificity and institutionalized cooperation—the ethos of a "civilian power." Shrinking steadily, European armies are no longer repositories of nationhood (and ladders of social advancement), but organizations with as much prestige as the post office or the bureau of motor vehicles.

If this is postmodern, then America is premodern in its attachment to faith and community, and modern in its identification with flag and country. In the postmodern state, "the individual has won, and foreign policy is the continuation of domestic concerns beyond national borders. . . . Individual consumption replaces collective glory as the dominant theme of national life [and] war is to be avoided."[35] The modern state fused power to nationhood, and mass mobilization to a mission. Still, the difference between Europe and the United States is not one of kind. After all, Americans are just as consumerist and preoccupied with self and family as are Europeans, nor do they exactly loathe the culture of entitlements that spread throughout the West in the last half of the twentieth century. If the "statist" Europeans invented social security, the "individualist" Americans invented "affirmative action" as a set of privileges for groups defined by color, race, sex, or physical disabilities. "Political correctness," the very epitome of postmodernism, is an American invention.

But if we subtract the postmodern from the modern in the United States, a large chunk of the latter remains. For all of its multiethnicity, America possesses a keen sense of self—and what it should be. Patriotism scores high in any survey, as does religiosity. There is a surfeit of national symbols throughout the land, whereas no gas station in Europe would ever fly an oversized national flag. With its sense of nationhood intact, the United States is loath to share sovereignty and reluctant to submit to dictates of international institutions where it is "one country, one vote." The country still defines itself in terms of a mission, which Europeans no longer do—though the French once invented a *mission civilisatrice* for themselves, and the British the "white man's burden." The army, though digitalized to the max, can still draw on remnants of a warrior culture, especially in the South; as was once the case for the "Fighting Irish" of the Civil War, the army still offers newcomers one of the swiftest routes to inclusion and citizenship. America's armed forces, unlike most of their counterparts in Europe, are central tools of statecraft. American bases are strung around the globe, and no nation has used force more often in the post–World War II period than has the United States—from Korea to Vietnam to Iraq, and in countless smaller engagements from Central America to Lebanon and Somalia.

But whatever the distribution of pre-, post-, and just modern features may be, the most critical difference between America and Europe concerns power and position in the global hierarchy. The United States is the nation that dwarfs the rest. With its planetary clout, its location athwart two oceans, and its global interests, it remains the universal intruder and hence in harm's way. Its very power is a provocation for the lesser players, and, unlike Europe or Japan, No. 1 cannot huddle under the strategic umbrella of another nation. Nor can it live by the postmodern ways of Europe, which faces no strategic challenge as far as the eye can see. (Neither would Europe be so postmodern if it had to guarantee its own safety.) The

United States is the security lender of last resort; there is no ISF, or International Security Fund, where the United States could apply for a quick emergency loan. And so, the United States must endure in a Hobbesian world where self-reliance is the ultimate currency of the realm, and goodness is contingent on safety. The anatomy of the international system, to borrow once more from Sigmund Freud, is destiny. Where you sit is where you stand—postmodernism, post-nationalism, and all.

But a predominant power that wants to secure its primacy can choose among various grand strategies. While anti-Americanism has been, and will remain, a fixture of the global unconscious, it need not burst into venomous loathing. Nor is the fear of American muscle necessarily irrational when that power seems to have no bounds. It is not anti-Americanism when vast majorities, ranging from 59 percent in Germany to 80 percent in Canada to 82 percent in France, believe that the United States does not pay attention to their countries' interests.[36] Power unbound also suggests why 50–73 percent of the people in key NATO countries prefer more independence from the United States, why even larger majorities throughout the world (from 58 percent to 85 percent) don't want the United States to remain the one and only superpower.[37]

"Oderint, dum metuant"—"Let them hate me as long as they fear me"—the Roman emperor Caligula is supposed to have said. Fear is indeed useful for deterring others, but it may turn into a vexing liability when great power must achieve great ends in a world that cannot defeat, but can defy, America. What, then, is the appropriate grand strategy for the twenty-first century's überpower? The options will be explored in the next chapter.

5

A Giant's Grand Strategy

Models from History

NO OTHER POWER has ever loomed as large as did the United States at the beginning of the twenty-first century. If we liken the games played by nations to poker, and the various sources of power to chips, then the United States commands the biggest pile on the table. No rival can hope to match the sophistication, firepower, and mobility of America's armed forces. Its economy is not only the world's largest, it dwarfs the next-biggest one, Japan's, by a factor of almost three. If there is a global civilization, it is Made in U.S.A. Cultural domination is not just a matter of film, pop, and fast food. Of the world's thirty top-ranked universities, only seven are non-American.[1] The globe's largest official language, used by 1.4 billion, is English. Whether the spelling is "labor" (U.S.) or "labour" (Britain), English is the gateway for the advance of all things American. The United States is indeed a *hyper-puissance*, an überpower.[2]

History has known nothing comparable, but History also whispers that this cannot last, as it recalls the fates of the Roman and Habsburg empires, of Napoleon's France and Hitler's Germany—the Soviet Union being the most recent case in point. Power will inevitably generate counterpower, and the wider the gap, the harder the other players will seek to balance or best No. 1. This is the invariable logic of Nos. 2, 3, 4, et al. Naturally, the "positional logic" of No. 1 is the very opposite. Naturally, a giant like the United States, which exceeds all the others in strength and sweep, will want to secure its exalted position. The last remaining superpower will strive to remain precisely what it is.

How? What is the appropriate grand strategy for the twenty-first century's Mr. Big? Grand strategy is a design that relates means, and not just military ones, to ends, and ambitions to outcomes—what must a nation do in order to get what it wants or keep what it has? A paramount power has three, and only three, choices short of self-abdication. The first two strategies are merely theoretical; only the third one is practicable. The first choice of no practical value is *supremacy*. That ambition—lording it over each and all by sheer force—would stultify even a behemoth like America. Even a more modest variant of the supremacy gambit—keeping rivals from rising to the top—would founder on contemporary realities. To "keep others down" ultimately requires preventive war, a very costly, if not suicidal, approach in an age of nuclear second-strike capabilities.

Even preventive war against a third-rate power like Iraq, fingered as a possessor of weapons of mass destruction, proved neither cheap nor efficacious, given the "asymmetrical warfare" inflicted on the United States by a smallish number of underequipped insurgents and foreign terrorists. It took only three weeks in 2003 to slice through Saddam's armies. However, in the second part of the war, which began in November 2003, the enemy simply sidestepped America's overwhelming military advantage and fell back on the oldest tricks in the book: dispersion, concealment, terror, and tactical surprise. Moreover, the United States will not rush into preventive war against would-be nuclear powers like Iran and North Korea, because it is more economical to deter than to defeat them. The United States could destroy them both, as Rome obliterated Carthage, but total war would require an existential threat to the United States that these two nations do not pose. Without such a threat, a democratic nation will not lightly endorse a precautionary principle that demands catastrophic violence.

The second nonstarter—*isolation*—would be the opposite of the first. A near-autarkic power, the United States could trade with some, but treat with few, while withdrawing into nuclear-armed isolation. This is equally unpromising because the country would have to let go of those vital interests that transcend physical safety, renouncing its stake in order beyond borders. That is not the American way. Even before the country emerged from its nineteenth-century cocoon, it had stressed what the political scientist Arnold Wolfers called "milieu goals" as opposed to "possession goals"—a benign setting that would allow American interests and values to flourish.[3]

When the Republic was still very young and weak, it made the milieu point in all its (foolish) glory by taking on mighty Britain in the War of 1812 in order to assert the freedom of the seas. Eleven years later, the Monroe Doctrine pronounced as ambitious a milieu goal by declaring the Western Hemisphere off limits to the European powers: the Americas for the Americans, north and south. Several generations later, the Monroe Doctrine was followed by the Open Door policy, which demanded equal access to the far-flung markets of the Pacific. America's twentieth-century interventions in Central America and in the Caribbean were likewise milieu driven. The object was to "teach the South American republics to elect good men," as Woodrow Wilson famously put it—or, more accurately, to keep "bad men" out of power in America's backyard.

Defining the country's well-being in terms of a favorable environment is quintessentially American, as exemplified by Wilson's Fourteen Points, Roosevelt's Atlantic Charter, and Bush the Elder's "making Europe whole and free." Sweeping as these milieu goals were, they were still restricted to a narrow chunk of the world: the Atlantic area. Bush the Younger, however, outdid all of his predecessors by defining America's well-being in terms of planetary democracy. America, decreed George W. Bush, will "support democratic movements" everywhere because "the advance of freedom will lead to peace."[4] Calling for an order without borders, this new definition of the right setting literally encompasses the entire world. Isolationism, in short, was but a briefly victorious reflex of the interwar period, and then only with regard to Europe. It was never a biblical commandment of U.S. foreign policy as such.

That leaves merely the third, and the only promising, strategy—*disaggregation*. The object is to keep players 2, 3, 4, et al. from uniting against No. 1, from undermining its interests and vitiating its goals. The "categorical imperative" for a hegemonic power that wants to avoid endless war, let alone encirclement and defeat, is this: "Act in such a manner as to keep others from joining forces to block or bloody you." Conceptually, the quest is for position rather than for possession. Operationally, the third option breaks down into two variants, which shall be labeled "Britain" and "Bismarck."

Why choose Britain, and why, even more outlandishly, Bismarck? These are models drawn from bygone eras—when Britain "ruled the waves," from the seventeenth century through the nineteenth, and when Otto von Bismarck, chancellor of the Wilhelmine Reich, tried to secure Germany's shaky new perch in the heart of the Continent. As they now recede into the mist of history, how can these grand strategies provide insights for twenty-first-century America? With all its unprecedented power, the United States finds itself in a similar position today. It is No. 1, but not master of the diplomatic universe. It can deter and defeat any combination of rivals, but it cannot rule over them. Like Britain and Bismarck's Germany, the United States today enjoys primacy, but not supremacy, which is why "empire," in the strict sense, does not fit the American case. Hence, Britain and Bismarck lay out two very different paradigmatic choices for a power that has risen to the top and wants to stay there.

After the defeat of the Spanish Armada in 1588, certainly after the Treaty of Utrecht in 1713, which ended France's global ambitions under Louis XIV, Britain was for two centuries the leading actor on the great-power stage: virtually unassailable at home, though vulnerable abroad and unable to impose its writ on the rest of the world. At the end of the nineteenth century, Bismarckian Germany was a kind of Continental Britain: the richest player at the gaming board, a nation that would eventually surpass the United Kingdom in terms of raw economic power (like steel production) and defense expenditures.[5] But like Britain, it was only a "semihegemonial power,"[6] too weak to go it alone, too strong to be left alone. Like Britain, the Second Reich had to remain forever *en vedette* (vigilant) against encroaching coalitions, as both Frederick the Great and Bismarck put it, the two men who presided over the rise of German power in the eighteenth and nineteenth centuries, respectively.

Geography, however, had placed Britain and Germany at opposite ends of the spectrum of grand-strategic choices, and so Britain, an island power, and the Continent's new colossus mapped out two opposite escapes from the ubiquitous trap of encirclement. Britain capitalized on the great advantage of insularity and naval superiority. Its grand strategy was to stay aloof from the quarrels of Europe. Failing that, it would intervene—always with others—against the hegemonist du jour. But the main game was to reduce the other players' incentives to gang up on Albion, to use Britain's ancient name. An intruder only when other strategies had failed, Britain usually remained offshore while striking out on its farflung extra-Continental ventures, whether in Africa, the Middle East, India, North America, or the Far East. To defang hostile coalitions when they formed nonetheless, Britain harnessed superior ones—successively against Habsburg Spain, France, and Germany. But never did Britain embroil itself permanently in the rivalries of Europe, let alone lay claim to its leadership. Britain in short, was always the balancer, never the "balancee," to coin a phrase.

Such a grand strategy—watchful aloofness—was not an option for the Second Reich. Squeezed by mighty neighbors to the east (Russia), west (France), and southeast (Austria), Bismarckian Germany went off into the opposite direction. If Britain refused entanglement, Bismarck turned bonding into a lasting obsession. The game was not intermittent intervention but enduring commitment. To banish the "nightmare of coalitions" (Bismarck's term for "ganging up"), the "Iron Chancellor" sought to cement better relations with all contenders than they might establish among themselves. As long as all these relationships converged in Berlin like spokes in a hub, Germany would be the manager, not the victim, of Europe's great-power diplomacy.[7]

The point of this foreshortened story is "one problem, two solutions." The problem is primacy without supremacy—precisely the issue the United States confronts today. Which shall it be for the twenty-first century's überpower—Britain or Bismarck? Or a grand strategy that harnesses the best features of both?

Balancing à la Britain: The Principles

Henry VIII, for example, was the first monarch to render his country's grand strategy explicit with the maxim "Cui adhaero praeest"—"Prevail shall those whom I support." By 1577, his daughter Elizabeth I was the "Umpire betwixt the Spaniards, the French, and the Estates," wrote an admiring chronicler. "France and Spain are . . . the Scales in the Balance of Europe, and England the Tongue or the Holder of the Balance."[8]

To balance is to do battle when neither dynastic marriage nor diplomatic maneuver rights the scales. When Philip II of Habsburg Spain, the "empire on which the sun never set," dispatched his mighty Armada against England eleven years later, Elizabeth, the "Virgin Queen," launched the grand strategic tradition Winston Churchill would describe thus:

> For four hundred years the foreign policy of England has been to oppose the strongest, most aggressive, most dominating Power on the Continent. . . . Faced by Philip II of Spain,

> against Louis XIV under William III and Marlborough, against Napoleon, against William II of Germany, it would have been easy . . . to join with the strongest and share the fruits of his conquest. However, we always took the harder course, joined with the less strong Powers, made a combination among them, and thus defeated and frustrated the Continental military tyrant whoever he was, whatever nation he led. . . . It has nothing to do with rulers or nations; it is concerned solely with whoever is the strongest or the potentially dominating tyrant.[9]

This is the prototypical, if also idealized, rendition of British grand strategy throughout the ages, which Third Viscount Palmerston, the conservative foreign secretary, in 1840 characterized as a general law of his country's foreign policy. It enjoined the country to "watch attentively and to guard with care the maintenance of the Balance of Power." In particular, Her Majesty's government would not accept any "attempt of one nation to appropriate to itself territory which belongs to another nation," because such a move would constitute a "derangement of the existing balance."[10] This is the golden thread that runs endlessly through the debate on British grand strategy, whether enunciated by Tories or by Whigs. In 1852, Lord John Russell, Whig prime minister, used virtually the same language as had Palmerston, the conservative: any "territorial increase of one Power, any aggrandisement which disturbs the general balance of power in Europe . . . could not be a matter of indifference to this country [and might] lead to war."[11]

In the great European struggles for supremacy, Britain engineered those Continental coalitions that laid low one would-be hegemonist after the other: Habsburg Spain, the France of the Bourbons and Bonapartes, and the Germany of the Hohenzollerns and Hitlers. Nor was Britain finicky when it came to choosing allies. To be sure, against the Most Catholic King of Spain, Philip II, Protestant England supported the Dutch Calvinists and the French Huguenots. But when the Huguenot leader Henry of Navarre turned Catholic (explaining that "Paris is worth a mass"), England did not recoil from the newly minted papist but continued to fight on the convert's side, now renamed Henry IV, against his Spanish coreligionist. The enemy, in other words, was not Catholicism but the Habsburg Empire, the most fearsome power in sixteenth-century Europe, which also happened to be Catholic.

Yet half a century later, in the aftermath of the Thirty Years' War, Britain took on Louis XIV, sole ruler of France from 1661 to 1715. With Spain in decline, it was now the Sun King's turn to "unify" Europe under the knout of a single power. Setting the model for Napoleon 130 years later (the hegemonist always rings twice), Louis unleashed four wars of conquest, and each time Britain forged those coalitions that, in the end, overwhelmed the would-be supreme power of seventeenth-century Europe.

When Louis in 1667 invaded the Spanish Netherlands, which belonged to Britain's arch-enemy of the preceding hundred years, Britain naturally took on the new rival, masterminding a triple alliance with the Dutch Republic (United Provinces) and Sweden against France in the War of Devolution—never mind that Britain had just finished fighting its second maritime war against the Dutch, and would fight the third one a few years later. The coalition forced Louis to sue for peace at Aix-la-Chapelle (Aachen) in 1668. The respite did not last. Four years into this tenuous peace, Louis tried again, invading the Spanish Netherlands once more. This time England fought together with Protestant Brandenburg (the forerunner of Prussia), its old Catholic nemesis, Habsburg Spain, and the princes of the Holy Roman Empire. The war ended in a draw in the Peace of Nijmegen in 1678–79. Louis's third try was a thrust against the Palatinate (Germany), which he sought to seize in 1688. For the next eleven years, England recruited the Empire, the Dutch Republic, and Savoy against the usurper of the European order.

The coalition against the Sun King became practically European-wide during the War of the Spanish Succession (1701–13), which Louis unleashed by claiming Spain for his grandson Philip after the last Habsburg on the Spanish throne had died. Since Philip of Anjou, if successfully installed, was also slated to rule France and the overseas possessions of both countries, Her Majesty's government was not amused. Again, previous enmities or religious convictions did not matter. In addition to the Holy Roman Empire (minus Bavaria), England recruited Austria, Portugal, Savoy, Brandenburg, Naples, and Sardinia, as well as the Dutch, against whom it had fought three wars for maritime supremacy between 1652 and 1674.

And so England's strategic master plan continued to unfold: never to be of Europe, but always in Europe when a "derangement of the balance" (Palmerston) required it—whatever the "coalition of the willing" (Don Rumsfeld). Britain fought with Austria against France and Prussia in the War of the Austrian Succession (1740–48) and then *with* Prussia and *against* Austria in the Seven Years' War (1756–63), which had actually begun as an Anglo-French colonial contest in North America two years earlier. Known in America as the French and Indian Wars, the Seven Years' War was actually the *real* first world war—prosecuted in Europe, India, and North America, as well as in the Pacific Ocean. "The question," notes the historian Niall Ferguson, "was simply this: Would the world be French or British?"[12] The answer, provided by the Peace of Paris in 1763, was British. The French were extruded from both India and North America. The tools of victory proved to be a finer navy, vast shipyards, and the Bank of England as well as the London Stock Exchange, where the government could sell (freely tradable) long-term debt at more favorable rates than could the French kings, lacking such modern instruments of finance, in their own country.

In 1763, the world beyond Europe became British, but the French, following in the footsteps of the Valois and Bourbon dynasties, would again try to "unify" the Continent four decades later—

this time not under the emblem of the royal lily, but under the *bleu-blanc-rouge* of the revolution. By 1793, France, striking out in all directions and fortified by a universalist democratic ideology, once again became Britain's European enemy no. 1. At one time or another, British diplomacy mobilized virtually the entire Continent against Napoleon, with Austria, Spain, the Netherlands, Russia, Portugal, Sardinia, Naples, the German Reich, Turkey, and Prussia all involved at one time or another. At Waterloo, French imperial ambitions were shattered once and for all, and only on the eve of World War I, almost a century later, would France become Britain's ally for the first time since the two started dueling in the Hundred Years' War (1337–1453).

By 1914, another "military tyrant," in Churchill's words—Imperial Germany—was reaching for the hegemonial crown, but British grand strategy remained the same: "to oppose the strongest, most aggressive, most dominating Power on the Continent." Against the Kaiser, Britain fought with France, Russia, Italy, Japan, and the United States—an alliance that would eventually encompass twenty-eight nations and force Germany to sue for peace in 1918. The same pattern was repeated twenty years later against Hitler's Germany when Britain at first stood alone and then passed the crown of the grand balancer to the United States.

Balancing à la Britain: The Means

The basic principle of Britain's strategy can be reduced to three words "antihegemonism without entanglement." It was nicely rendered by Castlereagh, the secretary of foreign affairs, in the wake of the Napoleonic Wars: "When the Territorial Balance of Europe is disturbed," Britain "can interfere with effect, but She is the last Govt. in Europe, which [will] commit Herself on any question of an abstract character. . . . We shall be found in our Place when actual danger menaces the System of Europe; but this Country cannot, and will not, act upon . . . Principles of Precaution."[13] By this he meant membership in an alliance that faced no clear and present adversary. His negotiating brief for the Congress of Aix-la-Chapelle in 1818 warned that regular meetings with the other great powers would "necessarily involve us deeply in all the politics of the Continent, whereas our true policy has always been not to interfere except in great emergencies and then with a commanding force."[14]

His successor George Canning would oppose even the Holy Alliance, which was neither holy nor an alliance. It was merely a loose compact—actually a royal talking shop—that Austria, Prussia, and Russia had formed after Napoleon's final defeat in order to hold the line against further assaults on the monarchical order. To Canning, even the irregular meetings of the trio smacked of too much Continental amity, a coalition in the bud that had to be undone before it could blossom into something more serious. And so, Canning wrote proudly in 1826, "[The Holy Alliance] no longer marches *en corps* [in formation]. I have resolved them into individuality. . . ."[15] To dissolve *any* formation into "individuality" is the best one-sentence description of British grand strategy throughout the ages—a reflex that continues into the very present, where Britain fitfully seeks to dilute Franco-German designs for a more "federalist," that is, centralized, European Union.

In terms of means, British grand strategy was characterized by four preferences: sea power over land power, flexible combinations over permanent alliances, balancing over conquest, and intervention over enduring intrusion. This strategy was extraordinarily successful, securing Britain's exalted status as the only truly global power for 250 years. Until World War I, when the country lost virtually an entire generation in the trenches of Flanders, the strategy was also enormously economical. As Spain, France, Prussia, and Austria exhausted themselves in an endless series of Continental (as well as overseas) wars, Britain played out the essential advantages of an island-based sea power.[16]

Insularity granted Britain the rarest gift of international politics: immunity from direct attack as long as the Royal Navy controlled the Channel and the North Sea. If that advantage reduced the demand for security, Britain's dominance of the seas increased options and drove down costs. Compared with the expense of keeping and moving large armies, the dispatch of the fleet was more than just cheap; it was also highly profitable. Maritime power yielded speed, hence strategic surprise at points chosen by the attacker. When fighting alone, Britain won its decisive battles at sea, notably against the Spanish Armada and Napoleon's fleet at Trafalgar (as was America's battle at Midway, which turned the tide against Japan in World War II), and at far smaller cost than, say, Napoleon's victory against Russia at Borodino. Outnumbered at Trafalgar, Admiral Nelson did not lose a single ship.

Balancing rather than conquering added to economy. Tipping the scales (exploiting "synergy") is obviously cheaper than providing the full weight of countervailing power. The no-conquest rule reduced future costs, maximizing alliance options in the next round by avoiding the kind of eternal enmity that embroiled Frederick the Great in permanent conflict with Austria after he had robbed Maria Theresa of her Silesian province in 1740. Territorial conquest in the end would also undo the Wilhelmine Reich, which had grabbed Alsace-Lorraine in 1871, leaving France plotting for *revanche* until the opportunity arose on the eve of World War I.

As a result of self-restraint in victory, Britain could assume the role of arbiter (or "umpire" in the Elizabethan terminology) far more naturally than France, which would always have to fight the next war to defend its gains of the last one, or later the Wilhelmine Reich. Of course, the no-entanglement rule carried few risks for the extra-Continental power. As long as several great powers were crowding the European chessboard, mutual stalemate was the likely outcome, sparing Britain the necessity of calculating the balance too closely or of intervening too obsessively.

Is there a model in this tale for the United States? Surely, some of the analogies are striking. The United States, too, need not worry about "core security," that is, its ability to deter or defeat an all-out attack on its territory. Indeed, since the War of 1812, when the British burned down the White House, no foreign power has ever set foot on American soil. Though a small group of Islamist terrorists did bring down New York's Twin Towers in 2001, that threat will turn into a strategic one only if terrorists can bring many weapons of mass destruction into the country. By contrast, the British Isles were seriously threatened thrice: by Spain's Armada, Napoleon's fleet, and Hitler's bomber wings.

With the largest navy in the world, the United States duplicates Britain's classic edge as a sea power that can project force over a long distance faster than any land army. This advantage is compounded by a vast "navy in the air" that allows the United States to intervene anywhere in the world within hours and without recourse to bases. America's technological superiority may be likened to Britain's maritime dominance. Throughout the sixteenth, seventeenth, and eighteenth centuries, British ships may have been smaller, and its cannon lighter, than those of its enemies. But speed triumphed over size, while the accuracy of British gunners trumped the caliber of their foes, not to speak of the superiority of naval tactics. Blessed with a deterrent power Britain never had, the United States could even more easily follow a grand strategy of *garder les mains libres*—of keeping its hands untied.

In contrast to Britain, which could never do without coalitions, the United States does not really need allies to assure its physical safety. It needs them even less now than in the bipolar era when allies were valued more for the strategic real estate they provided as a glacis against the Soviet Union than for their actual fighting strength. Self-sufficient as Britain never was, the United States could play out the British game with even greater equanimity. It could safely wait out the formation of a hostile trend before committing itself to one or the other side in order to apply force synergistically rather than massively and unilaterally. In short, the United States is Albion writ large—an XXL Britain.

Balancing à la Britain: The Problem

To list the analogies between Britain and the United States is also to recognize their limitations. Britain, seemingly a consummate calculator of the balance, was actually not always prescient in identifying serious future threats. Was it Spain or France that posed a more serious threat in the decades before Elizabeth took on Philip II? Was it wise in the second half of the seventeenth century to fight three maritime wars against the diminutive Dutch Republic before zeroing in on the hegemonic ambitions of the French Sun King? Why did Britain support Frederick the Great in the middle of the eighteenth century while Prussia, an upstart if ever there was one, was taking on established great powers like France and Austria? Indeed, these two old-timers were much better than Britain at identifying the new threat from Berlin. In 1757, one year into the Seven Years' War, France and Austria in their treaty of alliance, pointedly sought to reduce Frederick's power "within such boundaries that he will not in the future be able to disturb the public tranquility."[17] What state was the gravest threat to Britain in the last third of the nineteenth century? France, which pressed on Britain in the colonial arena? Russia, which meddled in the Balkans, in the Near East, and in the Middle East? Or was it Germany, recently unified and forging ahead toward economic and military primacy? It turned out to be Germany, which Britain treated with nonchalant goodwill until the beginning of the twentieth century—and again in the 1930s, which was the gravest mistake of all.

Indeed, at least thrice did Britain unwittingly promote the rise of Prussia-Germany. The first time was the Seven Years' War

(1756–63), when Britain helped Frederick keep the Silesian booty he had wrested from the Austrian empress Maria Theresa in his previous foray; these were the humble beginnings of a power that would twice threaten the United Kingdom's very survival in the twentieth century. Britain miscalculated again during Bismarck's wars of unification a century later. London looked on idly as Prussia and Austria took on the Danes in 1864, easily relieving Denmark of Schleswig-Holstein. Nor did Britain move when Prussia defeated Austria in 1866, extruding the Habsburgs once and for all from the affairs of Germany. In the Franco-Prussian War of 1870–71, Britain practically held the ring for Bismarck. When the war was over, Prussia had demoted France and conquered Germany, so to speak, by unifying twenty-five city-states, duchies, and kingdoms under the Prussian Hohenzollerns. Within the next thirty years, this new player moved into a commanding position on the Continent, while Britain kept focusing on Russia—an incredibly obtuse mismeasure of the European balance of power. That failure, though, paled against the third instance—the aftermath of World War I. Instead of keeping a tight rein on a resurgent Weimar Germany, the British resumed its old balancing game against a mortally weakened France.

As France was desperately trying to preserve the World War I entente during the illusory peace of the 1920s, Britain tacitly supported revisionist Weimar Germany by committing itself, along with Italy, to guarantee the country's redrawn borders with Belgium and France (this was the gist of the fabled Locarno Treaty of 1925). That pledge marked the end of the Franco-British alliance because the guarantee cut both ways: against Germany if it attacked west, and against France if it invaded Germany. In a fit of absentmindedness, Britain had suddenly turned into an implicit partner of Weimar Germany. Not surprisingly, after Hitler became Reich chancellor in 1933, he went for massive rearmament and then territorial conquest by grabbing the Czech Sudetenland with Britain's blessing. Approval was given at the Munich conference of 1938, which has come to epitomize the very essence of appeasement. It took Britain six years—from 1933 to 1939—to recognize the deadly menace, and when it did, by declaring war on Hitler in 1939, it was too late. Britain was not up to the match. Just three years later, Britain's century-old nightmare became true: from Portugal and Spain, ruled by Fascist dictators, to the gates of Moscow, the Continent was unified under a single "military tyrant."

How to balance against whom and when is an issue as old as the state system itself, especially on a quickly shifting stage. Moreover, the United States has never been immune to failure. It was folly to take on Britain in the War of 1812 when the former mother country was fighting for survival against Napoleon. It was more foolish still to ignore Germany's strategic challenge in the run-up to two world wars. The United States intervened very late in the First World War—not at the beginning in 1914, but close to the very end in 1917. A generation later, Franklin D. Roosevelt's America joined the fray in the next round only in the last days of 1941, and then because Japan had attacked at Pearl Harbor and Hitler had declared war first. Today, the task of grand strategy has become a lot more complicated for the United States than it was for Britain in centuries past—for three reasons.

One: The Nature of the Playing Field Has Changed. It is a segmented, rather than a single, arena. Britain faced only one deadly threat, and that emerged in changing guises from one location only: Europe. Even better, Britain did not have to shoulder the burden of the balance all by itself; its weight could be distributed on many shoulders. A "coalition of the willing," in contemporary parlance, was always to be had. And so, Britain could apply its military might intermittently and on the margin. Today, there are at least three arenas of concern, and the connections among them are either loose or latent: Eurasia, the Middle East, and the Far East.

Apart from the pursuit of commercial gain, Europe takes only a passing interest in the Far East. It cannot and will not contribute its strength to the containment of China. That task rests squarely on the shoulders of the United States, with India and Japan, local powers both, in the second row. Nor does China look to the European Union as a strategic partner against its Russian neighbor. If Europe ever resumes balancing against Russia, it will look for help from across the Atlantic. In the Middle East, none of the "candidate members" of the superpower club—EU, China, Russia, Japan, or India—plays a significant, that is, strategic, role. It is the United States that guarantees the security of Israel, Saudi Arabia, Jordan, Iraq, and the Gulf States. The point here is a conspicuous mismatch between economic and strategic globalization. Economically, it is "a small world, after all," as the Disneyland song has it. Militarily, the name of the game is compartmentalization. And so, there is at present only one player capable of managing all three segments, and that is the United States.

Two: Intraregional Balances Are Shaky. By itself, Europe is not capable of restraining a resurgent Russia, and the Greater Middle East is unable to balance itself, as three Gulf wars have shown: Iraq against Iran in 1980, Iraq against Kuwait in 1990, the United States against Iraq in 2003—not to speak of three major Arab-Israeli confrontations. In all cases, the United States had to intervene from the outside. In the first Gulf war, it supported Iraq sub rosa; in the next two, it switched sides to take on Saddam Hussein. Earlier, the United States had intervened indirectly against Israel by pushing its army out of Egypt after the 1956 Suez War, and in favor of Israel by deterring the Soviet Union during the Six-Day and Yom Kippur wars. Syria got away with the de facto annexation of Lebanon in 1990;* no Arab nation complained, though none could have been

*In 2005, Syrian forces withdrew from Lebanon under American and French pressure.

assured by the grab. The balance is rendered more precarious still by the wobbliness of regimes. Domestically, all Arab states are explosions waiting to happen, while the private armies of terror are busy laying the fuses.

In the Far East, a quadripartite balance is theoretically possible among the United States, China, Russia, and Japan. But it is far from mature. Though North Korean nuclear weapons threaten all these powers, China, Russia, and Japan have been content to let the United States carry the main burden of antiproliferation. Japan is worried about the rise of China, but even though it has assembled the world's third-largest surface navy, it continues to huddle under a security umbrella Made in U.S.A. While Russia must also worry about the ascendancy of China, it pretends not to notice or may be too weak to react. Only the United States can organize the balance *within* these three areas, but that implies that it does not have the great advantage of Britain: the option of aloofness. The United States is at once fortunate and cursed. It is fortunate, because it alone has the wherewithal to manage balances regionally and to tie them together globally. And it is cursed because, unlike Britain, it cannot withdraw from the game and return only fitfully to apply its might on the margin. There is no safe haven to which the last remaining superpower can withdraw. The United States is entangled in the world not just by choice but by globe-encircling might.

Three: The Game Has Changed. As long as there are states, they will be condemned to live in a self-help system without an ultimate court of appeal and an enforcer that guarantees the security of each and all. Hence, power will remain the final arbiter, no matter how many "soft issues" like AIDS or climate control have crowded into the agenda. But the traditional enactment of the contest has changed beyond recognition.

In the past, peace was just a break between two great-power or even global wars. Fighting was the full-time occupation of princes and potentates, and so was expansion. Reading a diplomatic history of the eighteenth and nineteenth centuries is as unnerving as watching the chaotic and totally unpredictable course of a hurricane. Will it collapse, pick up, or suddenly change directions? Crises erupted daily as a minor move by one nation was transmuted into a cosmic menace in the imagination of another. What was the true import of an envoy's trip or a monarch's throw-away line? Everything mattered, no matter how remote. Threats and counterthreats were flung on a daily basis and forces dispatched, until a third nation offered mediation or support.

The problem, to recall Palmerston, was always the "attempt of one nation to appropriate to itself territory which belongs to another nation." Today, territorial conquest has lost its luster because territory itself has lost its shine, at least among the great powers. Land and people were the two great sources of a nation's strength in the past; hence these assets were constantly grabbed or defended. Today, other riches matter more among the great powers, as capital is being substituted for the land, and brains are for muscles. The "derangement" of the balance is measured not in square miles but in terms of economic growth, Security Council votes, arms technologies acquired or denied, and domestic regimes sustained or toppled.

War was the constant companion of traditional power politics, but since 1945 no great power has clashed directly with another—unless one wants to count Red China as a great power in 1950, when it took on the United States in Korea. There have been a hundred wars in the wake of World War II, but they were all peripheral or civil ones, which, crucially, did not spread in the way the Anglo-French duel in North America segued into Europe's Seven Years' War. It was Israel against Arabs, Arabs against fellow Muslims, and Africans against Africans. It was India against Pakistan, and India against China, but in tightly limited encounters. It was the United

States against North Korea, North Vietnam, Afghanistan, and Iraq, and Soviet Russia against Afghanistan. There were three Soviet interventions against disobedient allies in Eastern Europe in the 1950s and 1960s. Count also NATO's three-month bombardment of Serbia in 1999 as a war of sorts. But since the Iraq–Iran war of 1980–88 (with casualties said to amount to two million), the most horrifying bloodshed has occurred *within* countries: in Rwanda, Bosnia, Algeria, Chechnya, or Sudan.

Relative peace (defined as absence of major-power war) is a key feature of the contemporary world, and it explains why the kaleidoscopic formation of alliances and counteralliances, the central issue of British grand strategy, is not the most pressing one for the United States now. Today's No. 1 faces denial or defiance by old friends and new rivals, but not the real thing—a formalized alliance of major players—which so obsessed Britain.

Old allies like France and Germany have become ad hoc adversaries, and yesterday's enemies like China and Russia have become ad hoc cohorts. But more important, the strategic game is not yesterday's zero-sum version ("my gains are your losses"), but decidedly mixed, as cooperation always vies with confrontation. Nor should this come as a surprise when the stakes are tallied. In the days of yore, the obsessive quest was for physical security, and the object of the game was territorial or maritime gain. How shall we count the ways in which not only the stakes but also the prizes for cooperation have multiplied in the contemporary world? "Old Europe" might dream of turning the EU into a superpower rival of the United States, but its would-be leaders, France and Germany, must not damage the largest trading relationship in the world, which is the trans-Atlantic one. The EU can defy the United States on tariffs and protection, it can oppose the United States in Iraq, but it cannot do without the United States when it comes to chastising a fourth-rate power like Serbia.

The United States might wish to organize an anti-Chinese

alliance in the Pacific, but it cannot do so too blatantly, because China, holding hundreds of billions of dollars in U.S. debt, might just decide to drop these on the market as the financial equivalent of a thermonuclear weapon. Conversely, China would not want to press its strategic advantage against Taiwan too hard, because it might lose a trade surplus with America worth $160 billion. In its pursuit of global democracy, the United States must denounce Russia's neotsarism softly because it needs Moscow's help in the battle against Islamist terrorism. To generalize the point: balancing in the way of Britain is a blunt, if not useless, sword when it comes to all those major American interests that demand sturdy cooperation from others: from dollar stability via the spread of nuclear weapons to healing the political pathologies of the Arab Middle East.

The traditional tools of statecraft will remain on the table as long as there are states in the world. But the parsimony of old-time power politics—thrust and parry, collaborate and quit—no longer takes care of the rich reality of international life this side of existential security. Above all, the United States lacks the option of aloofness in a world where it is present everywhere. If these are the limits of the British model, what about the Bismarckian one, which was born not in the battle against the Armada but three hundred years later when Germany, victorious and unified, suddenly advanced to the head of the great-power class.

Bonding à la Bismarck: The Stage

The opposite of the British model was designed by Bismarck after Germany's unification in 1871. This new player, born from the fusion of twenty-five lesser German states, was suddenly the most populous country in Europe, and between 1885 and 1913, its industrial production grew at twice the British rate, eventually outstripping everybody else as an economic power.[18] Yet this towering figure on the Continental board suffered from three grievous handicaps that would haunt Bismarck without end.

First, this new Germany was a latecomer, an arriviste to the great-power club, and so it lacked the legitimacy that stems from sheer longevity. Britain, France, Austria, Russia, Turkey—great or still-great powers then—had been around for centuries. Whether at war or at peace, they had a seat at the table. But the Second Reich was an intruder, indeed a potential usurper. It was mighty, but not yet "clubbable," and thus a designated target of envy and suspicion.

Second, Bismarck's creation unhinged an ancient distribution of power predicated on a weak European center. Since the late Middle Ages, "Germany" was more or less coterminous with the "Holy Roman Empire of the German Nation," but, as the quip goes, that entity was neither holy, nor Roman, nor even strictly German, but multiethnic, and certainly not a real empire. The last point was proven beyond a doubt by the Thirty Years' War (1618–48). Purportedly fought for reasons of faith, the war was in fact an all-out power struggle in and over Germany that wiped out one-third of its population. When it was over, the emperor was but a figurehead, and the Empire a bunch of weakling states closely supervised by its stronger neighbors. Until Bismarck's Second German Reich bestrode the stage 223 years later, Germany was but a power vacuum and an object of desire at the crossroads of Europe. No more. "What had become clear to Europe was that primacy had passed from France to Germany," the British historian John A. Grenville has noted, with a view to Bismarck's war of unification in 1870–71, and he quotes Disraeli to make the point: "You have a new world. . . . The balance of power has been entirely destroyed."[19]

Destroyed? Not quite—and that leads to the Reich's third handicap. Muscular it was, but vulnerable, too, which Britain was only in the direst of straits. There was no North Sea moat to still the hands of would-be conquerors. So isolation à la Albion was impossible for the new colossus, encircled as it was by four great powers. And one of them, France, burned with a thirst for *revanche*. Or as Leon Gambetta, founder of the Third Republic, famously put it with an eye on Alsace and Lorraine, Germany's booty in the war of 1870–71: *En parler jamais, y penser toujours*—we will never talk, but always think, about our sacred loss.

France was Bismarck's lasting obsession. As he wrote in 1874, "Nobody ought to harbor any illusions; peace will end once France is again strong enough to break it."[20] Yet France was only one part of his problem; the rest was geography. Frederick the Great's term for "geography" was the *cauchemar des coalitions*—the nightmare of coalitions. Obsessed by Frederick's near-demise in 1762, Bismarck kept harping on *die Kaunitzsche Politik*, his shorthand for the almost fatal all-European coalition Maria Theresa's chancellor Kaunitz had masterminded against the Prussian upstart in the Seven Years' War. As a semihegemonial power, Germany could hold off any one challenger, but not all of them together. Worse, long unguarded frontiers meant that Germany had to fend with a destabilizing mix of capabilities: it was much better at offense than at defense.

This yawning gap between offensive and defensive could hardly escape Germany's neighbors, because it implied a permanent temptation to go first—recall more recently Israel's preventive war against Egypt in 1956 and its three-pronged preemptive strike in 1967, both of which were driven by long, vulnerable frontiers and the lack of strategic depth. This built-in temptation could not reassure Germany's neighbors; in fact, "striking first," and then in all directions, was precisely Berlin's strategy in 1914 and 1939. In short, though the biggest player on the board, Germany was also the most exposed—a perfect target of "ganging up" that Britain never presented. If Britain was the balancer, Germany was the balancee. And so, Bismarck's Reich faced a grand-strategic problem of frightful magnitude.

Bonding à la Bismarck: The Means

In 1877, five years after the birth of the new Reich, Bismarck noted, "A French newspaper recently wrote that I suffered from '*le cauchemar des coalitions*'; this kind of nightmare will plague a German minister for a long time, perhaps forever." The solution was limned in the same document, the famous "Kissinger *Diktat*" of 1877. In this "memo to himself," Bismarck formulated the very core of German grand strategy, which, as we shall argue, might offer a model for the United States, as well. The object was "not territorial acquisition but a general political constellation in which all the powers except France need us and, by dint of their mutual relations, are kept as much as is possible from forming coalitions against us."[21] If Britain's motto was "anti-hegemonism without entanglement," Bismarck's was soon to read, "Bonding beats balancing."

It is important to note that Bismarck's task was more demanding than just the containment of France. To begin with, a German-led alliance against Paris was not to be had. Austria, Russia, and Britain had their quarrels with France, but mainly with each other, especially in the Balkans and Near East. And for all of them, the new German heavyweight was at least a latent problem—as America, its might untrammeled, is for Europe, Russia, and China in the twenty-first century. Unable to harness Austria et al. in a stable foursome, Bismarck clad his strategy in a metaphor: Germany as "Bleigewicht am Stehaufmännchen Europa," as deadweight at the bottom of the tumbler doll that was Europe. To use more familiar language: if Europe was the ship, the Reich was to be the lead-filled keel that would defy any gust and so keep the vessel from capsizing. The tumbler doll simile implied that acting as "Tongue or the Holder of the Balance"[22] was not enough. Germany had to exert the gravitational pull that would keep everybody else in proper orbital alignment. Concretely, Berlin had to neutralize the rivalries that drove Russia and Austria toward collision in the Balkans, that threatened to embroil Britain and Russia in the nineteenth century's arc of crisis running from Turkey to Afghanistan, and that might tempt each of the three to look for help in Paris.

Initially, Bismarck actually tried his hand at the classic British game, maneuvering between the big three and manipulating them all without committing himself fully to any one. That heady moment came to an end at the Congress of Berlin (1878), which Bismarck had convened to contain yet another eruption of the "Eastern question": Who would get what and how much of the dying Ottoman Empire, which at that point extended from Bosnia in the Balkans to Basra on the Persian Gulf? With each power threatening war if any of the others seized too much, Bismarck interposed himself as "honest broker" who wanted nothing for himself, except, of course, the obeisance due to those who dole out indispensable services.

Alas, when the Congress of Berlin opened, the honest broker found himself outmaneuvered by the British and the Russians, who preferred to settle their quarrels without paying any commission to their German host and would-be intermediary. As it turned out, two weeks earlier, Lord Salisbury, the foreign secretary, and Count Shuvalov, the Russian ambassador, had redrawn the map of the Balkans à deux. For good measure, London had also extended a secret side deal to the Austrians in order to keep them from running to Germany for compensation. Bismarck may have wanted to be honest, but as broker he did not shine. Germany's "deadweight" was not heavy enough.[23]

At that juncture, Bismarck must have grasped that Balancing à la Britain could not be translated into German. So he changed the strategy, but not the purpose. If Berlin could not play the sun to Europe's great-power planets, if Austria, Britain, and Russia veered off on their own orbits, where they might collide with each other or collude against Germany, then Bismarck had to try the opposite of the British game. Now it was bonding rather than balancing, and so Bismarck contracted a lasting case of pactomania.

One year after the Congress of Berlin, Bismarck unveiled the new strategy in a dispatch to the Kaiser: "Further proof is not needed that we, located in the heart of Europe, must not risk isolation. But in my opinion, we will court this risk if we do not preempt it through a defensive compact with Austria."[24] It was concluded in 1879, just eight years after the birth of the new Reich. The Dual Alliance between the Habsburgs and Hohenzollerns was the centerpiece of the new system; it bound Germany and Austria to aid each other in case of an attack by Russia. Considering the age-old struggle between Prussia and Austria over the control of Germany, the realignment was just this side of revolutionary, leaving Russia out in the cold.

To keep St. Petersburg from slipping into the French orbit, Bismarck in 1881 revived the Three Emperors' League with Russia,* under which each guaranteed benevolent neutrality in a war with a fourth power, that is, France. Under the new dispensation, the imperial trio also tried to smooth over Austro-Russian quarrels in the Balkans and Near East by making any change in the status quo contingent on tripartite agreement. Bismarck now had two of his most dangerous neighbors on a leash. But how strong and how short was it? To Bismarck that mattered less than his success in adding the "Saburov rule" to the injunction of the Kissinger *Diktat*. "All politics," he told the Russian ambassador in Berlin, "can be reduced to this formula: Try to be in a threesome as long as the world is governed by the precarious equilibrium of five great powers. That is the true protection against coalitions."[25]

But three out of five was not enough for the man who lived in constant fear of encirclement. By 1883, Bismarck's alliance system covered half of Europe. Serbia and Romania were drawn into the Austro-German orbit by subsidiary alliances in 1881 and 1883. Italy

*The first Three Emperors' League (1873) was no more than a contractual commitment to mutual consultation.

joined Vienna and Berlin in the Triple Alliance concluded in 1883. Finally, after the Three Emperors' League collapsed under the pressure of Austro-Russian rivalries in the Balkans, the (albeit shaky) capstone of the structure was set in place in 1887: the legendary Reinsurance Treaty with Russia. It was exactly what the name implied: a mutual (and secret) pledge of benevolent neutrality in case either party suffered an unprovoked attack from its primary potential foe, that is, Germany from France and Russia from Austria.

What was the purpose of Bismarck's pactomania? He has often been attacked for casting a net of contradictory commitments over the Continent that was useless in case of war. Yet that is as true as it is beside the point. Bismarck constructed his system not in order to aggregate power but in order to *devalue* it. Like Britain's, his object was to stalemate the power of rivals, but he played the game in totally un-British ways. If Britain tried to keep its hands free, Bismarck was willing to tie his own in order to tie those of his rivals.

Above all, Bismarck dreaded the marriage of Germany's flanking powers; unlike Wilhelm II and Hitler, however, he understood Germany's limits too well to dare destroy them. Hence the web of entangling fetters and counteracting commitments that would preserve Germany's position by making hostile coalitions—indeed, war itself—impossible. If all but France were bound to Germany, if none could move without being tripped by the net weaved in Berlin, each would stay in place—and with it, the European status quo so profoundly destabilized by that enormous, but not supreme, power that was the Second Reich.

"Bonding beats balancing" was not all. Recall the Kissinger *Diktat,* which laid out the more ambitious part of the agenda. That was "a general political constellation in which all the powers except France need us and, by dint of their mutual relations, are kept as much as is possible from forming coalitions against us." The appropriate metaphor here is that of "hub and spokes." It implies two things. First, Berlin was the "hub," where all of Europe's major relationships were to converge like spokes. Second, Germany had to maintain better relations with the "tips"—Austria, Russia, Britain, Italy, and the lesser players—than they had among themselves. By definition, they would have little reason to "gang up" on Germany.

This was an ambitious, but not excessive, objective for a leader who kept professing that Germany was "satisfied," "saturated," "pacific," and "conservative."[26] The claim also was less duplicitous than it sounded, though duplicity was certainly a blatant feature of the hub-and-spokes gambit. For instance, when Bismarck shifted from balancing to bonding by concluding the Austro-German alliance of 1879, he laid it on thick. As A. J. P. Taylor put it,

> The French were assured that his object was to prevent the dismemberment of the Habsburg monarchy—a cause in which they also were deeply interested. The British were told that the alliance would create an unbreakable barrier against Russia; the Russians that it would sever Austria-Hungary from Great Britain—"I wanted to dig a ditch between her and the Western powers." No doubt there was some truth in all these stories. It was part of Bismarck's strength that he always believed what he said, at any rate while he was saying it.[27]

Yet it was certainly true that Bismarck did not want to play for the territorial stakes that kept embroiling Austria, Russia, and Britain. The "Eastern question," he told the Reichstag in 1876, was not "worth the healthy bones of a single Pomeranian grenadier."[28] (To the United States, the current "Eastern question," that is, the Greater Middle East, was worth three wars between 1991 and 2003.) Bismarck did not want to contest Britain's overseas possessions. He did not want to vie for colonies in Africa. When pushed by a colonial enthusiast, he snapped, "My map of Africa is in Europe. Here is Russia, and here is France, and we are in between; that is my map of Africa."[29] In fact, he positively encouraged Germany's arch-enemy

France to expand into North Africa. Given Austrian, British, and Russian rivalries in the Balkans and beyond, given Britain's, Belgium's, France's, and Portugal's "scramble for Africa," Bismarck played his very own game by three rules: "Keep out," "Keep them busy," and "Keep them away." The object was to divert the other powers' attention from the European center and to tie them down in faraway disputes. Self-containment spelled out the biggest prize of them all. Since the Reich took no direct interest in these quarrels, it could all the better play hub to a multitude of spokes. As long as they all looked outward, they would not cast an invidious eye on Berlin.

Disinterest and self-restraint is what keeps such a hub well greased. It lends credibility and legitimacy to those who want to hold the reins rather than own all the carts. And so the grand manipulator succeeded for twenty years in staving off the "nightmare of coalitions." Only in 1892, when France finally managed to draw Russia into an alliance, did the ganging-up process against Germany begin in earnest. And it took another fifteen years, until 1907, before Britain, previously a "sleeping member" of the Bismarckian system, would finger Germany as "military tyrant" and public enemy no. 1. With Italy in tow, the Triple Entente (Britain, France, and Russia) completed the Reich's encirclement. And by 1918, after utter defeat, the Reich was no more.

That Bismarck's pactomania succeeded for so long is testimony to the efficacy of his hub-and-spokes model. But why did it collapse? One classical answer is the stupidity of his successors and the boundless ambitions of Wilhelm II, who had acceded to the throne in 1890. A few months after Bismarck's dismissal, the Foreign Office's Paul Kayser remarked, "After a quarter of a century of genius, it is a real blessing to be able to be as homely and matter of fact as other governments."[30] Bismarck's heirs certainly lived up to that sigh of relief. The first blow against complexity was struck when the new regime refused to renew the Reinsurance Treaty with Russia, because that secret compact conflicted with Germany's pledges to Austria.

What else was new? The new chancellor Leo von Caprivi was heard to confess that he simply could not keep several balls up in the air, as Bismarck had done.

A more profound answer was offered in Sir Eyre Crowe's famous memorandum of 1907. There were two possible interpretations of German strategy, the foreign service officer argued in his dispatch to Britain's foreign secretary, Sir Edward Grey. Either the Kaiser was reaching for hegemony or "all her excursions and alarms, all her underhand intrigues do not contribute to . . . a well-conceived . . . system of policy." Bismarck's self-containment, which is the essence of any hub-and-spokes strategy, had given way to a naval race with Britain, to forays into the Near and the Middle East, to meddling in North and South Africa, to the quest for colonies in East Asia and Central Africa. Once "saturated" and "pacific," Wilhelm II's Germany suddenly demanded a "place in the sun." So what was it, Crowe's memorandum asked, hegemonial or haphazard? Intentions simply did not matter, Crowe concluded. The critical point was the relentless growth of German material power that would feed Germany's ambitions, turning it into a "formidable menace to the rest of the world" even without "malice aforethought."[31] In other words, for Britain it was back to Castlereagh, Palmerston, et al. The "derangement of the balance" called for containment and ganging up. Today, one might surmise that similar memoranda have circulated through the French Foreign Office, with *les Etats-Unis* substituting for Imperial Germany. Benign or not, American intentions do not matter, an analyst in the Centre d'Analyse et de Prévision might have penned. What counted was the enormous increase in American power, compared with all the rest.

A third problem with Bismarck's system was Germany's precarious position as semihegemonial power: strong enough to hold off anyone, but not all. To keep all spokes centered on Berlin required a strong, even impervious hub. Without that strength, Germany could not keep the rods in place forever. Russia was encroaching on Austria in the Balkans. France, eager to undo the defeat of 1871, was determined to break the entire wheel. Thus, an alliance between Russia and France, the two revisionists, was an ever-present threat. And materialize it did—not least because Europe's would-be manager became Europe's main problem when it began to grope for mastery after 1890. If Bismarck, fully cognizant of Germany's inherent liabilities, merely wanted to hold the baton, his successors wanted to play first fiddle and bang the kettledrum, too. That was the end of the concert that had blessed Europe with forty years of great-power peace.

What, if any, are the lessons for the United States in the twenty-first century?

"The United States of Bismarckia"

"Bonding beats balancing" and a "constellation in which all the powers except France need us" were the barebones of Bismarck's grand strategy. Changing only one word—"Soviet Russia" for "France"—produces an equally parsimonious description of American grand strategy after World War II. Pactomania was surely the hallmark of U.S. policy during the Cold War. Recall the alphabet soup of acronyms that stand for America's alliance network: NATO for the North Atlantic area, CENTO for the Middle East, SEATO for Southeast Asia, and ANZUS for Oceania, plus a host of bilateral alliances, the most important of which still is the U.S.-Japanese Security Treaty. Embedded in these formal compacts was a system of implicit or tacit alliances by which the United States came to guarantee the defense of states like Israel, Saudi Arabia, Jordan, Pakistan, and Taiwan.

Add to these security ties a whole slew of international institutions sponsored by the United States in the aftermath of World War II: the United Nations (UN), anchored by five great powers, which evokes the "Concert of Europe" of the nineteenth century; the International Monetary Fund (IMF), which was to manage the world's currencies;

the Organization for European Economic Cooperation (OEEC), which would expand into the OECD (for Economic Cooperation and Development); the General Agreement on Tariffs and Trade (GATT), now the World Trade Organization (WTO), which sets global trade rules; and the World Bank, which funds Third World development. Add also regional compacts like the OAS (Organization of American States) or NAFTA (North American Free Trade Agreement).

It was bonding *über alles*, and the purpose—directly or implicitly—was a "constellation in which all the powers except Soviet Russia need us." What France was to the Reich, the Soviet Union was to the United States: an implacable foe and target of isolation. Soviet power and ideology were the core issues of the Cold War. But the magnificent spin-off of this struggle was the golden age of American diplomacy, with the United States playing Bismarck on a planetary scale. None of these wondrous institutions would have arisen, let alone endured, if the United States had not acted as "lead financier" and indispensable impresario. What Bismarck had merely limned in one sentence of the Kissinger *Diktat,* post-1945 America turned into a towering global edifice. Because the United States had opened the richest bazaar of political goods the world had ever seen, everybody except the Soviet Union and its hapless vassals flocked aboard.

"If you build it, he will come" was the mantra of the 1989 movie *Field of Dreams*. The golden age of American foreign policy, circa 1944–1971,* obeyed precisely this principle: supply will create its own demand. Long before supply-side economics became a household word, the United States practiced supply-side diplomacy: produce goods and services like free trade or regional security, and "all

*Why 1971? In that year, the United States abruptly suspended the convertibility between gold and the dollar by closing the Federal Reserve's "gold window," at which other nations could convert their dollar holdings into gold at $35 per ounce. In doing so, the Nixon administration said good-bye to institutionalism and to the fixed exchange rate system that lay at the heart of the U.S.-sponsored International Monetary Fund (IMF). The United States was now free from the monetary discipline

powers but the Soviet Union will need you." The United States, in effect, "supersized" Bismarck by crafting not just a European but a global hub-and-spokes architecture.

What other parallels might be drawn? "Pacific," to recall Bismarck's soothing invocation of the 1880s, this American hub was not. Indeed, no nation has resorted to force more frequently in the aftermath of World War II than the United States. But like Bismarck's Germany, it was "saturated" and "conservative." For all its ideological fervor, which dates back to Woodrow Wilson's "making the world safe for democracy," the United States was a status quo power. It went to war in places like Korea and Vietnam not to redraw borders but to restore them. "Rollback" in Europe was a campaign shibboleth of the 1950s, not a policy, as the scrupulous avoidance of real confrontation in every East–West crisis demonstrated. When the United States broke the Soviet blockade of West Berlin in 1948–49, it resorted to an airlift, not to a bombing campaign. When the Berlin Wall was built in 1961, American tanks rolled up to the edge of the Soviet sector, but not one foot beyond the line of demarcation. When the United States almost did go to war over Cuba, the purpose was not to grab the island (as in the Spanish-American War of 1898) but to force the withdrawal of Soviet nuclear missiles that spelled a serious "derangement of the balance."

"Pacific," no—"conservative," yes. Postwar America also followed in Bismack's footsteps when it came to the use of alliances. Like the Reich, the United States amassed allies not to aggregate power for offense but to stalemate it. This is how George F. Kennan, the drafts-

---

that was to force countries with high inflation and current-account deficits to raise interest rates and taxes to uphold the external value of their currencies. Rather than risk a grave recession at home, the administration shifted the burden of adjustment to its main trading partners. As the dollar plunged, their currencies soared. This made their exports dearer and America's cheaper, improving the latter's trade position.

man of the containment policy, rendered the gist of America's Cold War strategy: the purpose was "a policy of firm containment, designed to confront the Russians with unalterable counter-force at every point where they show signs of encroaching upon the interests of a peaceful and stable world."[32] Russia was to America in the twentieth century what France was to the Reich in the nineteenth: the main threat to the status quo. By contrast, Germany and, in the twentieth century, the United States represented the "deadweight" powers in Bismarck's vocabulary. But how to act out this role when their enormous strength posed a latent threat to all the other players? How could the custodians avoid looking like housebreakers themselves?

To play the hub to Europe's spokes, Bismarck instinctively went for a strategy of self-containment. Having bested Denmark, Austria, and France in Germany's wars of unification, he argued against further expansion, but failed to resist the nationalist fervor that exacted the annexation of Alsace and Lorraine. He refused to meddle in Germany's "Near Abroad," in the Balkans and in eastern Europe. And he managed to halt the drive into Africa in order to avoid collision with France and Britain, though under his aegis, the Reich did acquire a handful of out-of-the-way colonies in Africa.[33] Nor did he challenge Britain's maritime supremacy. Germany, as Bismarck never tired in pointing out, was "satisfied" and "saturated."

"Self-containment" does not accurately describe Cold War America, which did meddle in Central America, its own "Near Abroad," and tried to topple or prop up regimes across the world. But the status quo outcome was not that different. If Bismarck opted for self-restraint by reasoned choice, the United States had no other choice, given those many lines in the sand drawn by its mortal rival, the Soviet Union. "Containment," the application of "unalterable counter-force at every point," evidently went both ways—with *both* superpowers caught in an endless ballet of thrust and counterthrust. True, the Soviet Union was always No. 2 in every category of power—"soft," economic, or diplomatic. But America's edge was always blunted—not least because of the vast nuclear overkill both giants held in reserve. The United States may have had the better guns, but it had to travel gingerly because a suicidal shoot-out lurked just around the next corner. "Mutual assured destruction" was the best guarantor of self-restraint. It imposed an existential check on U.S. power that reassured everybody else—foes as well as allies.

This ballet of containment and countercontainment suddenly stopped with the self-destruction of the Soviet Union on Christmas Day 1991. When terror struck New York's Twin Towers ten years later, fear and anger combined with unshackled strength, and the "United States of Bismarckia" was no more. The country went to war twice in short succession, first in Afghanistan, then in Iraq. The purpose was not to safeguard the existing order of things, but to transform it. As the United States shrugged off institutional restraints like those of the UN Security Council, it laid down an ambitious agenda of regime change, which, rhetorically at least, knew no bounds. By middecade, the United States was spending almost as much on its military as all other nations combined. America presented itself as a giant both fearsome and unfettered. The golden age of U.S. diplomacy had come to an end. How could it be restored?

6

A Giant's Perch

First among Nonequals

TO AVOID THE fate history holds in store for No. 1, Britain balanced and Bismarck bonded. These are the two historical models for a power that wants to stay No. 1. What shall it be for the United States as it peers into the twenty-first century?

Grand strategy is about the proper fit between means and ends, assets and ambitions. So any player, überpower or underdog, should begin by tallying its advantages and weaknesses and relating them to those of rivals, real and potential. Compared with those of Britain and Bismarck's Germany, America's advantages are awesome. Or as the grudging, hence sincere, compliment of the French foreign minister Hubert Védrine, has it, "The United States of America dominates in all arenas: the economic, technological, military, monetary, linguistic or cultural one. There has never been anything like it."[1]

America is a supersized No. 1, an überpower, when compared with the previous occupants of that perch. Britain ruled the waves, but never Europe, which, though a small patch of the planet, was then the central stage of world politics—the source of all great-power wars and the engine of material and intellectual progress. For all its far-flung might, Britain was never more than first among equals. In spite of the grand moat that sheltered the Isles, Britain could never assure security on its own, depending on allies always. It was remote, but not untouchable, as the invasions by Roman legions, Germanic tribes, and Norman conquerors had shown. And it was almost done in thrice: by Philip II's Spain, Napoleon's France, and Hitler's Germany.

Bismarck's Reich, though the biggest power in Europe, was more vulnerable still, as two world wars would prove. Just forty-seven years old, the Second Reich was smashed in 1918. Its Nazi successor, the Third Reich, was not just defeated but dismembered in 1945, though it had advanced to the gates of Cairo and Moscow only three years earlier. As last remaining superpower, the United States is not merely an XXL version of these two previous "semi-hegemons"; it plays in a different league altogether.

To begin with, the United States cannot be defeated in any meaningful way. Russia and soon China could obliterate the United States with the weapons of thermonuclear overkill, but only at the price of swift and certain suicide. Nor can any conceivable coalition of nuclear powers change this basic fact of post-Hiroshima life. Even if Russia, China, et al. joined forces, the United States could deter them all as long as it could inflict deadly damage on them. In the nuclear age, even the most oppressive "nightmare of coalitions" does not threaten America's core security. Indeed, because they can deter all comers, nuclear weapons are an isolationist's dream. "So long as it is clear that they will be employed only in the direct defense of the homeland," Robert W. Tucker has noted, "they confer a physical security that is virtually complete, and that the loss of allies cannot alter."[2]

In the conventional arena, numbers, hence allies, mattered; on the nuclear chessboard, it is the speed, reach, and invulnerability of retaliatory weapons and global battle-management systems.[3] Once thermonuclear missile weapons are in the game, quality trumps quantity. Nuclear weapons have severed the tight link between mass and mayhem. Because so few of them can wreak so much havoc, they provide an existential deterrent no coalition can overwhelm. Nuclear weapons simply cannot be "summed" like the armies of yore, and so more of them cannot provide the strategic edge that once handed victory to the side with the most.

Add to nuclear deterrence an unprecedented measure of geographical security, that is, protection from invasion. What Tocqueville had to say about the young Republic almost two hundred years ago, still holds true today. "Separated from the rest of the world by the ocean . . . , it has no enemies."[4] Later, he wrote, "Placed in the center of an immense continent . . . , the Union is almost as much insulated from the world as if all its frontiers were girt by the ocean." And so, "the great advantage of the United States . . . [consists] in a geographical position which renders . . . wars extremely improbable."[5]

In the meantime, the terrorist attacks on New York's World Trade Center and Washington's Pentagon in 2001 *did* break through Tocqueville's protective bubble. But such "asymmetric warfare," horrifying as it might yet become, does not change the basics of Tocqueville's insight. No conceivable coalition, fighting with conventional weapons, can assemble an invasion force capable of defeating the United States on its home grounds. Nor will such a coalition have the wherewithal for a long time, given that no potential rival possesses, or plans to acquire, the indispensable projection forces—the navies and the armadas of the air that would dominate the approaches and spew forth millions of assailants on American soil.

In other words, the United States deters just by being there. Size and location provide a kind of existential deterrent that makes conquest extremely costly. And nuclear weapons raise these costs exponentially. Nor is this the end of the story. Should the threat of mutual assured destruction lose its deadening grip, strategic defense—a missile shield in the sky—will deliver a backup within the next quarter century. The point here is not the dawning of the age of absolute security, which will remain elusive forever, but the distance the United States has already traveled. Having invested (and burned up) tens of billions of dollars in the search for a missile defense since the mid-1980s, the United States is far ahead in the race, and practically in reach of a point-defense system. Though the ability to shoot down a single missile is to a nationwide cover what an umbrella is to a stadium roof, numbers—that is, dollars that have been and will be spent—do matter at this juncture.

Let us now examine *relative* power, that is, America's position compared with other nations'. First, let us look at the numbers that distinguish the U.S. defense budget from those of its rivals, be it Russia, China, the EU, or the "candidate members" of the superpower club like India and Japan.

To stay ahead in the next "revolution in military affairs" (the current shibboleth is "network-centric warfare"), money matters. Four percent of the GDP has been the average share of U.S. military in the past half century. Now, 4 percent of $12 trillion is close to $500 billion. Compare this volume, about one-half of the world's total military spending, with the outlays of America's rivals. Russia is said to spend around $65 billion and China (according to official testimony) $30 billion,[6] which would be 2 percent of a $1.5 trillion economy. For the sake of realism, double this to $60 billion and assume that Chinese defense spending continues to grow at 10 percent, as it has been since the turn of the millennium. At this rate (compounded), it would take thirty years to reach the current American level.

Let us now look at the trends from the GDP side. Assume that the Chinese economy keeps growing indefinitely at a rate of 7 percent, the average of the past decade (for which history knows no example, not even in the halcyon days of the late nineteenth century).* At that rate, China's GDP would double every decade, reaching parity with today's United States ($12 trillion) in thirty years.

*The assumption of a 7-percent long-term rate seems more realistic than the actual figure of 9 percent, since history knows no example of such growth over the course of decades.

But the U.S. economy is not frozen into immobility. By then, the United States, growing at its long-term rate of 2.5 percent, would stand at $25 trillion. Now assume a 3 percent rate for U.S. growth. In that case, the U.S. GDP in 2035 would amount to $30 trillion, while China's would have reached $12 trillion—but only on the assumption that China's growth rate of 7 percent extends endlessly into the future. Cut that rate in half, which is the highest long-term trend the industrial world experienced in the past, and China's current GDP of $1.5 billion will be only twice that much in 2025, and $6 billion in 2045.

Such are the games that compound interest plays, but whichever way we cut these numbers, even if we substitute PPP (purchasing-power parity), which favors low-wage countries with undervalued currencies like China, the United States will stay way ahead of the pack as far as a hand-held calculator can see.* What about a resurgent Russia? Its current GDP stands at $400 billion, and its recent growth rate has oscillated between 4 percent and 7 percent. Let's put the best gloss on it and posit 7 percent in perpetuity. In that case, it will reach the current level of the U.S. GDP in fifty years. Then posit the historically normal rate of 2.5 percent for the United States. Under this dispensation, the U.S. GDP will have grown to $50 trillion in 2055, which would be more than four times the Russian GDP. Of course, these compound-interest games proceed under the

*Wages will rise, and PPP will fall, as China continues to integrate into the global economy. PPP will also fall relative to nominal GDP because China's predatory exchange-rate policy, a classic of an export-led growth strategy, cannot last forever, as the examples of Japan, Germany, and South Korea show. (In fact, in mid-2005, China loosened its tight link to the dollar by floating its currency, though within very narrow bounds.) These countries, too, unleashed their "economic miracles" with the help of artificially depressed currencies, but with domestic demand claiming its due, and integration into the world economy proceeding, their currencies eventually rose to market levels. West Germany started out with a parity of 4.20 deutsche marks to the dollar in 1949; by the 1990s, it had risen to 1.5 to the dollar, almost tripling in value.

biggest assumption of them all: ceteris paribus, all other things being equal. They do not take into account one likely and one certain scenario.

The likely scenario pertains to China, where rampant economic growth has gone hand in glove with tight one-party control. History whispers that these are two tectonic plates moving toward collision—in which case 7 percent growth may well turn into stagnation or even contraction, not to speak of the political toll such a clash might inflict on the country. The real-life analogy is China's Cultural Revolution, which destroyed the educational system, sent millions of knowledgeable workers to the boondocks, and set back economic development for an entire decade (1966–76). "Enrich yourselves, but leave the driving to us" is the motto of China's one-party dictatorship. It is a formula that has been tried in the West as a rising bourgeoisie and a dislocated peasant class moving to the city began to clamor for political and social rights. The outcome, from the French Revolution onward, was endless turmoil. "Leninist market economics" is a self-contradiction that cannot endure. According to Chinese police documents obtained by the RAND Corporation, there are now fifty thousand public protests per year in China.[7]

The certain scenario is already visible in today's Russia. The birthrate of 1.3 percent is among the lowest in the world; in Europe, only Italy, with 1.2 percent, has a lower one. Life expectancy in Russia is sixty-five years, and falling. In the recent past, the Russian population has shrunk by half a percent per year. One way in which population intersects with power is in the number of military-age young men. The projection for Russia is absolutely staggering: while that number is expected to rise by 23 percent in the United States, and to decline by 22 percent in the EU-25, it is slated to plunge by nearly one-half in the Russian Federation—leaving Russian male manpower in this age group at one-fourth the level of either the United States or the EU.[8] Also, given the historical link between demographic and economic growth, a shrinking population does not presage ballooning economic performance. Nor does the Kremlin's tightening grip on the economy promise sustained capitalist development in the decades to come. Neotsarism, as practiced by the successors of Mikhail Gorbachev, does not favor the energies only a free market can unleash. Neither can the curtailment of property rights attract the currents of foreign capital a developing economy needs the way a sprout needs water.

Superpower Europe?

Economically, there is only one player on the field able to hold its own against the United States. That is the European Union with a matching GDP of €10 trillion* and a population of 456 million, which compares to 291 million in the United States, a number growing at 1 percent per year. Yet, for all its gargantuan potential, there are three problems that stand between the EU and true great-power status.

Military. First, the EU does not spend enough on defense. The two best performers are Britain and France, which each invest up to 2.5 percent of GDP in their militaries. During the Cold War, the medium powers Britain, France, and West Germany allocated between 3 percent and 5 percent to their armed forces. Now, the biggest player, Germany, spends as much as the tiniest, Luxemburg: 1.5 percent of GDP. The next two middleweights, Italy and Spain, pay out 1.9 percent and 1.2 percent, respectively. Altogether, EU-Europe devotes 1.9 percent of domestic output to its military, which is half the American ratio and about one-half of U.S. spending in absolute terms.[9] Europe has cashed in its peace dividend, and likes

*Given the gyrating fortunes of the dollar-euro exchange rate, €10 trillion was $8.5 trillion in mid-2000 and 12.5 trillion in mid-2005.

it. Absent a new strategic threat, the EU will stick to its cozy post–Cold War posture, especially since the old gun-versus-butter quandary will take on an ever nastier edge.

Outside Britain, which took the harsh medicine of microeconomic reform in the 1980s and has enjoyed single-digit unemployment in the 5–6 percent range since the 1990s, the large countries of the EU have been battling with stubborn unemployment since the mid-1990s. An honest measure, which would classify hidden joblessness—retraining, early retirement, and subsidized jobs—as the real thing, would reveal that unemployment among the big three (France, Germany, Italy) has been welded into place at the 12 percent level throughout the new century. Politically, the remedy prescribed by British Thatcherism has remained hard to swallow for nations weaned on generous social protection. Eventually, "Old Europe," the EU of the fifteen, will come out of its structural slump because it has no other choice than to take up the gauntlet flung down by the low-wage competition in Eastern Europe and Asia, and the more adaptive economy of the United States. But change is slow in political systems—usually coalition governments—where power is too closely balanced to generate decisive majorities and clear mandates. In the meantime, high government deficits in the 4 percent range of GDP will ensure low military budgets.

Moreover, the fitful fusion of national foreign and security policies does not promise relief. Adding deficits does not a surplus make, and so the European Rapid Reaction Force, conceived in 1999 and composed of national forces, will not exceed 60,000 soldiers. (The United States deployed 500,000 troops in the First Iraq War and 160,000 in the Second.) The defense ministers of the EU are buying modernization at the cost of mass, and shrinkage is the price of mobility and high-tech weaponry. That makes European armies more deployable than the tank-heavy forces of the Cold War; Germany, the most spectacular instance, has reduced its 5,100 main battle tanks to 360. But agility cannot substitute endlessly for numbers and punch. Again, take Germany. In the wake of the Bosnian and Afghan wars, it dispatched 8,000 troops halfway around the world—from the Balkans to the Hindu Kush. Yet that was the end of the tether for a country that in the 1940s managed to subjugate almost all of Europe.

Economy and Demography. "It's the economy, stupid," has become a household saying throughout the West since it was first coined by Bill Clinton's presidential campaign in 1992. The curse of underperformance will eventually lift from Europe. Yet in the longer run—say, beyond the decade or so that it will take to implement painful reforms—a more oppressive foe lurks at the doors of the EU. Its name is "depopulation and aging." If we use the UN definition of Europe, which includes Russia, Europe's population started to contract at the turn of the millennium. It will drop from 728 million in 2005 to 653 million in 2050. The share of those over sixty-five years old, the nonworking population, will almost double, to 28 percent. Unlike Russia, EU-Europe does not contend with plunging life expectancy. Paradoxically, though, good health and longevity have turned into a liability when juxtaposed with stubbornly low birthrates.

The replacement fertility rate that keeps a population constant is 2.1 offspring per woman of childbearing age. Only the United States comes close to that rate. In the EU of the twenty-five, the fertility rate stands at 1.4. In Germany, it has fallen from 2.16 in 1950 to 1.3 today, while the median age has risen from thirty-five in 1950 to forty-two today and is slated to reach forty-seven in 2050. The Italian fertility rate has dropped from 2.3 in 1950 to 1.2 today, while the median age, which stood at twenty-nine in 1950 will rise to fifty-two a hundred years thence. Only France does not fit into this dismal pattern. It will age almost as rapidly as Germany and Italy, but with a fertility rate of 1.9 and a steady influx of immigrants from North Africa (who have one or two generations to go before their birthrates drop to indigenous levels), the French are expected to profit from slight demographic growth into midcentury.[10]

By contrast, the American population is growing at 1 percent per year, which, all other factors remaining equal, implies the doubling of the population by 2075. This dynamic is due to a fertility rate almost at replacement level, plus steady legal and illegal immigration (about two million per year). Such growth implies a younger population and an expanding workforce. Now assume that demographics and economics in the West continue to correlate as well as they did in the past century, when the churning machinery of capitalist production was fed by tens of millions of people pushing from the countryside into the city. In this case, a rising proportion of younger workers in the United States will make for faster growth than in Europe, where the working-age population is contracting.

The logic is simple. The fewer people work and the more old people they must support, the lower the total output. By 2050, each worker will have to support one nonworking old person in the EU; the current ratio is three to one.[11] But this is not the end of it. The higher the share of GDP that must go to the elderly, the less is left for investment, civilian or military. As a result, Europe is bound to fall behind in the growth race—unless other things are *not* equal in the following four areas. First, Europe manages to boost fertility, which has been dropping for the last fifty years—not an easy thing when so many long-term factors, ranging from late childbearing to high housing costs, conspire against the Lord's injunction to Adam: "Be fruitful and multiply."

Second, Europe might change its work/leisure balance by reversing a trend that has steadily cut into lifetime working hours; although the weekly rates are creeping up, the de facto retirement age is stuck below sixty. Third, Europe could compensate for shrinking numbers by outstripping U.S. productivity growth, which is about the same per hour worked, but not per worker, because Americans put in three hundred more hours per year than Europeans do.

Productivity growth requires higher capital expenditures. But how to shift resources in democracies where the growing armies of the elderly will vote their economic interests? Finally, Europe could boost its labor-force participation rate—the share of the population that works, which is lower than in the United States and reflects both social choice and enduring structural unemployment.

All of these remedies call for a rewriting of the social contract that has favored leisure, be it enforced or voluntary, over (documented) work,* and social protection over swift adaptation. If that contract is not recast, then demography will be destiny. And if so, the EU economy, currently the equal of the American one, will necessarily fall behind, if ever so slowly, as population decline and aging take their toll. Even today, the EU spends fifteen times more on social transfers than on defense (as fraction of GDP). The moral of this tale of numbers and projections is that Europe will not be able to generate the "surplus" required for an expansive global role.

Culture. Europeans, especially in France, Germany, and Spain, dream of a "multipolar" world that will check the ambitions of Mr. Big. Yet it is not just the demographics that darken this dream but also the culture. Europe, once a continent of conquerors who roamed the farthest corners of the earth, is turning into a culture of "post" prefixes. These are "postmodern," "postnational," "postsovereign," and "postheroic."[12] Such qualities have served Europe well, as it expanded from the original six† countries to twenty-five today, with Romania and Bulgaria as candidates and Turkey and Ukraine

*The crucial qualifier here is "documented" work. Europeans may well work as hard as Americans, but since they do so in their ample leisure time—be it because of high marginal tax rates or endemic structural unemployment—that portion of work does not show up on the national income ledgers. A frequently cited German estimate of the "shadow economy" puts the total at $430 billion, that is, at one-fifth of the official GDP. In Italy, again an improvable guesstimate, extralegal economic activity is said to add up to one-half of the official GDP.

†Belgium, France, West Germany, Italy, Luxemburg, and the Netherlands.

eager to crash the EU's gate. Europe, the fountainhead of all significant wars in centuries past, is now a zone of perpetual peace (give or take the Balkans); for all its problems, it remains prosperous and well ordered. As such, the EU, which started out as remake of the Carolingian Empire and now encompasses the northern half of the Roman one, may justly claim to represent the future.

But in the present, the "postculture" does not bode well for a global player that would seek to match or top the United States. "Soft power," in the end, cannot do without "hard power"—otherwise the papacy would still be a great power. That steely quality requires a national rather than a postnational mind-set, and a single sovereign rather than twenty-five, and soon more. It is not just a matter of forging an *e pluribus unum*. It demands the close fusion of state and sovereignty, nationhood and democracy. Yet the overlap is partial at best. The European "state" is not the sovereign; it is suspended between its incomplete powers and the battered prerogatives of its twenty-five members. It lacks the clout of a real empire, and it lacks the legitimacy the democratic nation-state has amassed by harnessing the freely given consent of the governed to its purposes. The ultimate irony may well be that the EU, a haven of many stable democracies, will end up with neither a state nor a nation nor a democracy. So add "postdemocratic" to the list.

A "postdemocracy"? An experiment in transcendence, the European construction has many wondrous qualities; otherwise it would not shine forth as "empire by application" that draws ever more would-be members to its doorsteps. But it is not a democracy in the classical sense. The European Parliament is not the U.S. Congress, for it does not set the law of the land; the key decisions are made by the European Council, which represents member governments. (The analogy to the United States would be a legislature composed of the fifty state governors.) The EU president is not elected but the product of horse-trading between the member governments. Its "ministers," the commissioners, are selected by national quota. The

EU's subjects are not "Europeans" the way Californians are Americans. Though they all carry burgundy-colored EU passports, they remain citizens of their own countries, the names of which are embossed right underneath the "European Union" label on the cover. Worse, they have only the most tenuous say over the choices of their quasi-nation. And yet the EU is the most powerful influence over their lives, with national parliaments no longer sovereign in the business of national law-giving. A large part of their job is to add their stamp of approval, rarely withheld, to the union's directives, issued by the commission and approved by the council, that fill up more than half of their dockets. Nor will this strange animal soon mutate into a "more perfect union," for it lacks the most critical ingredient: "We, the People."

The EU is certainly not *anti*democratic; it is a most benevolent political being. It celebrates human rights, redistributes income, and promotes individual entitlements. Its edicts are issued in the name of efficiency and liberalization. It has a parliament of sorts, and an independent judiciary, the European Court of Justice, which boldly rules against member governments. But a real democracy requires more. First, democracy entails a demos, a nation or community. Second, it requires a mechanism by which the ruled bestow their consent, hence legitimacy, on their rulers. The core of such a system consists of elections and public debate. But Europe's rulers, representing the various *governments*, are not elected, and there is neither a European public nor a European debate—nor are there European-wide media. Ironically, it is U.S. papers and networks like the *International Herald Tribune* or CNN that provide a European-wide forum.

The hallmark of any state is sovereignty. In a democratic state, sovereignty is lodged in the people. In the EU, sovereignty is located . . . where? It is lodged neither in the people nor in the parliament, where it should be. Power, sovereignty, and consent are disjoined, but this seems to be just fine with the EU's 450 million quasi-citizens. In the history of the democratic state, there has never been anything like it. A collection of many democracies, this European polity is not itself democratic. For want of a better term, call it postdemocratic. "EUcracy" has replaced the classical model, but, strangely, it was not the target of revolutionary discontent for half a century. Grumbling there was, but it came with a shrug and not with a balled fist. When a national referendum on a more perfect union was lost, as in Denmark in 1992 and in Ireland in 2002, it was repeated until the ayes prevailed. The exception has always been Britain, the fiercest defender of sovereignty, nationhood, and ancient democratic habits.

No more. Fifty years into this wondrous process of transcendence, the revolt against postdemocracy finally did materialize. In 2005, the real demos—that is, the voters of two founding members, France and the Netherlands—rejected by resounding margins what was billed as Europe's "constitution" (technically, a "constitutional treaty" that was to shift more powers from the states to the whole). In the aftermath, several more member states canceled their referenda. Since ratification requires unanimity among the twenty-five, the largest leap ever into a "more perfect union" was frozen in time. The message was "Enough—at least for now!" Democracy had asserted itself against postdemocracy, and the nation-state against the superstate. It was as if Virginia and Connecticut, two avid signers of the U.S. Constitution in 1787, had turned against it with a vengeance in 1788.

Yet France and Holland were asked to cede far less than any of the thirteen original American states. They were not expected to lodge power in a popularly elected president, nor were they asked to let the congress be the supreme lawgiver of the land. They were not asked to yield citizenship to the "United States of Europe" or to demote their national leaders to the modest status of a state governor in the United States. It was just a bit more than in the past—a European foreign minister or a voting system in the European Council that allocated a bit more weight to the more populous states. And yet this proved too much for three-fifths of the voters in two key countries. A third one, Britain, postponed its own referendum sine die, and so did a number of others. Europe remains a would-be state.

How, then, will the EU assert itself in the world? During the heyday of the modern nation-state, power, sovereignty, and consent all went together. Sovereignty defined the "self" of a nation, the "vessel," so to speak. Patriotism and nationalism, still richly present in the United States, filled that vessel with emotion, loyalty, and a sense of mission. Democracy added collective will to the purposes of nations, a will that injected legitimacy into power and in the end proved stronger than totalitarian mobilization under Nazism and communism. If the fusion of democracy, state, and nation is the stuff of self-assertion, the EU is badly equipped to bestride the world stage as a global actor.

With its power so fragmented, the EU cannot make strategic decisions with "decision, activity, secrecy, and despatch," to recall the famous phrase by Alexander Hamilton when he argued for a strong presidency.[13] Without a demos, the EU cannot express a "general will." Europe cannot even unleash a public debate on the whys and wherefores of boosting defense spending or going to war. There is no European-wide agora, and even if there were, the language that once inspired sacrifice in the name of the nation, would ring hollow in twenty-first-century Europe. As a postheroic culture, Europe lives by the obverse of John F. Kennedy's fabled injunction, which now reads, "Ask not what you can do for your country, but what your country can do for you." The European welfare state may seize up to one-half of GDP, but that is not proof of vast power, because most of the take—about one-third of GDP—is disbursed by way of individual or group entitlement. In a postnational society, the "I" has trumped the "We," while self-fulfillment has pushed aside collective purpose.

How can the "postnational" label stick to nations that *reasserted* their nationhood when they rejected the EU constitution? It is imperative not to confuse the anticonstitutional revolt with a resurgence of traditional nationalism. That version was expansive, if not aggressive, but the nationalism that turned against a "more perfect union" was defensive and inward bound. The battle cry was "Leave us alone!," not "Let us forge ahead!" The impulse was not to scale walls but to draw them higher against whatever "Europe" suddenly threatened: less protection, more competition, more cheap labor from the east and fewer jobs kept in the west. Yet this self-centered nationalism—more accurately, anti-integrationism—does not presage a new patriotism, that is, love of country. Europe remains a postpatriotic space, with Britain the exception that proves the rule.

When Americans are queried on their attachment to the country, 95 percent are "very proud/quite proud" to be an American. In Europe, such admissions of national fealty drop dramatically. Highest on the "very proud" scale are the British (54 percent). Spaniards, Scandinavians, and Italians admit to "high pride" in the mid-to-low 40 percent range. Only 35 percent of Frenchmen are "very proud." West Germans came in lowest, at 20 percent.[14] As the national fervor of Europeans has waned, so has the use of once hallowed terms like "reason of state," which has practically disappeared from the European vocabulary. The "national interest" is invoked mainly when companies wave the flag to stir governments into action either to shelter them against foreign competition or to help them penetrate foreign markets.

"Strategic interest" has become a tattered concept, too. The postheroic European state intervenes abroad not in search of gain or fame but in the name of humanitarian duty—preferably where there is no fighting, as in the 2004 East Asian tsunami disaster. Or where U.S. airpower has broken the enemy's will, as it did with the bombing campaign against Serbia in 1999. In the nineteenth century, competitive conquest drove the scramble for Africa; today, national glory is sought in "competitive compassion." Make no mistake: it is still the rivalry for advantage—for prestige and influence—that motivates even the humanitarian game, but the fleets unload blankets, not battalions. It is not power politics but the politics of goodness.

Europe's nationalism is defensive. With the Soviet Union off the chessboard, the enemy is "other people." It is Bosnians or Kosovars who fled west to escape "ethnic cleansing," and Afghanis who ran from the religious totalitarianism of the Taliban. It is North Africans who flee from misery or oppression. It is Central Africans who fear war and tribal butchery. It is Pakistanis and Bangladeshis who come for menial jobs. It is Poles who repair the plumbing in Paris, and Ukrainians who work the building sites of Lisbon. These are the new substrategic threats Europe faces—people of different color, faith, and culture who strain the coffers of the welfare state and batter tightly regulated labor markets. If Europe's defense ministers gave a frank answer (as one of them did privately to this author), they would admit that the restructuring of their forces for humanitarian intervention has a novel, but hard-nosed purpose. It is to pacify, or at least quarantine, those areas from Africa to Afghanistan whence war and famine propel the multitudes to Europe's shores. It is a kind of "forward defense" against the twenty-first century's "poor and huddled masses."

A second kind of European nationalism is anti-Americanism (see chapters 3 and 4). Indeed, when the French government in 2005, seconded from the sidelines by Berlin, tried to plead for a *oui* to the EU constitution, it did so by invoking a Europe strong enough to assert itself against American power and "Anglo-Saxon capitalism." But that species of nationalism at heart is also defensive. It seeks to throttle the engine of unrelenting modernization that is America and that threatens to overwhelm old dispensations just as the immigrants from Eastern Europe and the Third World do. It is the fear of unbridled American power that fuels the resentment. But anti-Americanism comes as celebration of moral and cultural superiority;

it does not forge the nations of Europe into a strategic counterweight to the Behemoth, though the French have tried to do so since the days of Charles de Gaulle.

When modernity and power last swept into Europe on the bayonets of Napoleon's armies, France's neighbors responded with a very different nationalism. It was armed and assertive, and it coagulated into victorious alliances. Today, postheroic and postnational Europe would rather deploy the weapons of multilateralism and institutionalism, and the purpose is not to best Gulliver but to put the ropes back on him. After sixty years of peace, the longest in European history, the postnational imagination leaves little room for ideas of strategic competition.

Astride Two Worlds

In 1890, at the height of the European age, power among the key players was closely balanced, and so the ratios of defense spending among Germany, France, Britain, and Russia were 29:37:31:29.[15] Today, the United States spends almost as much as the rest of the world combined, and though Russia and China boast higher economic growth than the United States, they are dwarfed by a $12 trillion economy that is thirty times larger than the Russian one and seven times larger than the Chinese one, not to speak of the even vaster gaps in per-capita income. It is $1,100 for China, $2,600 for Russia, and $40,000 for the United States. Only the EU comes close with $28,000 (at 2005 exchange rates), but its economic strength does not translate into strategic clout, because it is beholden to twenty-five, and soon even more, national wills, not to a single sovereign.

Let us now shift from relative power to America's global role. With the Soviet Union gone, the United States is not only first among nonequals but also in a unique strategic position. If Bismarck tried to be hub to Europe's spokes and Britain the "Holder of the Balance," the United States is hub to the world, both geographically and politically. It lies athwart two oceans, its military deployments stretch westward to the Sea of Japan and eastward across Europe and the Middle East into Central Asia—all the way to the Chinese border. It is the only nation whose strategic interests and bases circle the globe. Yet singularity extends beyond mere geography.

Like the Colossus of Rhodes, one of the Seven Wonders of the World,* standing astride the island's harbor, the United States is the *only* actor that straddles the two main stages of world politics. They are loosely connected through the accoutrements of global civilization, ranging from satellite TV via globally traded goods to the sinews of information technology. Otherwise, they are separated not only by distance but also by economic performance, historical memory, and political culture. And so, two very different dramas are being acted out on these two stages. Let's call one the "Berlin–Berkeley Belt" and the other the "Baghdad–Beijing Belt." The former is almost perfectly pacified; the latter is a vast cauldron of conflict. If the Berlin–Berkeley Belt is the twenty-first century, the Baghdad–Beijing Belt stretches backward from the murderous fury of the twentieth all the way to the religious wars of the sixteenth and seventeenth centuries. The United States is the only actor with one foot planted in each of these incongruent worlds.

The Berlin–Berkeley Belt. It extends from the eastern border of Germany to the San Francisco Bay; another name for this segment is "the West." Outlying members are Australia and New Zealand; affiliate members are ex-Soviet satrapies like Poland, Hungary, Czechia, and Slovenia—the ten states that joined the EU in 2004.

*Dedicated to the sun god Helios, the statue took twelve years to build and was completed in 282 BC. Alas, it is a myth that the colossus straddled the harbor. Given his height—110 feet, or 33 meters—he could not possibly spread his legs across the wide entrance.

Israel, Japan, Taiwan, and South Korea are honorary members. Although they share such basic Western traits as democracy and economic modernity, and are tied to the United States by formal or tacit alliance, they are strategically part of the Baghdad–Beijing Belt, hence actors in a different drama.

What does the Berlin–Berkeley Belt look like? Economically, core membership is defined by the shift from manufacturing to information-driven production. Politically, equality has replaced hierarchy. In society, authority has yielded to individual rights and group entitlements. This is a world of defanged nationalism, where the nation-state is being denationalized and citizenship desacralized. There is the creeping divorce between citizenship and the "metaphysics" of nationhood—those exclusive identities and loyalties wrapped into myth, race, and faith. The nation-state in the Berlin–Berkeley Belt seems no longer willing to demand assimilation as condition of membership. Nationalism can no longer drive millions into the trenches; these blazes have collapsed into flickers. Where the West does fight, the scenario of choice is a short, spasmodic encounter, preferably with zero casualties and a quick exit strategy; the favorite means is a high-altitude bombing campaign followed by mop-up operations on the ground that capitalize on speed and superior technology.

Nobody has explained (or foreseen) the dynamics of the Berlin–Berkeley Belt better than the nineteenth-century French sage Alexis de Tocqueville. Democracy and development, he predicted, would change the nature of both the polity and the society. "The warlike passions"—another word for nationalism—he predicted, "will become more rare and less intense in proportion as social conditions are more equal." Democracy, he continued, leads to "ever increasing numbers of men of property who are lovers of peace, the growth of personal wealth which war so rapidly consumes, the mildness of manners . . . that coolness of understanding which renders men comparatively insensible to the violent and poetical excitement of arms. . . ."[16] Tocqueville had a keener eye for the future than the German philosopher Hegel, who wrote at the same time. For Hegel, the "true courage of civilized states" was the "readiness to sacrifice in the service of the state, so that the individual counts as only one among many."[17]

Yet the critical factor is neither economic nor cultural. It is security. The most economical definition of the Berlin–Berkeley Belt is "a world without war." It is a world where the "Clausewitzian continuum" has been severed precisely at the point that for centuries marked the passage from diplomacy to the "admixture of other means," as the most famous phrase of the Prussian strategist has it. All these arch-enemies of yore—Spain, France, Britain, Germany, Austria—will not even dream of taking up arms against one another again. This magical change did not come from nowhere; the wand was originally waved by the United States, Europe's mighty protector and pacifier after World War II.[18] Suddenly, there was a player in the game stronger than each and all, shielding the West Europeans not only against the Soviet Union but also against themselves. That made all the difference, and so the European Union, née European Coal and Steel Community in 1951, owes its life to American power. America's gift of safety proved to be the progenitor of European community.

France, Germany, et al. no longer had to worry about one another; instead, they could lavishly consume security Made in U.S.A. With the Great Underwriter in the wings, they could extend hands in cooperation without having to agonize over the price of misplaced credulity. European integration was born after the worst war in European history, courtesy of the United States. The seeds of the postmartial state were planted at the same time. Enjoying so much gratis security within and without, Western Europe could turn away from nationalist mobilization and toward the pacifism of those whose security is provided by others. Under this bubble, the best things in international life could flourish, and so institutionalism and multilateralism replaced "war-war" with "jaw-jaw," to recall the memorable phrase attributed to both Winston Churchill and Harold Macmillan.

Above all, liberal democracy and the habits of trust could sink sturdy roots in a soil poisoned by authoritarianism, fascism, and Nazism because guaranteed safety undercut the business opportunities of the Pied Pipers. Hawking security at the price of liberty rang hollow while the mightiest power on earth manned the Fulda Gap—the most likely breakthrough point for the shock armies of the Soviet Union. Today, the enemy at the gate is gone, and so the longest peace in history stretches out endlessly into the morrow. No wonder that at least "Old Europe" believes that it has transcended history—and that its communitarian ways are the wave of the future. Closer to Russia, "New Europe" is less sanguine, and so is the United States, because its second foot is planted in a world where Hobbes, and not Rousseau, calls the tune.

The United States is different for other reasons as well. As the Berkeley part of the label suggests, postnationalism and postmodernity are hardly alien to American society. Indeed, the denizens of Berkeley may have more in common with Berlin's than with their fellow citizens in "red" America, which stretches from the Rockies to the Appalachians (minus the big cities). Yet the hard core of American identity is not a bunch of "post" prefixes. Nationalism is alive and well in America, and so is religiosity, a mainstay of the country's exceptionialism. While Europe's warrior culture, again with the exception of Britain's, is down to a mere remnant, America retains the essentials of a military ethos that used to be the very pillar of European statehood for centuries. Sovereignty and the world's oldest Constitution sit right next to the Holy Grail in the nation's imagination; hence the Republic's reluctance to submit to international bodies—certainly to those it cannot dominate. America's root ideology is eighteenth-century liberalism and the limited state, Europe's is twentieth-century social-democracy and the providential state that distributes close to one-half of the national output. America is in and of the West, postmodernity and all, but when everything is weighed and measured, Atlantic civilization looks not like a church with a single steeple but like a cathedral with two towers, with Europe occupying one and the *novus ordo seclorum* the other. Sharing a common nave, the two towers, like Notre Dame's in Paris, remain separate and distinct.

Beyond culture, two additional differences are critical. First, the United States cannot outsource its security; second, it is always in harm's way. The United States cannot duck behind an even greater power; its security is Made in U.S.A., and in U.S.A. only. Though it is part of the Berlin–Berkeley Belt, No. 1 cannot afford to succumb to all of its new habits. Nor can it scurry out of harm's way. Take Islamist terrorism, which also threatens Europe, as the mayhem at Madrid's Atocha railway station demonstrated in 2004 and the bombing of London's transit system showed in 2005. But the menace to Europe remains derivative; the purpose of such attacks is to split Europe from the United States. Staged on the eve of the Spanish vote, the massacre turned the electoral tide. America's conservative allies lost power, and a few months later the new Socialist government withdrew its troops from Iraq. Like Spain, European nations can always try to flatten themselves as a target; as "Great Satan," the United States *is* the target because of its ubiquity, character, and clout. A founding member of the Berlin–Berkeley club, it is also the biggest contender in the Baghdad–Beijing arena. Rooted in both worlds, the United States can escape from neither.

The Baghdad–Beijing Belt. On the Baghdad–Beijing stage, the drama of nations follows a script very different from that in the pacified West. The platform is much wider than the Berlin–Berkeley Belt, and for accuracy's sake one should add Belgrade to Baghdad and Beijing. Belgrade stands for that stretch of Europe known as the Balkans. Though European, the Balkans are by no means pacified, postmodern, or postnational. Murderous passion in the name of *Volk* or faith is alive and well; it was merely suppressed by foreign intervention. Serbia was bombed into submission; Bosnia and its renegade Kosovo provinces have become a protectorate of NATO and UN. What do the troupe and the set look like in the Belgrade–Baghdad–Beijing Belt?

The largest part of the stage is occupied by post-Soviet Russia, stretching all the way to the Pacific. It is populated by ex-communists and would-be democrats trying to sing the Western tune, sullenly or desperately, but all remember the lost glory of the Russian empire. Behind them, pushing forward, is a much larger mass. Attired in Mao suits and Ray-Bans, they claim that center stage should be theirs; after all, they used to run the "Middle Kingdom," the oldest theater of them all. In the Berlin–Berkeley playhouse, ever more opera glasses are being trained on the children of Mao and Deng Xiaoping, while their cultural kin across East Asia keep shooting ever more apprehensive glances at them.

A third group, known collectively as the Greater Middle East, refuses to follow the Western score. Some of them, including the Palestinians and Iraqis, are trying, but their voices are drowned by fellow believers waving the green flag of the Prophet and popping off guns that look like real AK-47s. A motley fourth crowd occupies the space between Baku and Bishkek, the capitals of Azerbaijan and Kyrgyzstan. The turmoil unfolds between and within ethnic groups. Though the contenders look and talk alike, they are angrily trying to push each other off the stage. A similar, but far bloodier, subdrama unfolds in the African section of the platform, where the massacres never stop. Down below is the largest crowd of them all: the destitutes of the Third World. Dressed in rags and swirling around the stage, they seem too listless to mount the stairs.

We can also use more pretentious, Hegelian language to make the point by citing an untranslatable German term: *Gleichzeitigkeit der Ungleichzeitigkeiten*—the contemporaneity of the noncontemporaneous.[19] Or we can simplify it by invoking Lenin's "uneven development."[20] The point remains the same. Though our world seems to be unified as never before by technology, trade, and telecommunication, it remains politically segmented and culturally compartmentalized. The world of the twenty-first century is occupied by nations divided not only by language, creed, and race but also by their different positions on the ladder of development. But if we had to choose a single word to mark the difference between the Berlin–Berkeley and the Baghdad–Beijing worlds, it is "nationalism" broadly defined—ranging from the tribalism of Rwanda via Islamist terrorism to the great-power chauvinism of China. A more encompassing term might be "integralism." It denotes the individual's submission to a collective defined by nation, clan, or faith and his readiness to resort to murder for his community's sake. Rampant throughout the West in centuries past, this kind of devotion suffuses the entire Baghdad–Beijing Belt. This is not to ignore Basque terrorism in Spain or Catholic-Protestant bloodshed in Northern Ireland, let alone America's wars of choice in Iraq. But the willingness to kill and be killed for a self-transcending cause is no longer typical for the West. In the Baghdad–Beijing Belt, the phenomenon can be subdivided into five parts.

Bent-Twig Nationalism. First, there is the phenomenon of the "bent twig," as Isaiah Berlin calls it, the "wounded nationalism" that lashes back in fury when released.[21] The bloody drama of national revivalism is found mainly in the post-Soviet space left behind by an empire that had suppressed so many nations within its vast borders in the wake of the Crimean War (1853–56), and especially through Stalin's forcible Russification policy in the 1930s. Here is a short list: violent clashes in Moldova (between Moldavians, Gagauz, and Russians), war in Chechnya (between Muslim separatists and the Russian army), a three-way battle in Georgia (between Abkhazis, Ossetians, and the "titular" majority), the endless struggle over Nagorno-

Karabakh between Armenia and Azerbaijan, once forced to live together under the same imperial roof.

Though the former Yugoslavia is geographically not part of the Baghdad–Beijing Belt, it offers the best example of "bent-twig nationalism." It is not an ex-satrapy of the Soviet Union, but its collapse in the 1990s is part of the same postimperial, postcommunist story. Stitched together after World War I from various parts of the Ottoman and Habsburg empires, the "Land of the South Slavs" was in fact a Serb dominion. Held together by Tito's charismatic leadership, communist ideology, and Soviet pressure from the outside, this tenuous construction was destined to crumple after the marshall's death in 1980 and the collapse of the Soviet Union. The bent-twig backlash obeyed an almost mechanistic dynamic. Communism, a handy tool of the largest ethnic group (Russians in the Soviet Union, Serbs in Yugoslavia) had sought not just to repress but even to eliminate minorities in the greatest assimilationist project of them all. Forging a "new man," communism would demolish and replace all other identities with a single proletarian one. Once the ideology cracked, only force was left. Boris Yeltsin's and Vladimir Putin's war against the Chechens was cut from the same cloth as Slobodan Milosevic's against Slovenia, Croatia, Muslim Bosnia, and Kosovo.

Nor was the suppression of the Yugoslav war of succession, circa 1991–99, by NATO warplanes the end of the "wounded nationalism" story. When the tide of power turns, yesterday's victims return the favor to their former overlords, as the Croatians and Kosovars did to the Serbs once Belgrade's grip was broken by NATO. It is either submission or ethnic cleansing—or the international protectorate that has taken the place of Yugoslavia. In the post-Soviet space, there are bent twigs in every one of the fifteen successor republics—from the twenty million Russians, who still live there, to a multitude of ethnic minorities strewn across Moscow's former underbelly and within Russia itself.

But there is more. Invariably, the greater powers smell both risk and opportunity in these tortured climes, and so a widening conflict is the natural counterpart of local score settling. NATO was drawn into Yugoslavia to protect Muslims against Serbs, as well as itself against a tide of Balkan refugees. In the post-Soviet space, it is terrorist bases, on one side of the ledger, and oil and gas, on the other, that have sucked in Russian and American forces—sometimes, as in Kyrgyzstan, in one and the same country. Outside powers will naturally manipulate (and munition) local forces for their own ends, assuring the persistence of the conflict. And they might clash themselves. Thus bent twigs can eventually shake the entire tree, as so many peripheral conflicts have done by spilling out from the wings to center stage. (The best example is still the Seven Years' War, which had begun as a Franco-British colonial war over North America.)

Failed-Modernization Nationalism. This phenomenon is particularly virulent in the Islamic realm that stretches from the Maghreb via the Levant into the Persian Gulf and beyond to Pakistan and Afghanistan. Wounded nationalism in this part of the world flows from the failure of keeping up. It is compounded by the painful encounter of backward societies with the West—first France and Britain, then the United States and Israel—that is short on triumph and long on humiliation.

Israel is the only country in the neighborhood that has mastered the trials of economic and cultural modernization; hence it is an honorary member of the Berlin–Berkeley Belt. Starting out barely ahead of its Arab neighbors half a century ago, Israel has jumped from an agrarian economy to a high-tech one without passing through the intermediate stage of industrialization. Though born and weaned in war, the country has not succumbed to the "garrison state," evolving instead into a fractious, but stable, liberal democracy. The "Little Satan" has won every passage of arms with its Arab neighbors since 1948. Though tied by peace treaties to Egypt, Jordan, and the Palestinians, Israel remains a painful reminder of Arab weakness. Israel's

GDP is almost as big as that of the four Arab "front states" combined; its per capita income is fifteen times higher than Egypt's or Syria's.

The frustration inflicted by Israel is compounded tenfold by the United States, the power that casts the largest shadow over the Middle East. In the 1950s, the United States wrested the imperial mantle from Britain and France; by the early 1970s, when Sadat's Egypt sent Soviet troops packing, the United States had extruded its last great-power rival from the area. Ever since the mid-1950s, America has acted in the Middle East as Britain had in Europe: it has stymied the ambitions of whoever sought to unify Arabia under a single anti-American will.

The United States undid coups in Lebanon and Iran in the 1950s and discreetly helped its surrogate Israel beat Arab armies in the 1960s and 1970s. Having dislodged the Soviet Union from Egypt in the 1970s, Washington masterminded the containment of Iran throughout the 1980s, initially by aligning sub rosa with Saddam's Iraq. Thereafter, it recruited a global coalition against Iraq in the First Iraq War. In the Second Iraq War, the United States escalated from containment to regime change, a move that might yet go down in history as the most potent factor of transformation ever. Unlike eighteenth- and nineteenth-century Britain in Europe, the United States organized not only war but also peace on its Middle Eastern turf. From the Camp David accords in 1977 onward, Washington goaded Egypt, Jordan, and the Palestinians into accommodation with Israel while isolating or punishing those—Damascus, Baghdad, Tehran—that would rally the Arab-Islamic world against the Great and the Little Satan.

The failure to keep up has sharpened the frustration of societies that have stumbled on the path of modernization. The natural fall-back position was aggressive nationalism. Syria, Egypt, Iraq, Libya, and Algeria have been the classic instances of failure, with Iran arriving at calamity from a different ideological direction. The five Arab states all tried Soviet-style modernization with an Arabic script. "In an endeavor to copy the Soviet model, embryonic heavy industries were established from the banks of the Nile to the Sahara, but they soon proved incapable of competing on the world market and turned into financial black holes."[22] They tried one-party rule and totalitarian mobilization in order to raze religious, ethnic, and familial pillars of authority. To hold it all together, Nasser, Assad, Saddam, et al. wrapped themselves in the cloak of all-Arab nationalism on the well-tried theory that enemies abroad are a despot's best friends at home.

How shall we count the ways in which that part of the world warred against itself and against Israel, the stranger in its midst? In the name of the *umma*, the "Arab nation," the Egypt of Nasser confronted the West over Suez in 1956 and triggered war with Israel in 1967, while seeking to subvert neighboring regimes and intervening openly in Yemen. After coming to power through bloody coups, Hafiz Assad of Syria and Saddam Hussein of Iraq competed for the mantle of hegemony in the 1970s and 1980s, never mind that "Baathist" was the label of both one-party regimes. In the same period, Yasir Arafat's PLO tried to gain control over Jordan and Lebanon, only to be bloodily rebuffed by King Hussein in 1970 and the Israeli army in 1982. Iraq attacked neighbors twice: Iran in 1980, Kuwait in 1990. In the 1990s, Egypt and Libya kept skirmishing along their common border.

Mohammad Reza Shah Pahlavi, who ruled Iran from 1941 to 1979 with a short interruption,* came at the game from another direction. His was not a socialist but a "white" revolution. Like his Arab colleagues, he prescribed a regimen of state-sponsored industrialization. Like them, he suppressed domestic, above all religious, dissent, by disenfranchising the Shia clergy. Like the others, who were emulating Europe's totalitarians, he tried to catapult a back-

*He briefly fled the country in August of 1953, while his domestic enemy, Prime Minister Mohammed Mossadeq was reaching for dictatorial powers. A few days later, in the wake of a military putsch sponsored by the United States and Britain, the shah returned and Mossadeq was arrested.

ward society into modernity by leveling competing centers of traditional authority. The difference was the "white" coloration of a revolution that wagered on capitalist development and alliance with the United States on the road to regional mastery.

The outcomes, however, were not that different. Modernization—the forced march into industrialization and secularization—failed to triumph on all fronts: economic, political, cultural. At opposite geographical extremes, Iran and Algeria paid for the attempt with the "return of the repressed": with an Islamist revolution in Tehran, with an unending revolt of the faithful in Algeria. While Algeria resisted, Iran fell to the Khomeinist revolution of 1979. Afterward, a familiar pattern unfolded: revolutionary regimes naturally slip into revolutionary foreign policies. Like the Soviet Union of the Comintern period and revolutionary France, the Khomeinists resorted to the classic repertoire: subversion of neighbors, terror against dissidents abroad, financial and military support for insurgent forces, confrontation with the two "Satans," America and Israel.

Egypt keeps battling the Muslim Brotherhood in a country where population growth consistently outpaces economic growth. Beset by Hamas and Islamic Jihad, the secular (and once socialist) PLO sought to perpetuate its supremacy by way of patronage politics and police-state repression until the death of its leader-for-life, Yasir Arafat, when his successors began to experiment with democratic procedures under U.S. pressure. Syria's Hafez al-Assad dealt with his Muslim Brotherhood by reducing their stronghold Hama to rubble in 1982. Afterward, Syria retracted into totalitarian torpor; upon his death in 2000, when his son Bashir took power, it evolved into a dynastic dictatorship. The counterpart of frozen domestic politics was stony-faced hostility to Israel, even as other Arabs—Egyptians, Jordanians, Palestinians—moved toward accommodation with this Western wedge in their midst.

Iraq, another avatar of failed Soviet-style modernization, remained the victim of "socialism in one family," the Takriti clan, until the U.S. army destroyed that regime by war. To secure its hold on a country where power was monopolized by the minority Sunni (about 15 percent of the population), the Saddamite regime resorted to classic imperialism along the advice that Shakespeare's Henry IV gave to his son and successor: "busy giddy minds with foreign quarrels." Saddam attacked Iran in 1980, Kuwait in 1990—all the while wrapping himself in the banner of Arab nationalism. The Saudi Wahhabis hold on to power with a mix of cultural self-isolation, petrodollars, and reactionary clericalism. Politically, Pakistan is a bomb waiting to explode. Until dislodged by the U.S. military, the Taliban ruled Afghanistan with an ideology that made post-Khomeini Iran look positively progressive.

If failed modernization—the inability to combine development with ethnic inclusion and mass participation—has been the curse of the Arab-Islamic world, nationalism wedded to faith or ideology has served as the universal cure. For nationalism, especially when married to the other great integralist ideology—religion—is the mother of all identities and loyalties. The us-against-them mechanism insulates societies from change and discredits internal rivals. Nor is this an invention peculiar to this region; recall the similar drama that unfolded during the age of European nationalism, which reached its murderous climax in the fusion of communism, fascism, and Nazism—secular religions all—with xenophobia and chauvinism.

Fossil-State Nationalism. A third type of nationalism in the Belgrade–Beijing Belt is found in North Korea, Cuba, Libya, and Myanmar, countries that have dug in against the changes sweeping the world since the fall of the Berlin Wall. Their economic base is preindustrial. Their politics is totalitarian, ranging from the charismatic version of Castro's Cuba and Gadhafi's Libya to junta rule in Myanmar to the Stalinist personality cult of Kim Jong Il's North Korea. With the exception of Myanmar, these nations have typically resorted to aggressive foreign policies at one time or another. Cuba and Libya have gone through a typical cycle that mirrors the biology of their leadership. In their younger days, Cuba and Libya emulated revolutionary regimes throughout history, exporting their ideologies by open or covert intervention as far away as Angola. In their dotage, these revolutionary leaders swung to the opposite extreme: rigorous self-isolation, reinforced, it should be added, by the quarantine thrown up around them by the United States.

North Korea represents a different variant. Instead of bureaucratizing, diluting, or dispatching the totalitarian model, as the Soviet Union did in the 1980s, Kim Jong Il, who assumed power in 1996, tried to keep alive the revolutionary flame ignited by his father, Kim Il Sung, who had ruled since 1948. The result has been a virulent nationalism, as manifested in the bellicose confrontation with North Korea's neighbors and their American allies, as well as in Pyongyang's quest for nuclear weapons. Throughout the fossil-state segment, high-pitched nationalism serves a purpose that is both obvious and familiar. By conjuring up images of implacable foreign enemies—actually, by provoking real enmity—integralism abets the *Gleichschaltung* of the populace and secures totalitarian rule.

Failed-State Nationalism. A fourth type of integralism is found mainly in Africa—in those states (the vast majority) that arose from the ruins of colonialism after World War II. Virtually all of them lack a homogenous ethnic base, given that the carving up of Africa in the nineteenth century drew borders following the commercial interest and the military reach of the European powers rather than ethnic or tribal boundaries. The bill came due as soon as the foreign overlords had departed, first and most dramatically in the Congo war of the 1960s and the Angola wars of the 1970s, whose successors have continued to torture Central Africa all the way into the twenty-first century.

The general pattern has been endlessly repeated. In the institutional vacuum left behind by the former overlords, postcolonial power is assumed by an ethnically or tribally based regime, majoritarian or not. These regimes proceed to favor their own in the distribution of material and symbolic benefits while excluding other groups. In due time, armed insurrections follows, which leads to bloody repression. Both sides are typically armed and abetted by outside powers for motives strategic or economic—a dynamic that outlived the Cold War. If the insurgents win, the cycle is repeated with victims and persecutors changing places. If the test of strength remains inconclusive, domestic war turns into bloody routine, as in the former Congo, in Sudan and Angola. In the worst case, as in Rwanda in the mid-1990s, failed states resort to genocide by machete and machine gun.

The postcolonial mayhem that continues to tear apart Africa actually does not deserve the "nationalism" label. It is rather a subnational or intrastate phenomenon, be it ethnic, tribal, or religious. The battles normally unfold not between but within states, usually failed ones. The source of disaster is the inability to reconcile ethnic with political borders or to strike a balance between factions by admitting the rebels to the troughs of political and economic power. A rights-based democracy might help, as would an economy that mutes Hobbesian strife with the plenty generated by growth. Yet, economic performance and democratic institutions are routinely the first victims of tyranny and revolt.

Rising-State Nationalism. A fifth and final type of Belgrade–Beijing Belt nationalism is that of rising states. This phenomenon has a record, too, duplicating the experience of Germany, Japan, and the United States in the latter part of the nineteenth century. Simply put, it is a two-step pattern: a nation becomes rich, then rowdy; with affluence comes ambition. A critical intervening variable is the consolidation of state power.

In the late nineteenth century, the economic growth rates of Germany, Japan, and the United States all began to overtake those of the established great powers, especially in those sectors related to war making during the industrial age: iron, steel, energy—manufacturing in general. Take Germany: from unification in 1871 to the eve of World War I, German coal output rose sevenfold, approaching parity with Britain. Steel production grew tenfold, and exports leaped by a factor of almost five.[23] Eventually, iron and steel would be forged into guns and navies.

The pattern was reinforced by demographic expansion. Japan's population went from 30 million in midcentury to 45 million in 1900. The U.S. population quadrupled during that period, and Germany's went from 40 million at the time of unification to 60 million in 1900. All three also profited from surging food production. Rapid railroad construction brought the "breadbasket" of the Ukraine closer to Germany. In post–Civil War America, where the largest immigration wave ever, emanating from eastern and southern Europe, was washing ashore, the transcontinental railroad opened the West to the plow. Most important, all three countries managed to shake off their worst political handicaps: weak or conflict-ridden states. In the United States, the Northern victory certified the supremacy of the Union in 1865. In Japan, 250 feudal domains were fused under the Meiji restoration in 1871, in the same year the Bismarckian Reich had turned twenty-five states into one. In all three, the first fruits of political unification were an enormously enlarged single market. The way was now open for breathtaking economic growth and the rapid rise to global power.

Though these events unfolded oceans apart, the similarities were striking. As the landed aristocracy—a formal one in Germany and Japan, an informal one in the American South—lost its hold, power was concentrated in Berlin, Tokyo, and Washington. Industrialization—statist in Japan, laissez-faire in the United States, a blend of both in Germany—began to hammer agrarian economies into manufacturing ones. The Meiji administration literally invented a state religion, replacing Buddhism with a cult of national deities. In Germany, the Bismarckian state drew the Lutheran Church into an alliance of altar and throne by granting it official status and financial largesse. In the United States, it was the civic religion of "Americanness," celebrated on the altar of assimilation, which welded together state and secular faith. In all three countries, universal education sought to instill a nationalist ethos; in the United States, millions of schoolchildren began to recite the Pledge of Allegiance after 1892.

By the turn of the twentieth century, two to three decades after national and economic unification, the trio began to bestride the global stage as claimants to great-power status. Japan unleashed war against China in 1894, wresting trade and territorial concessions from the country one year later. To stop Russian advances in Manchuria and Korea, Japan attacked the Russian fleet at Port Arthur in 1904, which presaged the assault on Pearl Harbor thirty-seven years later. In 1905, Japanese forces sank the Russian Baltic Fleet in the Tsushima Strait. Korea was annexed in 1910; Manchuria was occupied in 1931. Six years later, Japan attacked China. And in 1941, the target was of course the United States.

In Germany, the "New Course" and the *Weltpolitik* of Wilhelm II were married to the First Naval Bill (1898), which was clearly directed against Britain, the guardian of Europe's balance of power. Six years later, the Second Reich began to build a new class of battleships that were bigger and better armored than anything in the British arsenal. As Wilhelmine Germany proclaimed its right to a "place in the sun," it began to meddle in Africa and the Middle East. In 1905, at about the same time that Japan sank the Russian fleet, Germany began to prepare for hegemonial war by basing its strategy on the notorious Schlieffen Plan: attack first in the west and then, after defeating France, in the east.

Curiously, a solid democracy like the United States, beholden not to the Kaiser but to a Constitution and to Congress, embarked on a similar road paved by prodigious economic growth since the Civil

War. What the ideology of *Weltpolitik* did for Wilhelmine Germany, Manifest Destiny did for the ebullient United States. Agitating for a naval buildup, the German *Flottenverein* found its American counterpart in the likes of Alfred T. Mahan, the naval theoretician who had an enormous impact on U.S. strategic thinking. Closely read in Germany, Mahan argued that greatness demanded a mighty bluewater navy with bases around the world. By 1898, myth and muscle would propel the United States toward real, not just rhetorical, empire. It took Cuba, Puerto Rico, and the Philippines from Spain, turned Panama into a protectorate, annexed the Hawaiian Islands, and sought to impose its Open Door policy on the European powers carving up China. Physical expansion was wrapped into an even more expansive ideological cloak.

Theodore Roosevelt, the new president, articulated it in a message to Congress in 1904: "Chronic wrongdoing, or an impotence which results in a general loosening of ties of civilized society, may in America, as elsewhere, ultimately require intervention by some civilized nation, and in the Western Hemisphere, the adherence of the United States to the Monroe Doctrine may force the United States . . . to the exercise of an international police power."[24] The Europeans, notes Ernest May, "had now to reckon with a seventh great power."[25]

Rising-state nationalism, so well-documented in the nineteenth century, is also the most dangerous variant of the twenty-first century. In the Baghdad–Beijing Belt, fossil states like Cuba, failed states like Rwanda, or botched modernization experiments in the Arab world make for mischief and misery. But they cannot unhinge the global order in the way Japan, Germany, and the United States did at the end of the nineteenth century—or a few decades later, the Soviet Union, which followed a similar trajectory. First, it was consolidation of state power under Lenin, then forced industrialization under Stalin. Forcible expansion completed the three-step process. The first victims were Poland and the Baltics at the outbreak of

World War II, the rest of Eastern Europe plus one-half of divided Germany followed at the end of the war.

Today, even a nuclearized Iran or North Korea cannot tilt the global balance in any appreciable way. For that, it takes more than nuclear weapons; otherwise, nuclear powers like Israel and Pakistan would have pulled off such a momentous feat already. In the twenty-first century, only China has both the assets and the ambitions to overturn the world's hierarchy of power. With one billion people and a surging economy, India is clearly a candidate member of the great-power club, but it is a reluctant giant, not yet a gate-crasher. China is the most obvious claimant because it approximates most closely the history of the nineteenth century's highfliers. Indeed, the parallels are uncanny. Like Germany, Japan, the United States, and Soviet Russia in the past, China first had to unify state and nation by surmounting fragmentation or internal bloodshed. The task was as gruesome in China as it had been in the United States and in revolutionary Russia, which were almost torn asunder by civil war. After a million deaths, the Chinese civil war ended with the Communist victory of 1949; the aftershock came in the guise of the Cultural Revolution, which raged through the country in the 1960s and 1970s. Like Meiji Japan, China opened up to world trade and foreign investment in the wake of Deng Xiaoping's rehabilitation in 1977. At the same time, Beijing began shifting from Soviet-style management toward fitful microeconomic and fiscal reform. Its highlights were the privatization of agriculture, the partial liberalization of manufacturing, and a tax reform that allowed (more or less) private enterprises to compete on a more equal footing with the state-run sectors. Unsurprisingly, these moves soon triggered stupendous economic growth.

Taking off in the 1990s, the Chinese economy has grown at an annual average of 7 percent, while growth in the industrial world was stuck in the 2 percent range (with the United States growing faster, and Europe and Japan more slowly). Chinese energy production more than doubled in the last fifth of the twentieth century. Exports rose sixfold from 1986 to 1997.[26] Yet as in nineteenth-century Germany and Japan, modernization remains incomplete; the very same conflicts that unsettled this imperial duo during their rise haunt modern-day China. It is the clash between country and city, old and young, nomenklatura and the rest, not to speak of the brutal repression of ethnic minorities like the Tibetans. The Tienanmen massacre of 1989 spelled out the bloodiest price yet of "uneven development in one country."

The most dangerous divisions that can undermine a society are widening income inequalities and mounting friction between two warring ideological groups, as in "Enrich yourselves" versus "Leave the driving to us." It is the age-old war between rising new classes and a static, premodern power structure. These trends closely duplicate those of Wilhelmine Germany, which unleashed breathtaking economic growth while squelching the political claims of an expanding bourgeoisie. The United States, the world's oldest democracy, was not spared these travails at the turn of the twentieth century. Cyclical depression and rural impoverishment pitted the agrarian West against the industrial East. Inside industrial America, an urban proletariat, swelled by millions of indigent immigrants, raised its fists against the nouveaux riches of the Gilded Age, circa 1890–1914. Fueled by layoffs and dropping wages, class conflict kept erupting into violent clashes between workers and police. Even today, Chicago's Haymarket Riot of 1886 and the Pullman Strike of 1894 are seared into the nation's memory.

Though oceans apart, the nations that rose rapidly in the nineteenth and twentieth centuries all dealt with their internal convulsions by resorting to the same remedy: clamorous nationalism, indeed the most powerful political glue ever invented. Its promise is the deceptive equality delivered by the one political good that comes with an inexhaustible supply: national identity, pride, and exceptionialism. Power and wealth are by definition limited assets; what I acquire, you cannot. Not so nationalism, a bottomless well that will never run dry. All can drink from it without clashing over who gets what and how much—there is more than enough for all. Even better, as they gulp down the intoxicating liquid, all persons are all alike. Whether rich or poor, mighty or meek, they are one another's equals in the community of fate that is the nation. Nationalism delivers an "us against them" creed that wraps strife in the vast cloak of a common identity. The promise of community on the cheap explains how quickly regimes resort to the tool of busying "giddy minds with foreign quarrels" and how eagerly such a heady brew is lapped up by a people tortured by deepening rifts of income and status.

In the United States, it was "jingoism"; in Germany it was *Deutschland über alles*. And so it is in China, whose nationalism comes with an even sharper edge. If German *Weltpolitik* and American Manifest Destiny reflected overconfidence, Chinese nationalism is powered by an overweening feeling of humiliation at the hands of foreign powers near and far, which stretches backwards for centuries. Add in the Chinese case, a generous dollop of Social Darwinism, the conviction that one's race or nation must prevail over lesser ones. These ideas also animated British and American nationalism in the late Victorian era, but their bloody consequences at the turn of the twentieth century were well-nigh modest when compared with Japanese and German imperialism a few decades later. Their chauvinism was fueled not only by past grievances—the forced "opening of Japan," the punitive peace of Versailles—but also by a consuming sense of racial superiority that would eventually set the world aflame.

Contemporary Chinese nationalism feeds on a similarly flammable mixture of shameful memories, cultural, if not racial superiority, and the battle cry of "Never again!" Add finally another combustible: the waning of communism as the country's reigning ideology. In 1999, an American China watcher warned, "Since the

Chinese Communist Party is no longer communist, it must be even more Chinese."[27] Fearful of losing its grip, the regime is appealing to wounded pride while conducting a foreign policy that is at once muscular and petulant. Slights, even inadvertent ones like the American bombing of the Chinese embassy in Belgrade in 1999, are pumped up into mortal insults, followed by frenzied demonstrations against the embassies of the enemy du jour. By wrapping itself in the flag, the regime dons a sturdy armor that defies dissent. The intimidating message is: Whosoever criticizes the Party, betrays the nation.

Is it just a "defensive nationalism," as other observers have claimed?[28] If it is, the "defensive perimeter" of Chinese grand strategy is drawn with ever bolder strokes. China not only threatens war over Taiwanese "secessionism"; it also lays claim to territories around Japan, Vietnam, and the Philippines. At a minimum, Beijing's signal to Washington is "Roll over, America; the Pacific from here to Midway is *our* lake." At a maximum, the best defense is hegemony, which is the oldest tale in the history of the world. From the Athenian empire to the tsarist empire, it was always defensive necessity that drove expansion. Claiming that he merely wanted to break Habsburg's encirclement of France, Louis XIV spent his whole life trying to conquer the rest of Europe. Similarly, Napoleon started out intending to safeguard the revolution against the monarchical powers and ended up at the gates of Moscow. When Stalin tried to lay his hands on all of Europe after World War II, he similarly invoked the sacred right of self-defense.

In short, East Asia contains all the ingredients for a remake of the nineteenth-century European drama. Though the United States is the paramount power in the Pacific, though it is allied to regional players like Japan, Thailand, South Korea, and Taiwan, the contours of a competitive security system, a.k.a. multipolarity, have been long in the making. The obvious revisionist in this game is China, a nation forging ahead along all dimensions of power: economic, military, and diplomatic. It sees itself surrounded by an alliance network woven by the United States. In the west, it faces the stirring giant of India, in the south a quietly rearming Japan (with the third-largest surface navy in the world), in the north a defrocked Russian superpower hankering for reinstatement. Apart from its territorial claims against lesser neighbors, it seeks to "bring home" Taiwan, a ward of the United States. (The "ingathering" of nationals under foreign rule has been a classic obsession—and pretext—of expansionist powers.) Finally, China faces a nuclear threat from all sides: globally from the United States, regionally from Russia, India, and Pakistan, and farther down the road from might-be nuclear powers like Japan and the two Koreas. All of this hardly makes for a status quo policy.

Will this new drama of rising powers end in the same way as its nineteenth- and twentieth-century predecessors—in the devastation of global war? First and foremost, the answer will have to be delivered by the last remaining superpower, the one and only actor that straddles both the Berlin–Berkeley and the Baghdad–Beijing belts. By dint of its singular power and position, the United States has in its grasp the capability to take the world of the twenty-first century on a road that will not double back to the late nineteenth and early twentieth. To prevail in this herculean task, what grand strategy should No. 1 choose? It will have to be a judicious blend of "Britain-plus" and "Bismarck-plus": more engaged and less skittish than Britain's, more generous and less self-serving than Bismarck's solution to the problem of primacy without supremacy.

7

A Giant's Task

In Frederick Forsyth's thriller *Avenger*, an old British spymaster explains to his young American colleague, "My dear boy, if you [Americans] were weak, you would not be hated. You can have supremacy or be loved, but never both. Never seek popularity."[1]

This would have been sound advice for an imperial power like Britain. In the days of dynastic politics, love surely was not given. The dispatches of ambassadors and the instructions of their superiors read like a manual of power politics. Statesmen addressed each other in the most deferential language, but betrayal was always assumed and obligation hedged. Though fleshed out in minutest detail, treaties were meant to be broken, and so armies were always poised to strike. Bismarck did not love his allies in Vienna and Petersburg; Palmerston and Disraeli did not yearn for popularity in Paris and Berlin. The game was strictly zero-sum, and its name was not affection but advantage.

The twenty-first-century drama of nations follows a more complicated script. At bottom, it remains a zero-sum contest: what I want, you cannot have, whether it is profit or prestige. But the ancient my-gain-your-loss game is enveloped in layer after layer of unavoidable cooperation because so many new stakes have been piled on top of the old ones. It is no longer just physical security, exclusive trade, or territorial control. It is a wealth of issues no nation can resolve by itself or attack with the traditional tools of statecraft. How shall we count the ways? Here is a short list: terrorism, floods of capital and people, currency crashes, multination trade disputes, exhaustion of the global commodities, international crime, pandemics from AIDS to avian flu, weapons of mass destruction, ethnic slaughter, natural disasters. Some of these are "soft" issues, but all of them have hard consequences for the wealth and welfare of nations.

To be sure, these threats have not leveled the nation-state. Except in Europe, sovereignty shows no sign of flagging; the opposite is actually true once we move from the Berlin–Berkeley Belt to the Baghdad–Beijing Belt. International politics is still neither lovefest nor popularity contest. But autonomy is waning, and so is self-sufficiency. What, then, separates today's game from the old pastime of princes and potentates, where cynicism passed for wisdom and betrayal for prudence? The difference is twofold. One is "institutions"; the other, "legitimacy."

Institutions. The United States is party to two dozen international institutions whose existence Bismarck and Disraeli could not have imagined. They would have understood NATO, but not the G-8, which tries to get a grip on the global economy. Castlereagh hated the very idea of the Holy Alliance, which he was always trying to "dissolve into individuality"; imagine his disgust if he had to face the OSCE, which encompasses all of Europe as well as the United States.* The World Bank or the World Trade Organization (WTO), let alone the Missile Technology Control Regime, would have stumped the most farsighted statesman of the nineteenth century. To these could be added two dozen conventions that the United States has joined—from the one on the "Suppression of the Financing of

*Organization for Security and Cooperation in Europe. With fifty-five members from Europe, Central Asia, and North America, it is the world's largest regional security organization.

Terrorism" to the "Convention against Torture." This is not the new essence but the new texture of international relations.[2]

The point about these institutions is not that they have shattered, or even cracked, the nation-state. If it suits them, nations will ignore, defy, or abandon them. Yet these regimes spell out two new messages. One is the planetary nature of the tasks states now face. The other is globalized cooperation—an urgency not felt in centuries past. Multilateralism is not muddleheaded idealism, but part of realpolitik, precisely when it comes to hard-core threats like terror, crime, and proliferation. As for the "softer" problems like the depletion of the global commodities, the solution is either global or none at all. Or in economics: when a country defaulted on its debt in the old days, a strong creditor nation simply took over its finances like an insolvency administrator; today, the International Monetary Fund resorts to multibillion-dollar bailouts to keep a single default from turning into an avalanche.

Institutions have by no means superseded the state system. As in all cooperative ventures, gain, and not goodness, is the object. Self-interest is still the key, and so nations will always want more for themselves than they will wish to grant to others. All these games, whether played out in the UN or the EU, are about relative advantage. Absolute gain for all is good, but more for me is better. Hence power matters as much as it did in the past, because it skews the terms of cooperation in favor of those who have it. But the critical point cannot be gainsaid: it is "jaw-jaw" and not "war-war"—a game of trade-off, compromise, and suasion among a host of parties. And preserving the institution, no matter how flawed it may be, is a value in its own right. Otherwise, the UN would have been ditched long ago.

Legitimacy. This concept must not be confused with legality under international law. Ensconced in treaties and conventions, legality is conformity with rules that nations have voluntarily accepted; it defines what is permitted or proscribed. Yet what the law is—what is legal or illegal—is an open question. For international law has always been Silly Putty in the hands of states, to be kneaded and pummeled until it fits their self-serving purposes—and no wonder. To be binding, international law would require an impartial judge and a supreme enforcer, neither of whom exists in the world of states. The UN Security Council, often billed as the world's arbiter, is neither impartial nor supreme. Its verdicts reflect the interests of its members, and it cannot enforce anything unless it can assemble a posse of the willing and able, who will decide by their own lights.

Legitimacy is vaguer than legality, and yet it may exert a stronger influence on world politics than international law. Though a normative concept, it is invariably bound up with interests and numbers. For instance, it was in the interest of a great many nations not to let Saddam Hussein get away with the rape of Kuwait in 1990, and so all of them supported the United States in one way or another. America's first war against Iraq was legitimate because it was "right," and it was "right" because it served the interests of eighty nations, large and small, distant and nearby. America's second war against Saddam was not so blessed, because it ran counter to the interests of most. Arab authoritarians did not like regime change, Russians and Chinese did not want the United States to recast, rather than just restore (as in 1991), the status quo, nor did the French and the Germans cherish the consecration of American supremacy over the world's most critical piece of real estate.

Though inseparable from interest, legitimacy also has a normative component. After the invasion of Kuwait and again in the wake of 9/11, the United States had no trouble mobilizing the world against Saddam Hussein and the Taliban, because it could invoke two reasonably sturdy values of international society: the proscription of unprovoked aggression and the right of self-defense. In 2003, the second war against Saddam met neither test. Iraq had not attacked anybody, and the idea of precautionary war was not compelling ex ante and certainly not convincing ex post, because no weapons of mass destruction were found. Instead, most of the world saw the unchecked power of the United States as the greater evil. Preemption without proof is like an indictment without a grand jury—an act of hauteur that makes the United States look like a "clear and present danger."[3] To preempt without proof is to indict. And so by hook or crook, by denial and sabotage, the very nations that had bonded with the United States in the First Iraq War would balance against it in the Second.

Norms do matter, certainly when bound up with national interests. How does power, the ultimate currency of international politics, relate to legitimacy? Henry Kissinger, a worthy heir to realpolitikers like Palmerston and Bismarck, has provided this answer: "American power is a fact of life, but the art of diplomacy is to translate power into consensus."[4] Consensus comes from consent, which is another word for legitimacy. Consent is not "popularity" but a crucial facilitator of power. At a minimum, consent spells acquiescence, a green light; farther up the scale, it delivers partners, who are indispensable even for the mightiest nation on earth.

Another way to relate power to legitimacy is to recall the distinction between force and influence. Force is coercion; influence is leadership. And leadership rests on legitimacy; otherwise bullies would be kings. Or to put it in practical, rather than normative, terms, "The United States does not need the world's permission to act, but it does need the world's support to succeed."[5] This is precisely the challenge of American foreign policy in the twenty-first century. Impressive as never before, America's freedom to act has leapfrogged its ability to achieve.

Legitimacy is another word for getting others to do your bidding without having to bribe, blackmail, or brutalize them. Once the issue is framed this way, America's problem at the beginning of the twenty-first century becomes glaringly obvious. It is the gap between power and legitimacy. America's power is at a historical high; its legitimacy is low when compared with the level in 1945, the year the United States bestrode the stage as a permanent global actor. But why harp on legitimacy? Doesn't strength conquer all? It matters for at least three, and then very hard-nosed, reasons.

First, coercion does not buy cooperation. It breeds resentment and resistance. Force wins wars; it does not win the peace.* Just assume that the United States had gained the consent of many when embarking on the Second Iraq War. A UN, that is, a great-power, mandate would have certified the justness of America's cause, just as the backing of NATO did when the United States led the bombing campaign against Serbia in 1999. Instead of sabotaging the American effort, France and Germany might have offered help. (Note that Paris had dispatched the aircraft carrier *Charles de Gaulle* to the Mediterranean, which it later recalled to Toulon for "repairs.") Syria and Iran might have closed their borders to arms smugglers and foreign jihadis. Nation building would have rested on many shoulders (and pocketbooks). Power that merely compels is like a consumption rather than an investment expenditure. Instead of adding to a nation's "capital stock," it draws it down, as the American experience in Vietnam and Iraq II has shown. Power that bears no profit is like money spent on drugs. It delivers a quick hit, followed by letdown and loss of respect. Power that fails spells overextension and damaged reputation, two nasty negatives in the business of nations.

*It might be argued that force won the peace in postwar Germany and Japan. This is true up to a point. In order for these two countries to be democratized, they had to be utterly defeated. But it was a benign occupation that delivered safety, economic assistance, an open American market, and the progressive return of sovereignty that turned former enemies into friends while securing their democratic evolution.

Second, and more harmful, power without legitimacy generates antagonism and resistance, a response known as "realignment," "arms racing," or "coalition building," the classic tools by which weaker states seek to tame the strong. Organized defiance does not improve America's leadership position, forcing it to expend ever more capital on "counterbalancing," that is, on breaking up the opposition and buying the allegiance of the uncommitted. Pure power politics—diplomatic promiscuity plus war—was a winning strategy for the British Empire all the way into the end of the nineteenth century. But yesterday's playing field has changed.

It is an arena that hosts many games, each one with different skills, stakes, and rules. Some matches are familiar enough; they run from chess as a metaphor for diplomacy to kickboxing—war—where force and stamina carry the day. Other encounters resemble the World Soccer Cup or Formula One racing. Played out worldwide, these obey global rules, also known as institutionalism. Then there is the bilateralism of pair skating, where neither can score without the other, and the multilateralism of bicycle racing, where teams must excel at large-group coordination. And all the players must guard against spoilers lurking in the bleachers. These are flesh-and-blood enemies like terrorists, nonphysical threats like currency crises, or natural disasters like pandemics and hurricanes, such as the ones that devastated the American Gulf states in 2005.

Third, pure power politics does not sit well with democratic electorates, and least of all with the imperial Republic America is said to be. Give Americans real foe, and they will fight as ruthlessly as any nondemocracy, in "hot wars," as against Nazi Germany, or in "cold wars," as against the Soviet Union. But democracies do not cherish the cynical, ever-shifting balance-of-power game where yesterday's friend is today's foe. They need to know that their cause is just, and in poll after poll, Americans have professed that, if fight they must, they would want to have allies on their side. There is reassurance in numbers, and so legitimacy matters for domestic reasons, too.

Elements of Grand Strategy: Balancing, Bonding, and Building

What is America's playing field in the twenty-first century? Power will continue to dominate the strategic contest, certainly in the Baghdad–Beijing Belt, where traditional stakes like security and expansion overshadow all others. But even there, and undeniably in the Berlin–Berkeley Belt, new stakes have complicated the traditional game and blunted the old tools of statecraft. How does the containment of Beijing fit in with one of the largest economic relationships in the world, where the United States absorbs a $160 billion trade deficit (2004), while China protects the value of the dollar by hoarding it?

Chapter 5 laid out the spectrum of choices open to a hegemonic power that wants to remain one; they range from "Balancing à la Britain" to "Bonding à la Bismarck." Chapter 6, measuring the distribution of global power, described the extraordinary assets of the United States, hence its unprecedented freedom of action. This concluding chapter will try to match freedom and power with necessity and responsibility. Briefly: the United States will have to balance *and* to bond in order to extend its lease on the top floor of international politics. But to beat the historical odds, it must do better than Britain and Bismarck. "Better" means not only "smarter" but also "wiser." A smart hegemon uses its power economically; a wise one does so responsibly.

To balance is to undo threats to oneself and to seek advantage—this is how states will always act. To bond is to keep such threats from arising by holding out the fruits of cooperation and undercutting incentives for ganging up on No. 1. But bonding and balancing are not enough. To play this game over the long haul, a wise hegemon will have to add "building." The purpose is to build (and maintain) a structure of international relations that transforms rivals into partners and keeps allies from turning into adversaries. The way to achieve this is to take care of oneself by taking care of others—call it supply-side international politics.

The Centrality of American Power. America is the "linchpin of global stability."[6] More modest than "hegemony" or even "primacy," this term evokes "indispensability": take out the pin, and the machinery will fall apart. To extend the mechanical metaphor: the United States is motor, brake, balance wheel, and rudder. Or quite simply: there is nobody else to take care of business. Why not go for management by committee? Nos. 2, 3, 4, et al.—Russia, China, and France, to name just three—never fail to celebrate the virtues of shared governance and to extol the superiority of a multipolar world. They should remember the ancient Greek curse "May the gods fulfill your wishes."

Would they really want to re-create the world of yesteryear, a world run, and more often ruined, by competitive committee? In centuries past, multipolarity did not serve as a pillar of peace. Its price was recurring war. Indeed, war signified that the system was working. The ultima ratio was the ultimate arbiter, the decisive ingredient of balance-of-power politics. Ambitions of nations bred fear, arms racing, and hostile alliances. To thwart conquerors, states banded together in order to deter or defeat them. So war was routine, not accidental. Diplomacy and force formed a seamless web. Some wars of the eighteenth century were limited and brief, yet the Seven Years' War was global, bloody, and long. In the seventeenth century, the Thirty Years' War degenerated into a murderous melee that devastated half of Europe. In the twentieth, another thirty years' war, also known as World Wars I and II, left seventy million dead. Even the nineteenth century, the heyday of the balance of power, was not an exemplar of pacificity; recall Napoleon's wars of conquest, the Crimean

War,* Russia's expansion into the Caucasus, Prussia's three wars of unification between 1864 and 1871, and a score of colonial and Balkan conflicts. Balance-of-power politics can be said to have "worked" only in a very generous sense of the term: conquerors were ultimately beaten back, but constant war was the price of functionality.

Put differently, the purpose of the Balance of Power was not peace but the preservation of the multipower system. Once peace (or order, or stability) moves upstage, however, international politics runs into a familiar problem of culinary politics: more cooks do not make a better broth. Peace is one of the greatest public goods, and a collective is not very good at producing them. Fred Zinnemann's classic 1952 movie *High Noon* makes the point very vividly. It is the story of a small western town awaiting the assault of a gang of revengeful outlaws. This is a perfect moment for producing the public good of security—one for all, and all for one. To beat them back, the sheriff, played by Gary Cooper, seeks to organize the good citizens into a posse, yet ends up fighting almost alone. Why? Wasn't it in the interest of all to resist the aggressors?

The answer is yes, but collective purpose does not necessarily make for collective action, and the theory of public goods explains why.[7] Once a public good like peace (or a park, road, or dike) exists, anybody can enjoy it without having to work for it; that is the definition of such a benefit. From this, it follows that goodness—in this case, civic duty—does not necessarily produce the goods. Precisely because a collective good like security against outlaws would allow everybody in the town to "consume" it for free once it was produced, nobody had a compelling incentive to contribute to it. When something is everybody's responsibility, it is nobody's responsibility.

*The Crimean War involved Britain, Russia, France, Turkey, and Sardinia-Piemont, the forerunner of united Italy.

Why so? Even though all the townspeople in *High Noon* cherished peace, each asked himself why he should assume the risk and bear the burden. "Well, whaddya want?" one of them whines. "Do you want me to get killed?" On the one hand, individuals will abstain from action because they count on others to do the job. This is the "free rider" problem in politics—"let George do it." On the other hand, they will desist precisely because they suspect *others* as free riders—he won't help, so why should I and allow him to enjoy the fruits of my labor for free? In addition to the free-rider problem, *High Noon* illustrates another endemic problem of collective action: a common threat does not affect everybody equally.

The desperadoes were gunning for the *sheriff,* hence the others might just be spared if they stayed out of the fray. So why commit and invite the wrath of the aggressors, especially once they have won? And so it is with states. To avoid the risks of engagement, some states will chose neutrality; to profit from abstention, other nations will try to play the broker to pocket a commission. Some will seek to propitiate the aggressor, which is known as appeasement. Others will hold back to see which way the battle is going, joining in only just before victory to grab a share of the spoils. In short, nations left to their own devices will not necessarily do what the common interest demands.

Public goods are thus rarely, if ever, produced in the absence of a Great Organizer. There has to be somebody who satisfies two conditions. He must have an extraordinary interest in the right outcome, and he must have ample means to afford a disproportionate contribution to the common effort. This member assumes the largest chunk of the start-up as well as of the operating costs. As in a grassroots movement, somebody will first have to make the calls, send out the fliers, and secure a meeting room. Having provided the seed resources, that somebody will also pay a disproportionate share of the running costs to make up for the indifference of some and the free riding of others. To keep the group in harness, he will reward cooperation and penalize the wayward.*

The Great Organizer will make such a lopsided contribution because he expects to profit most from the common cause and because he is the richest in the group. Hence public goods require a leader, and not a committee. This is why the EU and NATO squirmed and dithered in the face of war and ethnic cleansing in the former Yugoslavia of the 1990s. Only when Clinton's America took the lead, while providing the firepower, did the Europeans act. When there was no such lead power, as in Rwanda earlier in the 1990s, ethnic slaughter ran its course. Who will act as Great Organizer, if not the United States? Who has the money, the men, the guns, and, above all, the inclination to bear the greatest burden? Let us run through the list one by one.

Europe is prosperous and populous, but not a strategic actor, because it is not an *e pluribus unum* and will not be for a long time. Fabulously rich, it does not have the means for global power projection or the will, backed by funding, to acquire them. For all its wondrous expansion (from six members to twenty-five), the EU's ken does not extend beyond the Mediterranean basin and its hinterland. When it acts strategically, as in the Balkans or in Afghanistan, it does so with and behind the United States—and then not as "Europe" but as an ad hoc alliance of the willing (or coaxed). If Europe has a global vocation, it is an economic, not a strategic, one.†

Russia? The tsarist empire and, of course, the Soviet Union did have a global career that took them to the farthest corners of the

*A good example for such individual incentives and penalties is a wage settlement between a union and the company. All workers will enjoy the benefits of the new contract. But to make them join and pay dues, the leadership of the union may reward individual members with legal assistance in case of dismissal, or penalize nonjoiners by denying such help.

†See chapter 6 for an elaboration.

earth. From a backward economy, the Soviet Union used to squeeze out a military potential that rivaled the panoply of the United States. But it lacked then, as does Russia now, the *prise de conscience* of a global power. After the defeat of Nazi Germany, the Soviet Union defined itself not as guardian of world order but as contender against the United States. Its lodestar was the other superpower, whose assets and attraction Russia could never match. Russia vied for equality, not stability. Its purpose was to *change* the existing order. Coming from behind and craving more, the Soviet empire was a threat to stability—which has been characteristic of revisionist powers throughout history.

Having lost its messianic ideology, today's Russia has dropped out of the global game, acting like a very large regional power. At the top of Russia's agenda is the restoration of its influence in the area to the south that was once part of the Soviet Union—all those "-stan" countries that used to be Soviet republics. Farther afield, Russia will sometimes team up, especially in the war on terror, and sometimes tangle with the United States. When in a competitive mode, Russia will seek out regional partners against the United States, as it did by joining with France and Germany to stop America's march into the Second Iraq War. Or it will routinely proclaim a "strategic partnership" with China, which is always undercut by the fact that both nations, sharing a long border, are destined to remain rivals as far as the eye can see. Russia is a great power-in-waiting. In due time, Russia may revive its ancient ambitions while reacquiring the wherewithal for global power projection. But there is little in Russia's past or present to suggest a global vision fused to a sense of global responsibility. Whether it is trade or aid, diplomatic engagement or nuclear proliferation, Russia shows up, but does not wade in. Like its Soviet predecessor, Russia is not a producer of global public goods.

Today, the revisionist mantle has fallen on China, a giant with breathtaking potential and a massive sense of historical grievance. Whichever way it moves, it encounters the outposts of American power and interest. Whatever China covets is protected by the Pacific-wide umbrella of American might, from Thailand to Taiwan. China cannot "bring home" its renegade province as long as the U.S. Navy patrols the Strait of Taiwan. Farther back, there is the third-largest surface navy in the world. It belongs to China's historical foe Japan, America's closest ally in the neighborhood. Like Russia of yore, China is a revisionist power, but unlike Russia today, it is a rising power that seeks to change the "correlation of forces" across the board: in the trade and energy sector, in the diplomatic and strategic realm. Revisionist powers may be responsible powers in the sense of "prudent" and "cautious," but they are never responsible in the larger sense of the term. Their quest is for advantage and grandeur, not for a global order that promotes stability and the interests of all. Indeed, they want to change the existing order, not to protect it.

India, another candidate member of the great-power club, is at best a regional player. It is caught in an eternal rivalry with Pakistan that mirrors India's domestic fault line between a Hindu majority and a significant Muslim minority (150 million). To the northeast looms China, another nuclear power, which relies on Pakistan to encircle India in the west. The upshot is that this growing giant, whose population has already passed the one-billion mark, is far too preoccupied with security threats in its front and back yards to raise its sight above its fences. A country beset by nationalist-religious strife at home and by security challenges in the very near abroad will not soon invest in the order of the far abroad.

Japan is like Europe—enormously wealthy and with globe-circling economic interests. But like Europe, it lacks other ingredients that go into a truly global role. Its strategic culture was shattered by World War II; sown by defeat, its pacifist instincts were, and continue to be, nourished by a generous measure of gratis security delivered by the United States. While its rearmament is proceeding apace, it does so under the Pacific umbrella of the United States. Its population is aging even faster than Europe's, leaving ever fewer resources for an autonomous military role. Japan's security interests are regional, not global; its strategic ken does not extend beyond the western Pacific.

The Possibilities of American Power. By default and self-definition, it is the United States that will have to look out for order beyond borders. This is not just a matter of vast power, though it is the most critical ingredient. It is also the *character* of its power that sets America apart. Previous would-be hegemons—from Rome to the German Reich—were conquerors. The United States, self-righteous and assertive as it may be, does not seek to amass real estate. It is more like a giant elephant than a *Tyrannosaurus rex*, less like Napoleon's France and more like Palmerston's Britain, which sought to defang its rivals and not to destroy, let alone absorb, them. This decisive distinction explains why Bismarck's "nightmare of coalitions" has not materialized against the überpower. Rapacious nations are more likely to trigger hostile coalitions than those which contain themselves, so to speak.

The United States has intervened liberally all over the world since Jefferson took on the Barbary pirates in the very early nineteenth century. But the "Imperial Republic" has not conquered, which may have been owing less to superior virtue and more to superior location. After all, there was a huge continent waiting to be settled. Once that expansion was completed, land grabbing stopped.* Ever since, the Republic has been at times aggressive, but never voracious. This is the main reason why, in spite of its singular strength, the United States has not provoked countervailing alliances. For other states, the difference between an elephant and a *T. rex* is crucial. Pachyderms trample the grass and uproot the occasional tree, but dinosaurs kill

*Apart from the Virgin Islands and some islands in the South Sea, the major exception is the Philippines, which the United States occupied in the Spanish-American War of 1898.

and devour. Theoretically, the state system should have "kicked in" against this unfettered colossus long ago, right after the demise of the Soviet Union. But because the United States does not threaten the existence of other major players, it enjoys a respite from the age-old curse of excessive power. Instead, the United States is blessed with a margin of freedom not even enjoyed in its heyday by Britain, which always had to worry about deadly combinations of rivals.

A distinct lack of appetite for classic empire is just one part of this felicitous story. If the United States is an empire, it is a liberal one—a power that seeks not to grab but to co-opt. In terms of its ideology (not always of practice), the United States stands for values enshrined in international public goods rather than strictly national ambitions. Or let's put it this way: like other great powers, the United States has followed interest more resolutely than ideals. But, in the process, it did pursue universal goals, whether it was the freedom of the seas in the 1812 war against Britain or the freedom of nations in two world wars. To recall that the United States has often honored such principles in the breach, and more often in the era of George W. Bush than under previous post–World War II presidents, is not to invalidate three larger points.

First, the United States embodies values with a larger scope (and appeal) than those that have traditionally shaped the nature and the ways of states. Protectionism, mercantilism, or autarky are not the distinctive traits of a country that has been running a trade deficit every year since 1971 (with two exceptions), which would grow to $700 billion by 2005. Nor does the United States stand for authoritarianism and totalitarianism, which tormented the twentieth century, or for the fusion of state and faith, which is threatening the twenty-first. These are exclusionary principles that serve or extol the national self, whereas the United States keeps defining its *national* interests in a universal language. Woodrow Wilson's Fourteen Points[8] reach back to the beginnings of the Republic and forward to the second administration of George W. Bush.

Second, the United States is the only player with a global vision and vocation. It defines its own welfare in global terms, and no wonder. America, as already demonstrated, is the only actor that straddles two oceans and two stages—the Berlin–Berkeley as well as the Baghdad–Beijing Belt. This pivotal position leaves little room for indifference, let alone insulation. At a minimum, it makes for worldwide interests; ideally, for worldwide concern and obligation. Finally, with its surfeit of power, the United States is the only nation that can act on a planetary scale. None of its rivals, real or potential, shares all of these traits. The rest of the world might chafe under the weight of America's might, but it is a safe bet that it would rather have a voice in Washington than entrust the world to China, Russia, India, Japan, or France, or a combination thereof. America's rivals have found it easier to agree on restraining the überpower than on articulating an alternative concept of world order, let alone on how to underwrite it.

Yet America's fabulous assets, now liberated from the fetters of bipolarity, are also its great liability. The long shadow of its power instills fear, resentment, and hatred, as was analyzed in chapters 4 and 5, which deal with the rise of anti-Americanism. And its dominance across the board breeds resistance, the kind of "Balancing against Mr. Big" described in chapter 2. But there is also a bright side to the überpower coin—namely great opportunity. If fused to responsibility, power is to international politics what supply-side economics is to the market: it creates its own demand.

Balancing à la Britain

The demand for American power is hardly on the low side. Though vilified, it is indispensable because there is nobody else to take care of the world's risky business. As we go through the regions with an eye on security, the *conditio sine qua non* of global stability, the first commandment of American grand strategy will be "Balancing à la Britain," but with a new twist. It must be sustained rather than fitful and proactive rather than reactive. The task is not just to discipline or defeat the malfeasant du jour but also to put in place the building blocks of international order.

The Middle East. This is the world's most critical and perilous strategic region—an XXL version of the nineteenth-century Balkans plus oil. Modern terrorism was born in the Balkans, triggering World War I. Its twenty-first-century progeny is the Islamist version; compared to al-Qaeda et al., Gavrilo Princip and the Black Hand were pathetic amateurs.* But international terrorism is merely one item on the agenda. Middle Eastern borders are contested not just by Israel and the Palestinians but by practically everybody else: states and peoples, Arabs and Kurds, Sunnis and Shiites. Regime longevity is actually quite high, given the dynastic dictatorship of Syria (now ruled by the Assads in the second generation), the orderly (though not democratic) succession in Saudi Arabia, or the durability of Egypt's soft despotism. But regime stability, as measured by consent, is as low as ethnic, social, and religious grievances are high. Secularists fight believers, and believers fight among themselves. Ethnic minorities, as in Syria, lord it over the majority, and where majorities are on top, they are still down when it comes to asserting themselves against their own oligarchs. No region harbors more arms per square mile than the Middle East, with Iranian (and other) nuclear weapons lurking in the wings.

The potential threat of the Baghdad–Beijing Belt is most obvious in the area between the Levant and the Persian Gulf. It is a stage where one claimant after another has made its bid for hegemony: Egypt, Syria, Iraq, Iran. A second fault line is domestic strife, the

*The Black Hand was a secret Serbian society dedicated to destroying Austria's rule in the Balkans and to uniting the South Slavs into an independent state. It dispatched Gavrilo Princip to Sarajevo in June 1914, where he assassinated Archduke Francis Ferdinand on June 28, provoking Austria's declaration of war against Serbia on July 28.

most notable having been a fifteen-year civil war in Lebanon that was ended by Syrian occupation. Except in Israel, economic failure is everywhere as endemic as political repression. The area's main exports are oil, the most strategic of resources, and terrorism, the most frightful and elusive enemy of the West. The regional balance of power is shaky at best, as evidenced by five Israeli–Arab wars, Iraq's invasion of Iran and Kuwait, two American wars against Iraq, followed by an American counterinsurgency campaign inside the country, plus an endless series of border conflicts, coups, and interventions between Arabs and Arabs.

The moral of this bloody tale is the need for an extraregional balancer. That task fell upon the United States once it had extruded Britain and France from the area in the late 1950s, and Soviet Russia from Egypt in the course of the 1970s. The United States secretly supported Saddam's Iraq against Khomeini's Iran in the 1980s, and then fought openly against Saddam in the First and Second Iraq Wars. This was a textbook example of Balancing à la Britain, making sure that ambitions fail. To compensate for Arab numbers, the United States helps Israel maintain its qualitative edge; in the moment of truth that was the Yom Kippur War of 1973, the United States mounted a massive resupply effort in favor of Israel while deterring Soviet intervention. Kuwait and the other small Persian Gulf states are wards of the United States. In the domestic power struggles across the Arab world, America underwrites the life-insurance policy of the Saudi regime, and implicitly of Jordan's and Egypt's as well.

All Arab societies may hate America with a passion, but it is no less true that the United States guarantees everybody's security against everybody else, with the exception of Iran's. If its revolutionary fervor ever wanes, even Iran might rediscover the traditional geopolitical interests that nourished the shah's alliance with the United States. Indeed, situated between a Russian colossus to the north, a hostile Arab world to the west, and a nuclear-armed Pakistan to the east, Iran's natural extraregional partner is America. Nor is America's engagement merely a military must. Diplomatically, too, the United States acts as indispensable intruder, nowhere more so than in the Israeli–Arab contest over statehood and borders.

Peace between Egypt and Israel was brokered by President Jimmy Carter in Camp David in 1978. When Yasir Arafat shook hands with Israel's Yitzhak Rabin in 1993, and Jordan made peace with Israel in 1994, the signing took place in the White House Rose Garden. When Israel and the PLO tried to settle in 2000, they, too, went to Camp David at the behest of President Bill Clinton. When crisis escalates into open conflict, as it did during the intifada launched immediately after Camp David, Israelis and Palestinians carry their complaints to Washington, counting on the überpower to exact concessions that neither could extract on its own. These maneuvers cast a bright light on the indispensability of the United States. Why don't Arabs and Israelis take their quarrels to Paris, Berlin, or Moscow, let alone to Beijing or Tokyo? The answer is power and credibility. None of the other outside players can guarantee the security of local actors; America can, and so power talks even among those who dislike the Great Satan as much as the Little Satan. The United States can bear down on Israel precisely because it is the only security lender of the last resort. It is the only outsider that can reward the pliant and chastise the recalcitrant. When Jimmy Carter acted the broker in Camp David, he literally bought the peace by pledging generous arms and economic assistance to both Israel and Egypt.

East Asia. If the Middle East, rent by religious passions and power struggles between mosque and state, resembles sixteenth- and seventeenth-century Europe, the Far East looks like a replay of the eighteenth and nineteenth centuries. The familiar elements are security competition and the drama of rising states. The number of major actors also recalls the nineteenth century. Then, the stage was dominated by Britain (first among equals), Germany (rising), France (demoted), Austria (declining), and Russia (ambitious, but anxious). In the Asian theater, the starring role goes to the United States. China is the would-be superpower. Russia is the defrocked superpower; Japan and India are the could-be superpowers.

In this part of the world, the United States assumed the role of extraregional balancer long ago. In the 1940s, it fought to the death the usurper that was Japan. In the 1950s, it fought to a draw North Korea and China. In the 1960s, it fought two wars in one against North Vietnam. One was a regional war against an expansionist local power; the other, a surrogate contest against the Soviet Union and China, which sheltered and supplied North Vietnam. The United States lost, but was not defeated, which is not an overly subtle distinction but a critical one. Emerging with its power intact (and growing), it hardly missed a beat in resuming its role as offshore balancer.

As China is forging ahead, and Russia is watching from the wings, the United States is quietly masterminding the containment of the rising giant while doing its best to "socialize" rather than provoke a regime that is always ready to suspect slights and encirclement. It has retightened its military alliance with Japan, which is again looking to Washington for protection, as it did when Soviet Russia posed the prime security threat. But implicitly, the United States also provides a kind of counterweight against its friends, just as it did in Europe. And so much of Asia counts on the United States to keep Japan from converting its fabulous richesse into offensive military power. By extending its strategic roof over Japan, the United States denationalizes defense policy, so to speak, inhibiting arms races and security competition. Farther afield, the United States has drawn an old Soviet ally, India, into its own strategic orbit. The Seventh Fleet is the over-the-horizon presence that deters a Chinese invasion of Taiwan. Even Vietnam, America's arch-enemy of the 1960s and 1970s, is looking to Washington as an implicit partner against its historical nemesis China—and certainly as a preferred investor and trading partner. The smaller nations, like Thailand, would rather huddle under the American umbrella than be exposed to the larger Pacific powers.

The United States has been, and continues to be, the hub of the Pacific wheel. Following the logic of collective-goods production, the United States is the Great Organizer because it has the greatest resources and the greatest interest in stability. A perfect example is North Korea's nuclear program, where the United States has taken the lead in defanging Pyongyang's ambitions. From a strictly self-serving point of view, North Korean nuclear weapons could be a second-order concern, since deterring an attack on the American homeland is easy for a power with America's intercontinental overkill capacities. Yet, from a regional-order perspective, the United States is like the sheriff in *High Noon*. It is compelled to act as the Great Organizer because it has the most to lose from North Korean nuclear weapons. If North Korea acquires a serious nuclear arsenal, so might Japan. South Korea might either follow suit or shift toward appeasement, both of which would sever the security tie between Washington and Seoul. India might accelerate its own nuclear effort, and in response so would Pakistan. Since North Korea has acted as a willing, though underhanded, supplier of nuclear and missile technology to all kinds of unsavory clients, it might be emboldened to do so quite openly once it could credibly deter an American attack. In short, by interest and ability, the United States is "Britain" writ large in the Pacific.

Europe. The "Old Continent" is at first sight a less obvious playing field for an extraregional balancer. The great strategic threat that bound Western Europe to the United States has vanished along with the Soviet Union. Russian troops, once ensconced in the heart of Germany, departed in 1994, and Europe's waning strategic dependence has already led to the outcome history and theory would predict. Old adversaries (Russia) and old allies (France and reunited

Germany) have begun to experiment with a latter-day reversal of alliances by joining forces against the last remaining superpower (see chapter 2). Nonetheless, this game remains more simulated than real.

One reason is Russia, which is down but not out. And so neither France nor Germany has pressed the United States to remove the last of its forces from Europe, reduced to about 70,000 from 300,000 at the height of the Cold War. None has questioned the existence of NATO, the American-led alliance. And some are positively happy to have the United States remain a *European* power. Notably, "New Europe" cherishes an America in place. The closer these countries are geographically to Russia, the closer they want to be militarily and psychologically to the United States. Nor is this all. Just as in the postwar period the lesser nations of Western Europe looked to the United States as a reassuring counterweight to the large ones, so the newcomers in the east would not want to be left alone with France and Germany, the "tandem," which has regularly asserted its claim to leadership of the EU. Though much diminished in its importance, the "Great Pacifier-cum-Protector" continues to play its ancient role on an enlarged stage.

Bonding à la Bismarck

Describing America's role as Great Balancer in these terms leads automatically from Balancing à la Britain to Bonding à la Bismarck. Recall once more the essence of the Bismarckian game. The purpose was "not territorial acquisition" but a setting where all of Germany's rivals, except for France, would look to Berlin instead of coalescing against the giant in their midst.

This was "the image gestating in my mind," Bismarck noted. It evokes the metaphor of "hub and spokes." Berlin was the hub, the center of all things, where Europe's major relationships were to converge like spokes. And Germany had to forge better relations with the "tips"—Austria, Russia, Britain, Italy, et al—than they had among themselves, so that they would have little incentive to conspire against Germany. Berlin would be the manager, not the victim, of great-power diplomacy. Substitute Washington for Berlin, and the EU, Russia, China, Japan, and India for yesterday's major players, and you have both a diagnosis and a prescription. Today's hub is America, and to stay in that central place, the United States will have to sustain stronger ties with its rivals and allies than they might weave among themselves.

Note that this task is more demanding than merely Balancing à la Britain. Balancing is ad hoc and with no other purpose in mind than welfare and security for one's own nation. Bonding, on the other hand, is steadier and less self-serving. It requires an eye for the common interest and a commitment to cooperation. Or put it this way: the United States has to deliver the goods to those that it seeks to bind—a costly and onerous task. The upside is twofold: the United States is ideally positioned both as balancer and as bonder. And it stands to profit most from that role.

Despite all the resentment against this unchained giant, the United States remains central to world affairs. It has, or could have, better relations with all the "tips" than they have among themselves. China and Russia may be touting their "strategic partnership," but Russia will not deliver a market that would grant China the $160 billion surplus it enjoys in its trade with the United States. Developing nations both, China and Russia cannot attract from each other the kind of foreign capital and advanced technology readily available in the United States. It is true that China and America are security competitors in the Far East. But so are China and Russia, which share a long and unguarded border. Eying each other warily, both look to the United States as a tacit cobalancer against the other.

What is implicit in the American-Russian-Chinese triangle is glaringly explicit in the tie that binds Japan to the United States. Japan and Russia are separated by intractable territorial quarrels; Japan and China look back at an ancient history of enmity, and China remembers the traumatic Japanese occupation of the 1930s and 1940s. In either country, the other is the prime target of nationalist loathing. So while the Cold War is no more, Japan continues to cling to the U.S. security umbrella. Given its strategic dependence, Japan remains the perfect spoke to the American hub. A similar logic holds true for most of the lesser players in the neighborhood: Australia, New Zealand, Thailand, Taiwan, Malaysia, Singapore, Cambodia—even Vietnam, living as it does in uncomfortable proximity to China. The global No. 1 is the indispensable bonding partner against the region's No. 1, which is China.

Farther west, the United States has recruited India into its orbit while simultaneously extending a protective hand to India's arch-rival Pakistan. Again, the United States is the hub, and the hostile duo form the spokes. The moral of this tale is that the United States is to the nations of East Asia what the Federal Reserve is to America's banks—the lender of the last resort—except that the currency is security rather than dollars. It is not affection but the more reliable glue of necessity that toughens the bonds—and will continue to do so as long as the United States has the will and the strength to carry the burden.

Europe provides the most interesting test case. A client of the United States during the Cold War, it is no longer chained to its Great Protector. Yet NATO endures in the absence of the strategic threat that gave rise to it. Indeed, it keeps expanding eastward. Another paradox is that none of the European medium powers that took up (diplomatic) arms against the United States during the Second Iraq War has even intimated a desire to bolt from the alliance. They talk the talk of multipolarity, but don't walk the walk. They have limned, but not designed, alternative coalitions with Russia and China. It is not love but necessity that sustains the American connection. Would France and Germany entrust their security to Russia, let alone to China? Russia is not a partner but a latent problem. Europe remains a spoke, and within "New Europe" there are many smaller spokes that would rather insert themselves into the American hub than into the Franco-German hub.

The Responsibilities of American Power. By virtue of strength, interest, and location, the United States occupies a central perch between the Berlin–Berkeley and the Baghdad–Beijing Belts. No other nation or alliance has a foot planted in both worlds, and that is the critical distinction between this colossus and the competition. America has interests everywhere; it cannot withdraw into indifference or isolation, and so all the world's troubles land on its plate. It is also the lead player in every international institution of weight—from the UN to the IMF, from the G-8 to the World Bank.

From this it follows, or *should* follow, that America's obligations are also global. The planetary hub is where power meets responsibility. This is not a prescription for woolly-headed idealism, let alone altruism. It is in the coldly calculated interest of the überpower to shoulder the burden and pay the price. Why so?

Obligation, legitimacy's twin, is what makes hegemony tolerable, if not acceptable. The überpower can balance like Britain and bond like Bismarck, and do so better than anybody else in the twenty-first century. But both models, though indispensable classics in the repertoire of nations, do not quite add up to a grand strategy for the long haul. Take Balancing à la Britain. As it did in the past, it requires consummate skill and a sharp eye for small shifts that might turn into large threats. But it also demands a heavy dose of cynicism that enables states to break commitments, betray allies, and change friends and enemies like shirts. Such a grand strategy is better suited to princes and potentates than to democratically elected leaders, who must explain why they want to fight—especially inconclusive wars of choice like those in Vietnam and in Iraq II.*

*How is a war of choice different from its apparent opposite, a war of necessity? The distinction is not as obvious as appears at first sight. It may be argued that *all* wars are wars of choice. Was it really necessary for the United States to declare war on Imperial Germany in 1917, after the Kaiser had declared unrestricted submarine warfare on the Atlantic? No, the argument could run, because the United States was not physically threatened by the Reich and so could have sat out World War I, as it

The Second Iraq War

It was easy to retain the nation's consent to the limited interventions against Serbia and even to the much more costly operation of the First Iraq War, which involved half a million U.S. troops. In both cases, victory was swift and bloodless—a democracy's dream. Not so Iraq II. Though the victory against Saddam's armies met the test of speed, the post-2003 sequel failed on conclusiveness. Although Sad-

---

had ignored the sinking of the Lusitania in 1915. To push this argument to its outer limits, one could claim that the war against Japan was not necessary, either, because the United States could have chosen to absorb the loss and to accommodate Japanese interests in the Pacific. Hence, all wars can be depicted as wars of choice. When somebody points a gun at me, I still have a "choice" between giving in and fighting back. Under duress, a state can always choose to capitulate. But this would be an absurd use of the word "choice." States would rightly claim necessity when using force against those who threaten its security and vital interests.

Though the distinction between choice and necessity is fluid, if not tricky, it is an obvious one at the extremes of the spectrum. Israel's invasion of Lebanon in 1982 ranges close to the pole of choice because it was only vaguely related to the country's core security. The purpose was to install a friendly government in Beirut and to extrude the PLO, which did not pose a strategic threat to Israel. Yet the Yom Kippur War of 1973 was necessity squared because Israel had to beat back a two-fronted assault by its strongest enemies, Egypt and Syria.

The distinction between choice and necessity hinges on physical security and vital interests. The qualifier "vital" denotes interests that are critical for a nation's future survival. They range from the freedom of travel, trade, and navigation to the prevention of deadly military threats down the road. While it is true that acting against future threats involves choice based on judgment, some choices are more necessary than others. To expel Saddam from Kuwait in 1991 was closer to the pole of necessity than to the pole of voluntarism. Saddam's control of the Kuwaiti oil fields, abutting on the world's largest reserves in Saudi-Arabia, was a compelling casus belli. But to destroy his regime in 2003 was a benefit and not a necessity, given Iraq's reasonably effective containment and the degradation of its forces. Necessity warrants an all-out effort; benefits demand the close calculation of costs and staying power. Is it worth it, can I achieve my objective, can I stay the course—especially as a democracy? The best wars of choice are therefore quick, cheap and conclusive, which lends them an aura of necessity ex post facto. In recent times, alas, only regime change in Grenada and Panama has met this triple test.

dam Hussein was toppled after three weeks, the larger objective—democracy-cum-order—proved elusive. Why, then, continue to expend blood and treasure? Why, indeed, launch the war in the first place?

Since Iraq posed only a vague threat to America's security, the national interest was hardly compelling enough to warrant a massive, if not an open-ended, commitment. So Saddam Hussein had to be transfigured into a mortal foe to justify the most radical option of power politics, which is preemptive war. But how to make the case when Iraq was neither a sponsor of terrorism nor a producer of weapons of mass destruction? Hence, the casus belli mutated into the irredeemably evil nature of the Saddamite regime. The objective was neither balancing nor bonding but deliverance, which should only be a secondary concern of great powers. Invoking the democratization of Germany and Japan is misleading. For after 1945, the "reeducation" of these two countries was safely wrapped up in overwhelming strategic interest, which underwrote America's open-ended commitment throughout the Cold War. In fact, the United States had plenty of authoritarians in its camp in the 1950s and 1960s. Ruled by dictators, South Korea, Portugal, and Spain were welcome because their strategic worth trumped the unsavory character of their regimes.

How overwhelming was the strategic interest that Iraq II was to serve? Next to preemptive war, the central ideal of the "Bush Doctrine" was the "democratic peace." Democracy, so the theory runs, is not only good in itself but also good for security because since the Anglo-American War of 1812, no two democracies have ever fought each other. While this is a historical truth, democracies, unfortunately, can be just as aggressive and foolhardy as any despotism, as is shown by the many offensive wars they have fought—from Athens to America. The contemporary Middle East raises yet another problem: how to implant democracy in a hostile soil, which extends far beyond the borders of Iraq. This task obeys a timetable different from that of "network-centric warfare." Though the United States has performed brilliantly in Iraq, it has yet to find a swift answer to the "asymmetric warfare" exploited by Terror International and its Sunni allies. The United States also has to battle "asymmetric time," a problem as old as insurgency warfare itself. As the French sociologist Raymond Aron put it forty years ago, the insurgents win as long as they do not lose; the intruder (or government) loses as long as it does not win.

The price of this war of salvation was exorbitant. One was the loss of legitimacy abroad, followed by a harsh penalty. Allies, which were more critical for nation building than in the initial phase of the war, proved elusive, if not obstinate. Another price was the loss of trust at home, where the electorate turned restless two years after military victory, as always happens when a democracy is asked to support a war of choice with no end in sight. This is why one of the most intelligent advocates of the Iraq War intimated to this author as early as December 2002 that "we will not stay longer than eighteen months"—which was a sound wish but a grave miscalculation.

Above all, Iraq II was the wrong war in pure realpolitik terms, that is, as an attempt to right the regional balance of power, which America is sworn to uphold. Given the arms embargo and the "no-fly zones," Iraq's military capabilities had gone from bad to worse after the First Iraq War (1990–91). All of its neighbors, whether they hated the United States or not, shared America's interest in the containment of Baghdad. But regime change in a neighborhood ruled by despots and dictators? This could not buttress the bonding instincts of Middle Eastern potentates. Nor could regime change plus democratization strengthen America's role as balancer, which it had executed so skillfully during the First Iraq War. This time, the "coalition of the willing" was clearly on the small side.

Nor was this all. Ironically, the most serious revisionist power in the area, Iran, was the greatest profiteer of America's second war against Saddam Hussein. Khomeinist Iran, and not post-Kuwait

Iraq, was and is the greatest threat to American interests in the area. It has been assiduously assembling the many pieces that go into the making of nuclear weapons. It has sponsored or authored terrorism around the world—from Beirut to Berlin, from Hamas to Islamic Jihad. It has threatened America's ally Israel with incineration, and it is the most vociferous foe of Israeli–Arab accommodation. But courtesy of American power, Tehran's worst rival was suddenly laid low; thanks to America's democratic impulse, Iran's strategic position improved by leaps and bounds. As a result of America's victory, Shia power in Iraq was liberated from Sunni oppression, which presaged at least ideological kinship where irreducible hostility once separated the regimes in Baghdad and Tehran. Even worse, as long as the United States was entangled in an inconclusive insurgency war (which Iran subtly manipulated from the outside), it dared not—or could not—mount an attack on Iran's nuclear installations. From a coldly strategic perspective, the intervention in Iraq was a war against the wrong foe at the wrong time. America had targeted the lesser evil.

The Task of an Überpower. Worst of all, a surge of resentment strained to the breaking point many a spoke in America's global wheel. Though fitfully uttered, the message was that the mighty shall be thwarted if they do not use their power wisely. This is why, early on in Germany's imperial career, Bismarck shifted from a grand strategy of mediation and maneuver to one of hub and spokes. The purpose was to make everyone cooperate with the hub so that none would conspire against it. Yet while bonding is more stable than balancing, it has its own problems.

If balancing depends on speed and ruthlessness, for which democracies are not well suited, bonding is like a slow-motion film. Recall that Bismarck's game was to stalemate power, to cast an entangling net of alliances over Europe that would freeze history. If history is anything, however, it is fickle and ornery. Luckily, Bismarck was no longer alive in 1907 to witness how the spokes in the grand wheel had been broken and rearranged into a deadly alliance against the Reich, one that would destroy it in 1918. To bond, as the term implies, is to immobilize, but the essence of all politics is nicely summarized in Robert Burns's poem "To a Mouse": "The best-laid schemes o' mice an' men / Gang aft agley."[9] What is a spoke in America's hub today can turn into a spike tomorrow, as happened to the German Reich when Russia and Britain turned into implacable foes.

History, at any rate, whispers that primacy is not a fixture of international life. It has to be conquered anew every day. So balancing and bonding are not enough; these strategies have to be reinforced by building. Balancing dismantles threats; bonding keeps them from arising. But building an international order that turns rivals into stakeholders is the magic catalyst that transmutes raw strength into legitimate power. To dull the sting of its unprecedented might, the United States has to honor Uncle Ben's dying words to Spider-Man in the 2002 movie of the same title: "Remember, with great power comes great responsibility."

Why assume responsibility when America's powers are even more fabulous than Spider-Man's? Why worry, when the rest of the world cannot vanquish No. 1 in the way it crushed a long line of claimants, ranging from Spain's Charles V to Germany's Adolf Hitler? Why not opt for lofty indifference, broken by the occasional sally against the rogue state of choice? After all, Nos. 2, 3, 4, et. al. have no compelling incentive to conspire against a No. 1 that acts more like a restless elephant than a flesh-eating dinosaur. America irks and domineers, it tries to call the shots and bend the rules, but it does not inspire existential angst, except in the Milosevics, Bin Ladens, and Saddams of this world, who are a lot more terrifying than any American president could ever be.

"Pourvu que ça dure"—provided that it endures—was the wary counsel of Napoleon's mother, Leticia, when he boasted of his triumphs. Great power creates opposition willy-nilly, and a pachyderm, no matter how benign, is no pussycat. True, America was conceived as "empire of liberty," as Thomas Jefferson put it in 1780,[10] and it stopped conquering a hundred years ago. But for America's friends and rivals, the critical issue is not the virtue or the reassuring history of this beast but its behavior today and tomorrow. How, then, should a No. 1 act if it wants to remain one?

For centuries, Britain played the "Tongue or Holder of the Balance," opposing the "strongest, most aggressive, most dominating Power on the Continent."[11] Bismarck's grand strategic design was a constellation "in which all the powers except France need us." Guided by these principles, Britain preserved its primacy, while Bismarck managed to stave off the Reich's encirclement. Why not play the same games *à l'américaine*, especially since the United States has been quite successful at both over the last fifty years? These classics of statecraft—balancing and bonding—will persist as long as the state system persists. But there is a third and superior version that is far better suited to a liberal and democratic hegemon. Its purpose is to convert stalemate into order, and rivals into stakeholders. Britain and Bismarck had little else to invest in their strategies except manipulation, maneuver, and mendacity—and, of course, the threat of force. The payoffs were negative, and the message read: stick to the status quo in order to avoid worse, which is great-power war. Neither Britain nor Bismarck's Germany was an institution builder. They did not craft an order that gave all the other players *positive* incentives to stay in the game—and to stay there for the long haul.

What are these incentives? In the language of Hollywood, it is the motto of *Field of Dreams*: "If you build it, people will come." In more formal language, it is international public goods, hereafter abbreviated as IPGs. These come in all shapes and sizes, but they all share one defining characteristic: IPGs deliver benefits all can enjoy once they exist. The supreme IPG is stability or international order, a setting where disputes are resolved by the appeal to rules, and not to arms. Another is international institutions, which embody the mechanisms for the adjustment of conflicts. An alliance like NATO is an RPG, a "regional public good." Organized by the United States at the outset of the Cold War, it was a "perfect" public good in the sense that it extended a unilateral American security guarantee to its European allies—even to those who hardly contributed their own resources.* But IPGs need not be enshrined in institutions.

When the United States plays the extraregional balancer, it provides an IPG. By underwriting the security of its allies and clients in the Middle East—from Israel to Saudi Arabia—it delivers a precious IPG all of them can "consume" for free. Likewise in the Pacific, where the United States produces two IPGs at once. By subtly balancing against China, it adds to the security of everyone else; by explicitly protecting Japan, it slows the pace of Japanese rearmament and so inhibits arms races throughout the region. By acting as security lender of the last resort in Europe, America eliminates security competition on a continent that has seen history's worst wars, the two bloodiest of which required an enormous American intervention. This does not exhaust the list of collective benefits. After years of hand-wringing on the part of the EU, it was the United States that organized a posse against Serbia, which sought to absorb a large chunk of the former Yugoslavia. American cruise missiles forced Belgrade into the Peace of Dayton in 1995. In 1999, European NATO members took to the air only after the United States had come around to leading the charge.

The First Iraq War, in which the United States recruited the coalition and provided five-sixths of the manpower, was both an RPG and an IPG. By blunting Saddam Hussein's ambitions, the United

*Even after France opted out of the military integration in 1966, it continued to enjoy security Made in U.S.A.—and so did neutrals like Austria, Sweden, and Switzerland.

States bestowed the collective benefit of stability on the area. Removing Saddam's grip on Kuwait and his threat to Saudi Arabia, it did a favor to the rest of the world by securing the free flow of oil—the greatest strategic resource of them all. The War on Terror, declared by Washington after 9/11, is also an IPG, though an ambiguous one. The campaign is a collective good that not everybody wants to consume. Some nations may decide to forgo it in order to avoid retribution by al-Qaeda et al. To deflect Terror International's wrath, states have minimized their (public) contributions to the American effort.

The international economic arena abounds with public goods. Those who enforce free—or freer—trade provide a vital IPG that allows all nations to enjoy the benefits of comparative advantage and global economic growth. The same holds true for the IPG of monetary stability. Whenever the United States bails out a defaulting country—or presses the IMF to do so—it inhibits production of *negative* public goods like protectionism, competitive devaluation, or investment barriers. So Bill Clinton and his secretary of state, Madeleine Albright were not just boasting when they celebrated America as an "indispensable" power.

At this point in the story, analysis shifts into admonition. America *did* shoulder the burden and pay the price incumbent on a Great Organizer during the Cold War, when strategic necessity fed global goodness. That golden age of American diplomacy is no more, and so some dark patches of ignoble metal have broken through the once solid plating. Still, the golden age serves as a benchmark for what America's grand strategy in the twenty-first century *should* be. In the postwar era, America extended to the world not only the gifts of security, open markets, and financial liquidity. The country was also an institution builder extraordinaire, as illustrated by a whole alphabet soup of acronyms: UN, IMF, GATT (renamed WTO), OEEC/OECD, NATO, World Bank, NPT, and PfP, plus a host of subsidiary Cold War alliances like ANZUS, SEATO, and CENTO.* The United States bestrode the world as provider of international and regional public goods; this not only secured but also *legitimized* American power.

This was the critical difference between the United States and previous greats and would-be greats. All the way into the twentieth century, America's predecessors sought to conquer. The United States, on the other hand, has produced public goods—whether enshrined in institutions or policies. Even brilliant statesmen like Bismarck, Palmerston, or Disraeli never thought much beyond Germany or Britain. Their purpose was to do good not for Europe but for their own countries. Nor did they devise systems that would transcend the narrow purpose of dispersing or destroying the competition.† Previous hegemons were in business for themselves. But the genius of American diplomacy in the golden age was building an order that would advance American interests by serving those of others.

Why shoulder this costly task in the twenty-first century when the strategic threat of the Soviet Union is no more, and that of

*UN stands for the United Nations founded in San Francisco, IMF for International Monetary Fund, GATT for General Agreement on Tariffs and Trade, WTO, its successor, for World Trade Organization, OEEC for Organization for European Economic Cooperation (a.k.a. the Marshall Plan), OECD for Organization for Economic Development and Cooperation (a club of the industrialized states), NATO for North Atlantic Treaty Organization, NPT for the Non-Proliferation Treaty, and PfP for Partnership for Peace, which brought former members of the Communist Warsaw Pact into the Western fold. ANZUS stands for the alliance between Australia, New Zealand, and the United States. SEATO was the Southeast Asia Treaty Organization and CENTO the American-sponsored alliance of Turkey, Iran, Pakistan, and the United Kingdom.

†Britain must be partially exempted from this dour assessment. A liberal empire, it was the foremost champion of free trade and monetary stability (a.k.a. gold standard) in the nineteenth century, thus providing two vital public goods to the trading world.

China has yet to materialize? In the new, low-threat environment, the United States has flagged as an investor in global public goods. America's old penchant for free trade has been diluted by "managed trade"; its enthusiasm for multilateral trade rules has given way to bilateral deal making. If it cannot dominate international institutions, it will dodge or disregard them. If it cannot activate its longstanding alliances, it will recruit "coalitions of the willing." If it cannot tame its exploding trade deficit, it will argue that it is actually providing an international public good by boosting aggregate demand in the world economy, which is true, but self-serving.

In other words, the United States has been repatriating capital from its far-flung IPG enterprises. To be sure, the Great Organizer has not shifted into a free-rider role. How could it when its navies plow the oceans, its air forces patrol the skies, and its bases encircle the globe? It does lead the campaigns to discipline the Saddams of this world, defeat Terror International and stop nuclear proliferation. The United States is still the impresario of all crucial endeavors, but it is in a saving rather than in an investment mode when it comes to those parts of the global agenda that do not pose a clear and present danger to itself. And why should it continue to play the lead investor when the twenty-first century is no longer darkened by the grand strategic threats of the twentieth?

The answer consists of two words: "national interest." A nation that has always defined its own welfare in terms of the right milieu—a liberal order low on violence—will flourish when the rest of the world flourishes. Or to put it in still more hardheaded terms: goodness is good for a No. 1 that wants to remain one.

Nos. 2, 3, 4, et al. will invariably prefer cooperation with No. 1 to anti-American coalitions as long as the United States remains a reliable purveyor of global and regional public goods—and as long as nobody else steps forward to shoulder the burden. The contemporary state system with its two hundred members does not abound with understudies eager to slip into America's starring role. The essence of IPGs, to repeat, is that anybody can profit from them once they are on the market. Though costly to produce, IPGs are the greatest capital of the Great Organizer, frustrating though the free riding of others may be. It is in the nation's own best interest not to squander what it amassed in the golden age of American diplomacy. Its largesse is self-serving because it gives the lesser players a powerful reason to bond with the United States and to accord at least grudging acceptance to its towering position. At the same time, America's generosity mutes the traditional reflex of the weak, which is to tame, trounce, or topple the strong.

These nations will find it useful to have a special player like the United States in the game as long as the latter lives by the rules it itself has written or coauthored. Europe, Japan, and China routinely suffer from America's commercial hauteur, but they will not defect as long as the United States keeps its markets open and promotes freer trade. When violence racks the Belgrade–Baghdad–Beijing Belt, or when revisionists like Iraq, Iran, or North Korea reach for nuclear weapons, most will be only too happy to call on the Great Organizer. Who else has the will and the wherewithal to do what others cannot achieve on their own? America is indeed "indispensable," but only if it respects the interests of others while serving its own. In other words, with great power comes great responsibility, and if the giant falters in its responsibility, so will its power.

Or put it this way: responsibility breeds legitimacy, and legitimacy builds influence. Those who can draw on influence do not have to resort to force, whose payoffs are always uncertain. As Iraq II demonstrated, force can also be more costly than investing in global public goods, which tend to attract loyal clients. Besides, it is more satisfying to hold the helm than to hunker down in the hold, let alone jump ship. But primacy is not about pleasure. If the United States wants to retain its lease on the mountaintop of the international hierarchy, it must match self-interest with obligation. This is not an impossible task. As guardian of international security, the

United States buys security for itself. Stability is its own reward because it prevents worse: arms races, nuclear proliferation, conflicts that spread. Enlarging NATO, though costly to the American taxpayer, has brought profits to both Eastern Europe and the United States because anything that extends the liberal-democratic realm peacefully benefits the "empire of liberty." Respecting the WTO, even when it pronounces against Washington, is still good for America because, as the world's largest exporter, it has the greatest interest in freer trade. In short, by resisting the lure of its unprecedented power, the United States will husband its strength instead of squandering it on imperial ventures that provoke resentment and resistance.

As the United States peers into the twenty-first century, the choices are all too clear. Primacy does not come cheap, and the price is measured not just in dollars and cents but in the currency of obligation. Conductors manage to mold eighty solo players into an orchestra because they know how to soften the sting of discipline with the balm of dedication—because they act in the interest of all. Their labor is the source of their authority, and the reason why they keep possession of the baton. And so truly great powers must do more than merely break up the opposition, as they have done throughout the ages. They must also provide a public service, which is the best insurance against the "nightmare of coalitions." Those who do for others engage in systemic supply-side economics. They create a demand for their efforts, and that translates into political profits known as leadership.

With great power comes great responsibility. As long as this unbound giant lives up to its responsibility—or enlightened self-interest—envy and resentment will not escalate into fear and loathing. "Do good for others in order to do well for yourself" remains the most fitting maxim for an unchallenged No. 1. America was conceived as "cittie upon a hill," with "the eyes of all people uppon us"[12]—indeed, as "New Jerusalem." Four centuries ago, it was but a tiny settlement in a colony known as Massachusetts; today it is the mightiest power on earth. To continue on its path, to endure in the twenty-first century if not beyond, this hegemon must surely soften the hardest edge of its power, all with the world's assent. If it fails to act in such a manner, this "cittie upon a hill" will be a high, but lonely place.

Notes

Chapter 1

1. "The Sources of Soviet Conduct," *Foreign Affairs*, July 1947, p. 575. This article was based on the "Long Telegram" the author wrote to the State Department from Moscow on February 22, 1946.

2. *Democracy in America*, vol. 1 (New York: Vintage Books, 1954), p. 452.

3. Quoted in "Gorbachev and Kohl Strike NATO Deal," *New York Times*, July 17, 1990, p. 1.

4. As quoted in "Soviets Accept Wall's Fall, Not Reunification," *Washington Post*, November 10, 1989, p. A23.

5. Archie Brown, "Gorbachev and the End of the Cold War," in Richard K. Herrmann and Richard Ned Lebow, eds., *Ending the Cold War* (New York: Palgrave Macmillan, 2004), p. 49.

6. As recalled in Gorbachev's memoirs, published first in German as *Erinnerungen* (Berlin: Siedler, 1995), p. 926.

7. Milovan Djilas, *Conversations with Stalin*, trans. Michael B. Petrovitch (New York: Harcourt, Brace and World, 1962), p. 114.

8. "Radio and Television Address to the American People by President Kennedy on the Nuclear Test Ban Treaty, July 26, 1963," *The American Presidency Project*, http://www.presidency.ucsb.edu/ws/index.php?pid=9360&st=&st1=.

9. For an elaboration, see my "America's European Pacifier," *Foreign Policy*, Spring 1984.

10. "Shaping the World for 100 Years to Come," September 1, 1976, in Kiron K. Skinner et al., eds., *Reagan, in His Own Hand* (New York: Free Press, 2001), p. 10.

11. *Les cartes de la France à l'heure de la mondialisation: dialogue avec Dominique Moïsi* (Paris: Fayard, 2000), p. 9.

Chapter 2

1. As quoted in "The Road to War," *Newsweek*, January 28, 1991, p. 39.

2. Fully 65,357 combat sorties were flown during the three weeks of the entire campaign, including the land phase. See *Gulf War Air Power Survey [GWAPS]*, vol. 5, *A Statistical Compendium and Chronology* (Washington, D.C.: Government Printing Office, 1993), pp. 150 and 232–33. Compare this with 9,211 fighter/bomber sorties in Serbia during NATO's ten-week campaign in 1999; see U.S. Air Force, *Air War over Serbia Fact Sheet*, 31 January 2000, p. 6.

3. Christopher J. Bowie et al., *Future War: What Trends in America's Post-Cold War Conflicts Tell Us about Early 21st Century Warfare* (Washington, D.C.: Northrop Grumman Analysis Center Papers, 2003), p. 46.

4. Japan gave $10 billion and Germany almost $7 billion. Kuwait and Saudi Arabia handed over $16 billion each. Altogether, the rest of the world paid all but $7 billion out of a total bill of $60 billion.

5. As quoted in Thomas L. Friedman and Patrick E. Tyler, "From the First, U.S. Resolve to Fight," *New York Times,* March 3, 1991, p. A1ff.

6. For both quotations in this paragraph, see ibid.

7. For the following quotations, see "Excerpts from Pentagon's Plan: 'Prevent the Re-emergence of a New Rival,'" *New York Times*, March 8, 1992, p. 14.

8. Patrick E. Tyler, "Pentagon Drops Goal of Blocking New Superpowers," *New York Times*, May 23, 1992.

9. See Stephen Bowman, "Bosnia: U.S. Military Operations" (Washington, D.C.: Congressional Research Service, Library of Congress, 2003), "Summary."

10. "Excerpts from Pentagon's Plan," cited in n. 7, above.

11. "Remarks before the National Press Club," Washington, September 24, 1997, in USIA, *U.S. Information and Texts*, no. 39, October 2, 1997, p. 8.

12. "Statement before the House International Relations Committee, FY-98 International Affairs Budget," February 11, 1997, http://secretary.state.gov/www/statements/970211.html.

13. Confirmation hearing, "Statement before the Senate Foreign Relations Committee," January 8, 1997, http://secretary.state.gov/www/statements/970108a.html.

14. "Remarks by the President in Freedom House Speech, Washington, October 6, 1995, http://www.clintonfoundation.org/legacy/100695-speech-by-president-in-freedom-house-speech.htm.

15. "Acceptance Speech at the Democratic National Convention, Foreign Policy Excerpts," August 29, 1996, http://www.4president.org/speeches/clintongore1996 convention.htm.

16. All quotations from "Remarks by the President," cited in n. 14, above.

17. "Address and Questions & Answer Session before the Council on Foreign Relations," September 30, 1997, http://secretary.state.gov/www/statements/970930.html.

18. "Democracy and the National Interest: Remarks by Deputy Secretary of State Strobe Talbott to the Denver Summit of the Eight," October 1, 1997, http://www.mtholyoke.edu/acad/intrel/talbott.htm.

19. "Globalization and Diplomacy: A Practitioner's Perspective," *Foreign Policy*, Fall 1997, p. 70.

20. "Address to the U.N. General Assembly," September 22, 1997, in USIA, *U.S. Information and Texts*, no. 038/A, September 25, 1997, p. 2 (emphasis added).

21. Madeleine Albright, "American Leadership for the 21st Century: Doing What Is Right and Smart for America's Future," Jesse Helms Lecture at Wingate University, March 25, 1997, http://secretary.state.gov/www/statements/970325.html.

22. Ibid.

23. "Democracy and the National Interest," cited in n. 18, above.

24. In the first attack on New York's World Trade Center, a bomb killed six people. In 1995, five Americans died when a car bomb exploded outside the U.S. military headquarters in Ryadh. In 1996, an attack on the Khobar Towers in Saudi Arabia killed nineteen U.S. soldiers. In 1998, U.S. embassies in Kenya and Tanzania were bombed, leaving twelve Americans dead. In 2000, a suicide attack crippled the USS *Cole* in Yemen, killing seventeen.

25. Samuel R. Berger, "The Price of American Leadership," Washington, D.C., Brookings Institution, May 1, 1998, White House, Office of the Press Secretary, May 1, 1998, http://clinton6.nara.gov/1998/05/1998-05-01-remarks-by-sandy-berger-at-the-brookings-institution.html.

26. Martin Indyk, Clinton's Middle East expert, as quoted in Evan Thomas, "The 12 Year Itch," *Newsweek* (International), March 31, 2003, p. 56.

27. "Text of Second Bush-Gore Debate," Winston-Salem, N.C., October 11, 2000, http://www.cbsnews.com/stories/2000/10/11/politics/main240440.shtml.

28. "Address to a Joint Session of Congress and the American People," September 20, 2001, http://www.whitehouse.gov/news/releases/2001/09/print/20010920 8.html.

29. *The National Security Strategy of the United States of America*, September 2002, pp. 1, 29, and 30, www.whitehouse.gov/nsc/nss.pdf.

30. For accuracy's sake, these two terms ought to be carefully distinguished, especially since they were routinely scrambled in the Bushist rhetoric. "Preemption" means striking first when the other side is about to attack. "Prevention" implies going first in

a situation short of war—when the assailant still has the upper hand, but the balance of power is tilting in favor of its rival. It is the difference between the very short term and the longer term. Israel offers the best illustration for this distinction. Watching Soviet arms flow into Egypt, Israel attacked in 1956 while it was still favored by the "correlation of forces." In contrast to the Suez War, the Six-Day War was a classic instance of preemption. When Nasser's armies poured into the (demilitarized) Sinai, Israel interpreted this move as prelude to an attack and struck first in preemption.

31. *Democracy in America*, vol. 1 (New York: Vintage Books, 1954), p. 178.

32. *The National Security Strategy*, pp. 14, 31 (emphasis added).

33. During combat operations from March 19 to April 30, 2003. In the next two years, "post-combat ops," in the Pentagon's terminology, rose tenfold.

34. "President George W. Bush's Inaugural Address," January 21, 2001, http://www.whitehouse.gov/news/inaugural-address.html.

35. "Remarks by the President at 2002 Graduation Exercise of the United States Military Academy West Point, New York, June 1, 2002," http://www.whitehouse.gov/news/releases/2002/06/20020601-3.html

36. Ibid.

37. "President Thanks World Coalition for Anti-Terrorism Effort," March 11, 2002, http://www.whitehouse.gov/news/releases/2002/03/20020311-1.html.

38. "Remarks . . . at West Point," cited in n. 35, above.

39. Ibid.

40. "Remarks by the Vice President to the Veterans of Foreign Wars 103rd National Convention," August 26, 2002 (emphasis added), http://www.whitehouse.gov/news/releases/2002/08/20020826.html.

41. "The President's State of the Union Address, January 29, 2002," http://www.whitehouse.gov/news/releases/2002/01/20020129-11.html.

42. Thomas Paine, *The Rights of Man* (Harmondsworth, England: Penguin Books, 1984), p. 145.

43. This terse summation of the doctrine is taken from "President Discusses War on Terror," National Defense University, March 8, 2005, http://www.whitehouse.gov/news/releases/2005/03/20050308-3.html.

44. "Structural Realism after the Cold War," *International Security*, Summer 2000, pp. 27–28. To this should be added the ultimate method of balancing: a victorious war by the status quo powers against the usurper. For the general theory, see Waltz's seminal book *Theory of International Politics* (Reading, Mass.: Addison-Wesley, 1979).

45. On the theme of balancing short of alliance and war, see also my "Who Is Afraid of Mr. Big?: Balance and Power after Bipolarity," *National Interest*, Summer 2001.

46. "The Neoconservative Convergence," *Commentary*, July–August 2005, p. 22.

47. "France Is Not a Pacifist Country," interview with *Time* (International), February 2, 2003, p. 31; Jacques Chirac, "French Leader Offers America Both Friendship and Criticism," *New York Times*, September 8, 2002, p. A9.

48. "Wir müssen noch hart arbeiten," interview with *Welt am Sonntag*, May 19, 2002, p. 4.

49. "Dann lasst uns streiten," interview with *Der Spiegel*, April 4, 2003, p. 53.

50. "Europa und die Zukunft der transatlantischen Beziehungen," address at Princeton University, November 19, 2003. http://www.auswaertiges-amt.de/www/de/ausgabe-archiv?archiv_id=5116.

51. "Rede zur deutschen Außenpolitik vor dem deutschen Bundestag," Berlin, September 8, 2004, http://www.auswaertiges-amt.de/www/de/ausgabe-archiv?archiv_id=6131.

52. "The Last Word: Dominique de Villepin," *Newsweek* (International), December 15, 2003, p. 66.

53. "Wir können den Irak friedlich entwaffnen," interview with *Frankfurter Allgemeine Zeitung*, February 28, 2003, p. 5.

54. "La France s'oppose à une nouvelle résolution de l'ONU," interview with *Le Figaro,* February 24, 2003, p. 3.

55. "Today, I have given formal notice to Russia, in accordance with the treaty, that the United States of America is withdrawing from this almost 30 year old treaty. I have concluded the ABM treaty hinders our government's ability to develop ways to protect our people from future terrorist or rogue state missile attacks." "Remarks by the President on National Missile Defense," December 13, 2001, http://www.whitehouse.gov/news/releases/2001/12/20011213-4.html.

56. "Oh No, Kyoto," *Economist,* April 7, 2001, p. 81.

57. "Rede von Bundeskanzler Gerhard Schröder zum Wahlkampfauftakt in Hannover," August 5, 2002, pp. 7 and 8 of typescript. See http://www.spd.de. The chancellor's helpers depicted this sally as reaction to Vice President Cheney's regime-change speech. In fact, his address to the Veterans of Foreign Wars convention was delivered three weeks later, on August 26, 2002. See above, p. 47.

58. See "Schröder's Nein spaltet Europa," *Financial Times Deutschland*, January 1, 2003, p. 1. In January 2003, Germany entered the Security Council as a rotating member; in February, it became chair.

59. It is instructive to recall the fate of Chancellor Helmut Schmidt (1974–82), who stuck to the deployment of Pershing II and cruise missiles against the consuming hostility of his Social Democrats. No longer in control of his own party, he was abandoned by his Liberal coalition partners, who bolted to the Christian Democrats in 1982, helping to elect the conservative Helmut Kohl as chancellor.

60. As quoted in "Schröder macht den Atomstreit mit Iran zum Wahlkampfthema," *Frankfurter Allgemeine Zeitung*, August 15, 2005, p. 1.

61. As quoted in "Germany and France Draw a Line, against Washington," *New York Times*, January 23, 2003, p. A9.

62. "Schröder: Mut zum Frieden—Die Regierungserklärung des Bundeskanzlers," *Frankfurter Allgemeine Zeitung*, February 14, 2003, p. 6.

63. "Words of Refusal: Three Nations Say No," *New York Times*, March 6, 2003, p. A16.

64. "Conférence de presse de Monsieur Jacques Chirac," January 17, 2003, http:/www.elysee.fr/cgi-bin/auracom/aurweb/search/file?aur_file=discourse/2003.

65. This popular music hall song began with "We don't want to fight / But by Jingo if we do" and appeared at the time of the Russo-Turkish War (1877–78), when anti-Russian feeling ran high and the British prime minister Disraeli ordered the Mediterranean fleet to Constantinople.

66. As requested by the White House on February 14, 2005. See htttp://www.ngb.army.mil/ll/reports/ 06/whitehouse_suppreq_21405.pdf.

Chapter 3

1. *Stern* magazine, October 21, 2004, cover page.

2. For a short history of anti-Americanism, see James W. Creaser, "A Genealogy of Anti-Americanism," *Public Interest,* Summer 2003. For the best and most recent treatment of French anti-Americanism, see Philippe Roger, *The American Enemy: The History of French Anti-Americanism*, trans. Sharon Bowman (Chicago: University of Chicago Press, 2005).

3. François La Rochefoucauld-Liancourt, *Journal de voyage en Amérique et d'un séjour à Philadelphie* (Paris: Droz, 1940), as quoted in Roger, *American Enemy*, p. 36.

4. For the numbers, see "Krisengebiet Europa," *Financial Times Deutschland*, November 17, 2004, p. 9; for the citation, a paraphrase, see Mark Landler, "G.M., Struggling in Europe, Sets Big Job Cuts," *New York Times*, October 15, 2004, p. W1.

5. Heinrich Heine; "Ludwig Börne: Eine Denkschrift" (July 1, 1830), *Sämtliche Schriften*, vol. 4 (Munich: Hanser, 1976), p. 39.

6. As quoted in "Canadian Warm Front," *Wall Street Journal*, November 30, 2004, p. A18.

7. As quoted in Takis Michas, "America the Despised," *National Interest*, Spring 2002, p. 94.

8. "Kulturkampf? Ich bin dabei," interview with *Der Spiegel*, July 14, 2003, pp. 149ff. Earlier in the interview, Zadek had made the Nazi-America equation explicit, but a bit "cowardly" by putting it in the mouth of the British playwright Harold Pinter, who, according to Zadek, had said "that the Americans today should be compared with the Nazis." Then Zadek went further: "The difference is that the

Nazis planned to vanquish Europe while the Americans want to vanquish the entire world."

9. "What the World Thinks of America," *Newsweek* (U.S. ed.), July 11, 1983, pp. 44ff.

10. Andrew Kohut of the Pew Research Center, recounting the gist of the 1983 *Newsweek* poll, in *Anti-Americanism: Causes and Characteristics*, December 10, 2003, http://pages.zdnet.com/trimb/id214.html.

11. Ibid.

12. *American Character Gets Mixed Reviews* (Washington, D.C.: Pew Global Attitudes Project, June 2003), p. 23.

13. *World View 2002: European Public Opinion and Foreign Policy*, pp. 24, 25, and 15, http://www.worldviews.org/detailreports/europeanreport.pdf.

14. German Marshall Fund of the United States, *Transatlantic Trends 2005* (Washington, D.C.: German Marshall Fund of the United States, 2005), pp. 8 and 6 (chart 2), http://www.transatlantictrends.org/doc/TTKeyFindings2005.pdf. (See chart on p. 249.)

15. See n. 12, above. An interesting exception is the measurement of "American religiosity." A majority in France and Holland (61 percent and 57 percent) considers America "too religious." Since religiosity refers not to policy but to character, this variable might be seen as a measure of anti-Americanism, especially since U.S. religiosity, a cultural throwback in contrast to Europe's enlightened secularism, is a classic in Europe's indictment of American culture.

16. For this definition, see my "The Demons of Europe," *Commentary*, January 2004.

17. Here is a good working definition condensed from the *Encyclopaedia Britannica*: Obsessions are recurring words, thoughts, ideas, or images that seem to invade a person's consciousness. An obsession can take the form of a recurrent and vivid fantasy that is often obscene, disgusting, repugnant, or senseless.

18. Hardly had the rubble been cleared from Ground Zero than European bestseller lists were awash in books purporting to prove that the U.S. government had masterminded the 9/11 attack. A hit in France was Thierry Meyssan, *L'effroyable imposture: 11 septembre 2001* (Paris: Carnot, 2002), translated into 25 languages. In Germany, it was Mathias Bröckers, *Verschwörungen, Verschwörungstheorien und die Geheimnisse des 11.9.* (Frankfurt: Verlag Zweitausendeins, 2001), of which 100,000 copies were sold in the first ten months. A follow-up appeared in 2003.

19. On Al-Jazeera TV (Qatar), November 29, 2004 (emphasis added), http://www.memritv.org/search.asp?ACT=S9&P1=388.

20. "Saudi Princess Assails American History and Policy," as cited in Middle East Media Research Institute (MEMRI), Special Dispatch Series, no. 58, October 8, 2003, http://memri.org/bin/articles.cgi?Page=archives&Area=sd&ID=SP58503.

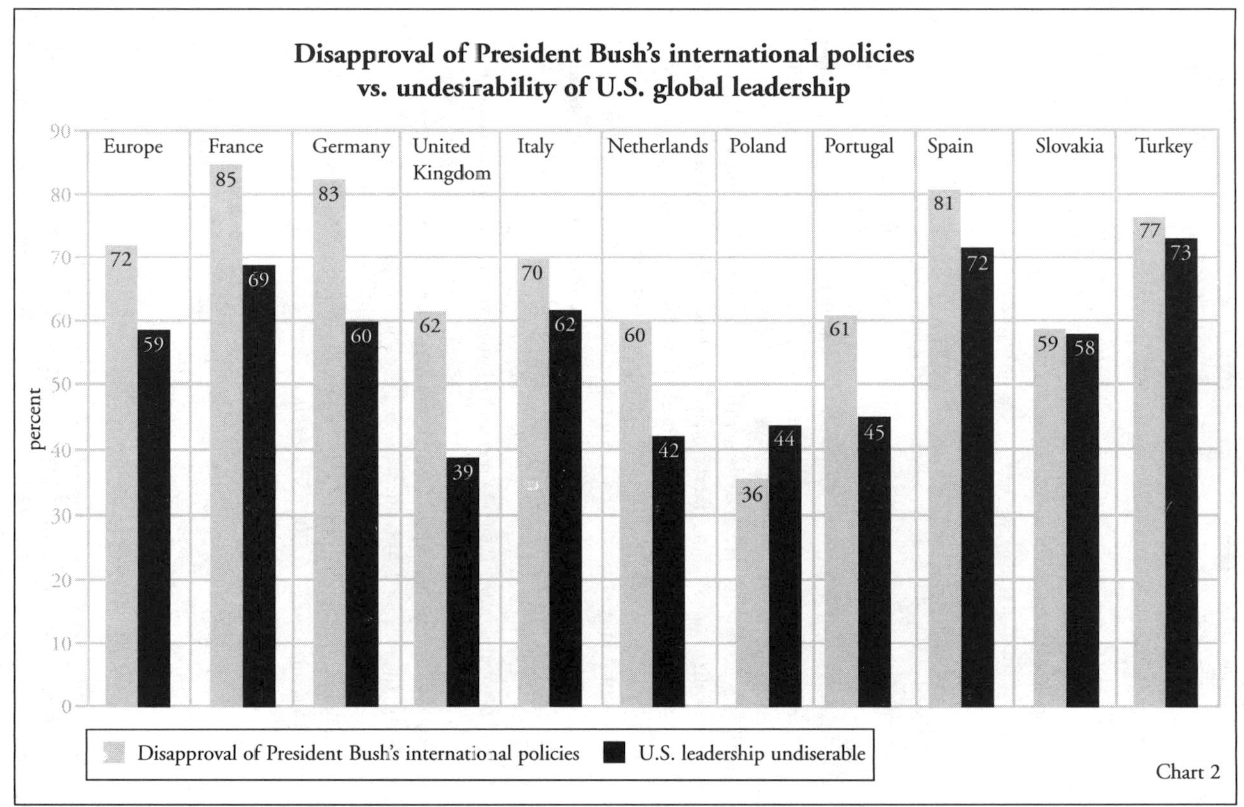
Disapproval of President Bush's international policies
vs. undesirability of U.S. global leadership
Europe
France
Germany
United Kingdom
Italy
Netherlands
Poland
Portugal
Spain
Slovakia
Turkey
72
59
85
69
83
60
62
39
70
62
60
42
36
44
61
45
81
72
59
58
77
73
percent
90
80
70
60
50
40
30
20
10
0
Disapproval of President Bush's international policies
U.S. leadership undiserable
Chart 2

21. Both quotations from *Al-Usbu* (Egypt), August 19, 2002, as cited in MEMRI, Special Dispatch Series, no. 413, August 21, 2002, http://memri.org/bin/articles.cgi?Page=archives&Area=sd&ID=SP41302.

22. All examples are from MEMRI, http://memri.org/bin/cartoons.cgi?cat4.

23. Jean-Claude Casanova, "Guantanamo, la force et la justice," *Le Monde*, February 26, 2002, p. 1. Casanova is a professor at various French universities, an editor, a quondam government adviser, research director of the National Political Science Foundation, and an avid contributor to the French media.

24. As quoted in Peter Finn, "Foreign Leaders Laud Move on Death Penalty in Illinois," *Washington Post*, January 18, 2003, p. A18. In Australia, this was echoed by an editorial in the *Age*: "The imposition of the death penalty is not the mark of civilized, enlightened or just society." "A Clean Sweep on Death Row," January 14, 2003.

25. Mark Thomas, "Britain's Anti-Americanism Is Blamed on Jealousy: This Must Mean We Want the Highest Obesity Rate in the World and Leaders Who Can't String a Sentence Together," *New Statesman* (London), July 22, 2002, p. 11.

26. When Tocqueville remarked on this gap, Europe still defined itself as a Christian civilization. For the facts today, see Pew Research Center, "Among Wealthy Nations . . . U.S. Stands Alone in Its Embrace of Religion," introduction and summary, December 19, 2002. Almost 60 percent of Americans think "religion very important." That is almost twice the figure in Britain, more than double the Italian number, almost three times the percentage in Germany, and almost six times that in France. See http://people-press.org/reports/display.php3?ReportID=167.

27. This theme figured in a dinner conversation with a highly placed German leader in Berlin, December 2002. As he mocked Bush, this author invoked live-and-let-live: "Though you and I are secular, why can't we respect the faith of those who believe in God?" The personage turned so angry that he almost left the table. Though strictly anecdotal, this incident tends to illustrate the intense antipathy Europeans harbor for the religiosity of America and its leaders.

28. "Die Komplizenschaft mit Gott," interview with Jean Baudrillard, *Berliner Zeitung Magazin*, March 16, 2002, pp. m4ff.

29. Thomas, "Britain's Anti-Americanism," p. 11.

30. Jennifer Monti, "Letter from Vienna: Anti-Americanism Gets Ugly in Central Europe," *Harvard Salient*, April 15, 1999, http://www.digitas.harvard.edu/~salient/issues/990415/vienna.htm.

31. "What We Think of America," *Granta*, March 2002, www.granta.com/extracts/1638.

32. See http://www.tns-sofres.com/etudes/pol/030704_etats-unis_r.htm#5.

33. "Rede von Bundeskanzler Gerhard Schröder zum Wahlkampfauftakt am 5. August 2002 in Hannover," http://www.spd.de/servlet/PB/-s/18xzsglpqhgcq1md8qev9b3tak1nt8tb5/menu/1011220/1019528.html.

34. See Gregg Easterbrook, *The Progress Paradox: How Life Gets Better While People Feel Worse* (New York: Random House, 2003), p. 58.

35. "Makes One Sad to Be British," *This Is London* (published in association with the *Evening Standard*), January 21, 2002. Wilson is an emblematic instance for the fusion of anti-Americanism and anti-Israelism in one and the same mind. See my "World without Israel?," *Foreign Policy,* January–February 2005, where Wilson denies Israel's very right to exist.

36. Thomas, "Britain's Anti-Americanism," p. 11.

37. Interview with Dag Herbjørnsrud and Stian Bromark, authors of an analysis of European anti-Americanism, *Frykten for Amerika: En europeisk historie* [*Fear of America: A European History*] (Oslo: Tiden, 2003), as cited in "Kan wi bli mer ydmyke, takk?," *Bergense Tidene,* November 4, 2003.

38. For instance, "Multiple Comparisons of Mean Performance on the PISA Scientific Literacy Scale (2000)," Chart A6.2, OECD Program on International Student Assessment 2000, http://www.oecd.org/dataoecd/21/14/12985310.xls. In PISA 2003, published in December 2004, the United States again came out in midfield, ahead of Germany, Spain, and Italy, on literacy skills. See figure 6.3 "Multiple comparisons of mean performance on the reading scale," http://www.oecd.org/dataoecd/58/58/33918060.pdf.

39. Jean Birnbaum, "Enquête sur une détestation française," *Le Monde*, November 26, 2001. These are not the opinions of the author, who adds that these are the "key themes that nourish the hatred of America."

40. *War Crimes in Vietnam* (London: Allen & Unwin, 1967), p. 112.

41. See Michael Elliot, "Europe: The Un-America," *Newsweek,* Special Davos Edition, December 2000–January 2001.

42. For a general and historical analysis of anti-Americanism, see Paul Hollander, *Anti-Americanism: Irrational and Rational* (New Brunswick: Transaction, 1995). By the same author, see also the edited volume *Understanding Anti-Americanism: Its Origins and Impact at Home and Abroad* (Chicago: Ivan R. Dee, 2004). For anti-Americanism in Europe and Germany, see Andrei Markovits, *Amerika, dich hasst sich's besser* (Hamburg: Konkret, 2004). For France, see Philippe Roger, *The American Enemy: The History of French Anti-Americanism*, trans. Sharon Bowman (Chicago: University of Chicago Press, 2005), and Jean-François Revel, *Anti-Americanism*, trans. Diarmid Cammell (San Francisco: Encounter Books, 2003).

43. Russell A. Berman, *Anti-Americanism in Europe: A Cultural Problem* (Stanford: Hoover Institution Press, 2004), pp. 34–35 and 60.

44. These are not real quotes, but the gist of countless conversations the author has had with Europeans.

45. "Amerikanisierung im Reich der Tiere," letter to the editor, *Hamburger Abendblatt,* February 28, 2003. I am indebted to Markovits, *Amerika, dich hasst sich's besser*, p. 154, for this example.

46. "Pop Anti-Americanism," *Foreign Policy*, January–February 2003, p. 16.

47. See n. 17, above.

48. As photographed by AP Worldwide, and reproduced in Daniel J. Goldhagen, "The Globalization of Anti-Semitism," *Forward*, May 2, 2003.

49. On the parallels between anti-Americanism, anti-Israelism, and anti-Semitism, see my "The Demons of Europe," *Commentary*, January 2004. French: "Antisémitisme et anti-américanisme," *Commentaire* (Paris), Summer 2004.

50. Ignacio Ramonet, in *Le Monde diplomatique*, March 2002, p. 1.

51. As quoted in Claire Trean, "Le réseau français . . . ," *Le Monde*, July 25, 2001.

52. Ramonet, "Vassalité," *Le Monde diplomatique*, October 2002, p. 1.

53. As quoted (from the *New Republic*, October 28, 2002) in Paul Hollander, "Introduction," in Hollander, ed., *Understanding Anti-Americanism*, p. 29.

54. "L'esprit du terrorisme," *Le Monde*, November 3, 2001.

55. (Paris: Gallimard, 2002); trans. C. Jon Delogu (New York: Columbia University Press, 2003).

56. *The American Enemy*, p. 24.

57. "The Unloved American," *New Yorker*, March 10, 2003, p. 34.

58. Berman, *Anti-Americanism in Europe*, pp. 34–35 and 60.

Chapter 4

1. This is the message of Alexis de Tocqueville's *Democracy in America* and of Louis B. Hartz's *The Liberal Tradition in America* (New York: Harcourt, Brace and World, 1955).

2. "Es gibt keinen Fortschritt," excerpts from a speech in Berlin, in *Die Zeit*, December 2, 2004, p. 43. Though the United States is not mentioned in the text, there is a telling clue. Residing in the United States, the author let it be known that he had not personally delivered the speech at a Berlin conference on world cultures, because he had "feared difficulties upon reentering the United States."

3. By 2002, almost half of the 18- to 45-year-olds celebrated Halloween in Germany, and 64 percent of the younger set, reports the German business magazine *Wirtschaftswoche*, adding, "The model is the U.S.A." Issue of October 21, 2002, p. 92.

4. Xinhua News Agency online 2003, http://www.china.org.cn/english/BAT/70112.htm, 11/2/04.

5. These four examples are taken from the January 31, 2005, issue of *Der Spiegel*. For more, see Christine Brinck, *Das Beste von Allem: Das Buch der Listen* (Hamburg: Rowohlt, 2005), pp. 42–43.

6. Though this count does not distinguish between "English" and "American," the overwhelming majority of them must hail from the United States, as a quick perusal of a German bookstore suggests.

7. Chap. 5, sec. 49.

8. Joseph S. Nye, *Bound to Lead: The Changing Nature of American Power* (New York: Basic Books, 1990), p. 188. Nye elaborated the theme in *Soft Power: The Means to Success in World Politics* (New York: Public Affairs, 2004).

9. Or, like *Lord of the Rings*, coproduced with foreign companies. International Movie Data Base, "All-Time Worldwide Boxoffice," http://www.imdb.com/box office/alltimegross?region=world-wide, December 4, 2004.

10. See the excellent essay by Wolfgang Pohrt, "Anti-Amerikanismus, Anti-Imperialismus," in his *Stammesbewußtsein, Kulturnation* (Berlin: Edition Tiamat, 1984), p. 79.

11. Lynn Hirschberg, "US &THEM: What Is an American Movie Now?" *New York Times Magazine,* November 14, 2004, p. 90.

12. "French Opinion and the Deteriorating Image of the United States" (MS, Georgetown University, n.d.), http://www.princeton.edu/~jjun/webs/PIIRS/papers/Kuisel.pdf. The data are from Pew Center Global Attitudes Project, *What World Thinks in 2002*, p. 63. http://peoplepress.org/reports/pdf/165.pdf. Kuisel's paper is one of the very best analyses of anti-Americanism in Europe and especially in France. The Pew report had this to say: "In general, people around the world object to the wide diffusion of American ideas and customs. Even those who are attracted to many aspects of American society, including its democratic ideas and free market traditions, object to the export of American ideas and customs. . . . Publics in every European country surveyed except Bulgaria are resentful of the American cultural intrusion in their country. The British have the most favorable view of the spread of American ideas, but even half of British respondents see this as a bad thing."

13. As quoted in Jim Hoagland, "The New French Diplomatic Style," *Washington Post,* September 25, 1997, p. A25.

14. Holger Liebs, "New York, New York," *Süddeutsche Zeitung,* February 17, 2004, p. 15. Werner Spies, "Die amerikanische Unfehlbarkeitserklärung," *Frankfurter Allgemeine Zeitung,* August 17, 2004, p. 35.

15. *Les cartes de la France à l'heure de la mondialisation: Dialogue avec Dominique Moïsi* (Paris: Fayard, 2000), p. 10.

16. For accuracy's sake, it should be noted that people do want to eat and dress like Italians and Frenchmen, and that Africans do court death on the Mediterranean when trying to get into Europe. But these forces of attraction hardly add up to the sum total of allures exerted by the United States.

17. *Who Are We?: The Challenges to America's National Identity* (New York: Simon and Schuster, 2004).

18. "Alien Scientists Take Over USA!" *Economist,* August 21, 1999.

19. Franz Müntefering, chairman of Schröder's Social Democratic Party, targeted "certain financial investors [who] do not care about the people whose jobs

they destroy. They remain anonymous, have no face, and fall like locusts over companies. These they graze bare and then move on." "Die Namen der Heuschrecken," *Stern*, May 3, 2005. The names of these equity funds were quickly published by the party. They were mainly American.

20. As quoted in "Onkel aus dem Westen," *Der Spiegel*, August 28, 2001, p. 29.

21. As cited in Josef Joffe and Elisabeth Niejahr, "Wie in einem Krämerladen," interview with chancellor candidate Edmund Stoiber, *Die Zeit*, July 25, 2002, p. 4. This was his response to the question "So no amerikanische Verhältnisse?"

22. As quoted in Claire Trean, "Le réseau français . . . ," *Le Monde*, July 25, 2001.

23. "Wir schicken Soldaten, um sie einzusetzen," interview with *Die Zeit*, February 28, 2002, p. 3.

24. "Deutscher Dienstleistungsmarkt soll geschützt werden," *Die Welt*, February 5, 2005, p. 5.

25. "Die Entdeckung Amerikas," April 1, 1997, p. 170.

26. The German business journalist Olaf Gersemann has pierced the usual arguments about Europe's better socioeconomic performance in *Amerikanische Verhältnisse: Die falsche Angst der Deutschen vor dem Cowboy-Kapitalismus* (Munich: Finanzbuch-Verlag), 2003. English edition: *Cowboy Capitalism: European Myths, American Reality* (Washington, D.C.: Cato Institute, 2004).

27. "Unsere Erneuerung: Nach dem Krieg—Die Wiedergeburt Europas," *Frankfurter Allgemeine Zeitung*, May 31, 2003, p. 33. Since this essay was written in the convoluted language of postmodernism, the author has taken some liberties with the translation.

28. *Les cartes de la France à l'heure de la mondialisation*, p. 29.

29. (Munich and Leipzig: Duncker und Humblot). The subtitle is *Patriotic Reflections*.

30. For a concise review of Sombart's thinking, see Colin Loader, "Weber, Sombart and the Transvaluators of Modern Society," *Canadian Journal of Sociology*, Fall 2001, pp. 635–53.

31. For instance, Paul Hollander, "The Politics of Envy," *New Criterion*, November 2002, and Paul Johnson, "Anti-Americanism Is Racist Envy," *Forbes*, July 21, 2003. Oscar Arias, former president of Costa Rica, opines, "People are envious of the United States. The images that flash across TVs all over the world portray a wealthy, comfortable society removed from the violence and misery so commonplace elsewhere." As quoted in "The Last Word: Why Hate America?," *Newsweek* (Atlantic Edition), September 9, 2002.

32. As quoted in Hoagland, "The New French Diplomatic Style," p. A25.

33. "L'ère des symboles est terminée," interview with Védrine in *Libération*, November 24, 1998. Also "Védrine critique la puissance américaine. Il faut un contre-poids, estime le ministre," *Libération*, December 25, 1998.

34. "Rede von Bundeskanzler Gerhard Schröder zum Wahlkampfauftakt am 5. August 2002 in Hannover." For full text, see http://www.spd.de.

35. The distinction between premodern, modern, and postmodern was borrowed from Robert Cooper, *The Breaking of Nations: Order and Chaos in the Twenty-first Century* (New York: Atlantic Monthly Press, 2003). This quotation is from p. 53.

36. The Pew Global Attitudes Project, *American Character Gets Mixed Reviews* (Washington, D.C.: Pew Research Center, 2005), p. 23.

37. Ibid., p. 30. Even America's best allies, the British—58 percent—want American power to be rivaled by another world heavyweight.

Chapter 5

1. According to the 2004 ranking by Shanghai's Jiao Tong University. The criteria used were Nobel Prizes and Fields Medals (the highest awards in mathematics) won by staff and alumni, highly cited researchers in twenty-one broad subject categories, articles published in *Nature* and *Science*, articles in Science and Social Science Citation Index. See http://ed.sjtu.edu.cn/rank/2004/top500(1-100).htm.

2. Thus the French foreign minister Hubert Védrine, *Les cartes de la France à l'heure de la mondialisation* (Paris: Fayard, 2000), p. 9.

3. Arnold Wolfers, *Discord and Collaboration: Essays on International Politics* (Baltimore: Johns Hopkins Press, 1962), chap. 6.

4. "State of the Union Address," February 2, 2005, www.whitehouse.gov/news/releases/2005/02/20050202-11.html.

5. See the tables in A. J. P. Taylor, *The Struggle for Mastery in Europe, 1848–1918* (Oxford: Clarendon Press, 1954), pp. xxviii–xxxi.

6. Thus Ludwig Dehio, *Deutschland und die Weltpolitik im 20. Jahrhundert* (Munich: Oldenbourg, 1955), p. 15. The English translation renders "halbhegemonial" as "semi-supremacy": *Germany and World Politics in the Twentieth Century*, trans. Dieter Pevsner (New York: Norton, 1959), p. 15.

7. The following draws on my "'Bismarck' or 'Britain'?: Toward an American Grand Strategy after Bipolarity," *International Security*, Spring 1995.

8. William Camden, *The History of the Most Renowned and Victorious Princess Elizabeth*, 4th ed. (London: M. Flesher, 1688), p. 233.

9. In a speech to the Conservative members of the Foreign Affairs Committee in March 1936, as reproduced in Winston S. Churchill, *The Gathering Storm*, vol. 1 of *The Second World War* (Boston: Houghton Mifflin, 1948), pp. 207–8.

10. In a dispatch to Russian emperor Nicholas I, December 22, 1840, as quoted in J. P. T. Bury, ed., *The New Cambridge Modern History*, vol. 10, *The Zenith of European Power, 1830–1870* (Cambridge: Cambridge University Press, 197), p.

258, from F. S. Rodkey, "Anglo-Russian Negotiations about a 'Permanent' Quadruple Alliance," *American Historical Review* 36 (1930–31): 345–46.

11. As quoted in *The New Cambridge Modern History*, 10:267, from *Hansard* (House of Common Debates), 3d ser., vol. 69, p. 552.

12. *Empire: The Rise and Demise of the British World Order and the Lessons for Global Power* (New York: Basic Books, 2003), p. 35.

13. "Lord Castlereagh's Confidential State Paper of May 5th, 1820," Appendix A in A. W. Ward and G. P. Gooch, eds., *The Cambridge History of British Foreign Policy, 1783–1919*, vol. 2, (*1815–1866*) (New York: Macmillan, 1923), p. 632. This quotation is taken from Henry A. Kissinger, *Diplomacy* (New York: Simon and Schuster, 1994), p. 88.

14. "Lord Bathurst to Lord Castlereagh, October 20, 1820," in *Correspondence, Despatches, and Other Papers of Viscount Castlereagh*, ed. Charles William Vane, vol. 12 (London: John Murray, 1853), p. 56.

15. As quoted in R. W. Seton-Watson, *Britain in Europe, 1789 to 1914* (Cambridge: University Press, 1945), p. 113.

16. I am indebted to my old teacher at Johns Hopkins University, George Liska, for many insights on European and American grand strategy in history, especially to his *Quest for Equilibrium: America and the Balance of Power on Land and Sea* (Baltimore: Johns Hopkins University Press, 1977), chap. 1 and passim.

17. Quoted in R. B. Mowat, *A History of European Diplomacy* (London: Edward Arnold, 1928), p. 142.

18. Taylor, *The Struggle for Mastery*, p. xxxi.

19. *Europe Reshaped, 1848–1878* (Hassocks: Harvester Press, 1976), p. 358.

20. Dispatch to the German ambassador in St. Petersburg, dated February 28, 1874, reproduced in Johannes Lepsius, Albrecht Mendelssohn-Bartholdy, and Friedrich Thimme, eds., *Die Grosse Politik der Europäischen Kabinette, 1871–1914*, vol. 1, *Der Frankfurter Friede und seine Nachwirkungen, 1871–1877*, 2d ed. (Berlin: Deutsche Verlagsgesellschaft für Politik und Geschichte, 1924), p. 240.

21. The *Diktat* (in the sense of "dictation") was formulated in Bismarck's summer retreat Bad Kissingen on June 15, 1877. See Lepsius et al., eds., *Grosse Politik*, vol. 2, *Der Berliner Kongress, seine Voraussetzungen und Nachwirkungen*, 2d ed. (Berlin: Deutsche Verlagsgesellschaft für Politik und Geschichte, 1924), p. 154.

22. Camden, *The History of the Most Renowned*, p. 233.

23. On Bismarck's failure, see Kissinger, *Diplomacy*, pp. 154–58.

24. "Der Reichskanzler an Kaiser Wilhelm I," August 31, 1878, in In Lepsius et al., eds., *Grosse Politik*, vol. 3, *Das Bismarck'sche Bündnissystem, 1879–1885*, 2d ed. (Berlin: Deutsche Verlagsgesellschaft für Politik und Geschichte, 1924), p. 27.

25. Quoted in William L. Langer, *European Alliances and Alignments, 1871–1890* (New York: Alfred E. Knopf, 1956), p. 199.

26. "Der Reichskanzler an den englischen Premierminister Lord Salisbury," November 22, 1887, in Lepsius et al., eds., *Grosse Politik*, vol. 4, *Die Dreibundmächte und England, 1879–1889*, 2d ed. (Berlin: Deutsche Verlagsgesellschaft für Politik und Geschichte, 1924), p. 378.

27. A. J. P. Taylor, *Bismarck: The Man and the Statesman* (New York: Vintage Books, 1967), p. 185.

28. "Address to the Reichstag," December 5, 1876, in Otto von Bismarck, *Werke in Auswahl*, vol. 5 (Stuttgart: Kohlhammer, 1973), p. 775.

29. As cited in Horst Gründer, *Geschichte der deutschen Kolonien* (Paderborn: Schöningh, 1985), p. 53. Self-denial, however, was not complete. Bismarck did not like, but he still presided over, the acquisition of German protectorates in today's Namibia, Cameroon, Togo, and parts of Rwanda, Burundi, and Tanzania, as well as various islands in the Pacific.

30. The head of the Colonial Section, as quoted by Walther Frank, "Der Geheime Rat Paul Kayser," *Historische Zeitschrift* 168 (1943): 320, citated in Gordon A. Craig, *From Bismarck to Adenauer: Aspects of German Statecraft* (New York: Harper and Row, 1965), p. 21.

31. For a lengthy exposition of the memorandum see Sibyl Crowe and Edward Corp, *Our Ablest Public Servant: Sir Eyre Crowe, 1864–1925* (Braunton: Merlin Books, 1993), pp. 110–19.

32. "The Sources of Soviet Conduct," in Kennan, *American Diplomacy, 1900–1950* (New York: New American Library, 1951), p. 104.

33. See above, n. 29.

Chapter 6

1. *Les cartes de la France à l'heure de la mondialisation* (Paris: Fayard, 2000), p. 9.

2. "Containment and the Search for Alternatives: A Critique," in Aaron Wildavsky, ed., *Beyond Containment: Alternative American Policies toward the Soviet Union* (San Francisco: Institute for Contemporary Studies Press, 1983), p. 81.

3. See the seminal contribution by Kenneth N. Waltz, *The Spread of Nuclear Weapons: More May Be Better*, Adelphi Papers no. 171 (London: International Institute for Strategic Studies, 1981).

4. Alexis de Tocqueville, *Democracy in America*, 2 vols. (New York: Vintage Books, 1954), 1:131.

5. Ibid., p. 178.

6. "China to Increase Defense Spending, Cut Troop Numbers," *Bloomberg.com*, http://www.bloomberg.com/apps/news?pid=10000080&sid=aFa8hc4mWGPA&refer=asia#, March 12, 2005.

7. As reported in Joshua Kurlantzick, "Red Herring," *New Republic*, June 6 and 13, 2005, p. 13.

8. Nicholas Eberstadt, "Population Power: Another Transatlantic Divergence?" (Washington, D.C.: American Enterprise Institute, 2004), p. 9.

9. The total for 2003, in constant dollars of 2000, is $163 billion for the EU-25, according to *SIPRI Yearbook 2004* (London: Oxford University Press, 2004), tables 10A and 10A3. Constant dollars give a more realistic measure than current dollars, which artificially inflate European defense spending because the euro has risen against the dollar by 40 percent since 2000.

10. These numbers are taken from United Nations, *World Population Prospects: The 2004 Revision*, http://esa.un.org/unpp. On EU data, see also the EU-funded report by Harri Cruijsen et al., *Demographic Consequences of Enlargement of the European Union with 12 Candidate Countries* (Voorburg: Statistics Netherlands, 2002).

11. Ibid., p. 45, table IV-11.

12. On the postmodern mind-set, see the trenchant work by Robert Cooper, *The Breaking of Nations: Order and Chaos in the Twenty-first Century* (New York: Atlantic Monthly Press, 2003).

13. *The Federalist Papers*, no. 70, March 14, 1788, fourth paragraph.

14. *Polls on Patriotism and Military Service* (Washington, D.C.: American Enterprise Institute, December 2004), p. 2, for U.S. data in 2000; pp. 7–8, for comparative data. The latter figures are from the *World Value Survey*, conducted 1990–93. Interestingly, German pride did not rise after the reunification of the country in 1990. "Since 1986, the share of 'very proud' Germans (West) has remained almost constant at one-quarter of the total." As reported by Dietmar Pieper, "Sehnsucht nach Moral," *Spiegel Special: Die Deutschen* (Supplement of *Der Spiegel*), April 1, 2005, p. 34.

15. A. J. P. Taylor, *The Struggle for Mastery in Europe, 1848–1918* (Oxford: Clarendon Press, 1954), p. xxviii, table IV.

16. *Democracy in America,* 2:279.

17. *Grundlinien der Philosophie des Rechts,* § 327, "Zusatz" (Frankfurt: Suhrkamp, 1970), p. 495.

18. For an elaboration, see my "Europe's American Pacifier," *Foreign Policy,* Spring 1984.

19. This is not Hegel's term, but a Hegelianism. The first to use it may have been the German art historian Wilhelm Pinder in *Das Problem der Generationen in der Kunstgeschichte Europas* (Berlin: Frankfurter Verlagsanstalt, 1926), pp. 67–69. Karl Mannheim picked it up in "Das Problem der Generationen," in his *Wissenssoziologie: Auswahl aus dem Werk* (Berlin: Luchterhand, 1964), pp. 517, 521. Ernst Bloch popularized the term in *Erbschaft dieser Zeit* (Frankfurt: Suhrkamp, 1985 [1935]), pp. 104–26. On the genealogy, see David Gross, *The Past in Ruins: Tradition and the Critique of Modernity* (Amherst: University of Massachusetts Press, 1992), pp. 94–95, 151.

20. Used throughout his *Imperialism: The Highest Stage of Capitalism* (Chicago: Pluto Press, 1996).

21. "The Bent Twig: On the Rise of Nationalism," in Isaiah Berlin, *The Crooked Timber of Humanity: Chapters in the History of Ideas*, ed. Henry Hardy (Princeton: Princeton University Press, 1998).

22. For an instructive account, see Gilles Kepel, *The Revenge of God: The Resurgence of Islam, Christianity and Judaism in the Modern World*, trans. Alan Braley (Cambridge: Polity Press, 1994), chap. 1, citation on p. 14.

23. For more details on these growth rates, see E. J. Passant, *A Short History of Germany, 1815–1945* (Cambridge: Cambridge University Press, 1969), pp. 105, 107, and 112.

24. Annual Message to Congress, December 6, 1904. This was the "Roosevelt Corollary" to the Monroe Doctrine. See http://www.historicaldocuments.com/TheodoreRooseveltscorollarytotheMonroeDoctrine.htm.

25. Ernest May, *Imperial Democracy: The Emergence of America as a Great Power* (New York: Harcourt, Brace and World, 1961), p. 218.

26. See Todd M. Johnson, "Foreign Involvement in China's Energy Sector," in Elizabeth Economy and Michel Oksenberg, eds., *China Joins the World: Progress and Prospects* (New York: Council on Foreign Relations Press, 1999), p. 270, and Margaret M. Pearson, "China's Integration into the International Trade and Investment Regime," ibid., p. 168.

27. Thomas Christensen, "Chinese Realpolitik," *Foreign Affairs*, September–October 1996, p. 46.

28. For instance, Suisheng Zhao, "Chinese Nationalism and Its International Orientations," *Politial Science Quarterly* 115 (2000): 1–33.

Chapter 7

1. Frederick Forsyth, *Avenger* (New York: St. Martin's Press, 2003), p. 245.

2. For a list, see Richard N. Haass, *The Opportunity: America's Moment to Alter History's Course* (New York: Public Affairs, 2005), pp. 212–19.

3. Thus John Lewis Gaddis, "Grand Strategy for the Second Term," *Foreign Affairs*, January–February 2005, p. 5.

4. "A Global Order in Flux," *Washington Post*, July 9, 2004, p. A19.

5. Haass, *Opportunity*, p. 27.

6. Thus Zbigniew Brzezinski, *The Choice: Global Domination or Global Leadership?* (New York: Basic Books, 2004), p. 17.

7. See the seminal work by Mancur Olson Jr., *The Logic of Collective Action: Public Goods and the Theory of Groups* (Cambridge: Harvard University Press, 1965), and, with Richard Zeckhauser, "An Economic Theory of Alliances," *Review of Economics and Statistics* 48 (1966): 267–79.

I first introduced the notion of collective or public goods into the analysis of U.S. foreign policy in "'Bismarck' or 'Britain'? Toward an American Grand Strategy after Bipolarity," *International Security*, Spring 1995, and "How America Does It," *Foreign Affairs*, September–October 1997. More recently, the theme has been elaborated by, inter alia, Michael Mandelbaum, "The Inadequacy of American Power," *Foreign Affairs*, September–October 2002.

8. For the Fourteen Points, see http://www.lib.byu.edu/~rdh/wwi/1918/14points.html.

9. Having inspired John Steinbeck's novel *Of Mice and Men* (1937), this line has evolved into the modern-day saying "The best-laid plans of mice and men often go awry."

10. "Jefferson to George Rogers Clark," December 25, 1780, in Julian P. Boyd, ed., *Papers of Thomas Jefferson*, vol. 4 (Princeton: Princeton University Press, 1951), pp. 237–38.

11. The first part of this quote refers to the origins of British grand strategy under Elizabeth I and is by William Camden, *The History of the Most Renowned and Victorious Princess Elizabeth*, 4th ed. (London: M. Flesher, 1688), p. 233. The second part is from Winston S. Churchill, *The Gathering Storm*, vol. 1 of *The Second World War* (Boston: Houghton Mifflin, 1948), p. 207.

12. This is the most famous phrase in John Winthrop's sermon "A Model of Christian Charity," delivered in the Massachusetts Bay Colony in 1630, ten years after the Pilgrims landed on Plymouth Rock.

Acknowledgments

A book like this one does not spring *ex nihilo*, and so I have drawn liberally from previous publications in *The American Interest*, *Foreign Affairs*, *National Interest*, *International Security*, *Foreign Policy*, and the *Washington Quarterly*, which reflect an enduring preoccupation with American foreign policy. But I have also drawn on the insights of others, and I want to recognize my debt to three scholars in particular.

One is Kenneth N. Waltz of Berkeley and Columbia, the man who first introduced me to the study of international politics at Swarthmore College and who has exerted a singular influence on the field. Call him the father of "neorealism," a school that focuses not on personages, policies, or ideologies to explain the world, but on "structure" defined as distribution of power. The second is George Liska, a Czech emigré, who taught at Johns Hopkins University. From him, I learned to appreciate an almost forgotten craft—diplomatic history—that is no longer part of the international relations curriculum at American universities. The third is Robert W. Tucker, also of Johns Hopkins, one of the most original minds in the field of

American foreign policy. For all three, received notions have been an irresistible target of intellectual attack, which is a scholar's most noble calling.

I also owe a debt to my students in 223 S at Stanford, an undergraduate seminar on U.S. foreign policy taught in 2004 and 2005. I learned from them, with their lively curiosity, as they learned from me—which is what the university is all about. Further, my thanks go to the Freeman Spogli Institute for International Studies and the Hoover Institution, which offered a hospitable setting for research and writing at Stanford, also known as "The Farm." Finally, three cheers to Robert Weil of W. W. Norton and to Otto Sonntag—two editors who did more to improve this book than an author can expect.

Josef Joffe
Spring 2006

Index

Abstract Expressionism, 105–6
Abu Ghraib prison scandal, 73
Adenauer, Konrad, 62
Afghanistan, 35
  Soviet invasion of, 19, 25
  Taliban control of, 27, 44–46, 48, 178, 192, 206
Afghan War, 27, 28, 34, 44–46, 47, 48, 53, 66, 81, 89, 161, 170, 206, 214
Africa, 22, 25, 154–55, 160, 177, 193–94
African Americans, 78, 84–85, 109
"Agenda 2010" program, 83
al-Qaeda, 42–46, 48, 64, 76–77, 220, 236
Albright, Madeleine, 36–37, 38, 39, 40, 41, 121, 236
Alsace-Lorraine, 138, 149, 160
American Enemy, The (Roger), 93
American Enterprise Institute, 91
American Forces Network (AFN), 98
anti-Americanism, 67–126
  "anti-ism" of, 73, 74, 75–77, 92, 106, 118, 121–22
  as anti-modernism, 95–97, 113–20, 178–79
  anti-Semitism compared with, 69, 74, 75, 76, 78, 79, 85, 87, 89, 90–91, 92, 94, 95, 96, 119, 120
  conspiracy theory and, 76, 87, 90–92
  cultural superiority assumed in, 85–87, 88, 93–94, 249*n*, 254*n*
  definition of, 69–73
  demonization in, 76, 77–79, 80, 87, 90–92, 106
  denigration in, 76, 77–79, 80, 85, 86–87, 106
  in domestic politics, 61–62, 83, 113–14
  economic basis of, 113–20
  "eliminationism" in, 76–77, 80, 92–93
  in Europe, 61–62, 67–68, 74, 80–94, 105–6, 108, 110, 112–26, 178–79, 249*n*, 254*n*
  growth of, 67–126
  Iraq War II and, 70, 72, 78, 79, 81, 89, 92, 104, 121, 122
  in Islam, 66, 76–79, 120
  language of, 73, 75
  moral superiority assumed in, 69, 76, 80–83
  obsession in, 76, 80, 87–90, 121–22, 249*n*
  opinion surveys on, 70–73, 82–83, 254*n*
  paranoia and, 121–22
  policy disagreements compared with, 71–77, 250*n*
  projection in, 83, 84, 106
  psychology of, 68, 75–79, 80, 83, 84, 85, 86–87, 90–93, 106, 108, 126
  seduction as factor in, 97, 107–13, 120
  social disparities in, 83–85, 113–20
  stereotypes as basis of, 76, 77, 80, 86–87, 94
  terrorism and, 66
  überpower status and, 97, 121–26
  ubiquity as factor in, 97, 98–107
Antiballistic Missile (ABM) Treaty, 58, 59, 89
Après l'empire (Todd), 92–93
Arafat, Yasir, 37, 74, 190, 191, 222
Aron, Raymond, 231
Assad, Bashir al-, 191
Assad, Hafiz al-, 190, 191
Athens, 20, 21, 22–23, 33, 201
Augsburg, Peace of (1555), 51*n*

Austria, 138, 140, 141, 150–51, 154, 155, 220*n*
Avenger (Forsyth), 203
Aziz, Tariq, 32

Baghdad-Beijing Belt, 180, 184–202, 204, 210, 219, 228, 239
Baker, James, 32
balancing, 51–66
  "Britain" strategy for, 130–47, 153, 162–63, 180, 202, 203, 210–12, 219–25, 226, 228, 230, 231, 232, 233, 234, 235
  by coalition, 61–63
  conceptual, 54
  by denial, 54
  institutional, 54, 57–61
  by locution, 56–57
  organized, 54
  symbolic, 54
  by terror, 63–66
Balkans, 35, 150–51, 152, 155, 156–57, 160, 173, 184–85, 187–88, 214, 220
Barbary pirates, 43, 44, 217
Barrès, Maurice, 119
Baudelaire, Charles, 93
Baudrillard, Jean, 80–81, 92
Beethoven, Ludwig van, 105
Beirut embassy bombing (1983), 64
Belgium, 61, 141
Berger, Samuel, 40
Berkeley free speech movement (1964), 103–4
Berlin, Isaiah, 186
Berlin Airlift (1948–49), 98, 159
Berlin-Berkeley Belt, 180–84, 185, 188, 202, 204, 210, 219, 228
Berlin Blockade (1948), 17
Berlin Hilton, 98–99
Berlin Ultimatum (1958), 17
Berlin Wall, 17, 18, 24–25, 39, 98, 159
Berman, Russell, 87
bin Laden, Osama, 64
Bismarck, Otto von, 52, 130, 131–32, 141, 147–61, 162, 163, 179–80, 196, 202, 203, 204, 207, 210, 217, 225–28, 230, 232–33, 234, 237
Black Hand, 220
Blair, Tony, 85
Bonaparte, Leticia, 233–34
Bosnia, 34, 170, 178, 185
Breytenbrach, Breyten, 96–97
Brezhnev, Leonid, 19, 25
British Empire, 15, 16, 27, 28, 36, 43, 120, 125, 130–32, 154, 203, 209, 217, 218, 237*n*
Burns, Robert, 233
Bush, George H. W., 30, 32, 49–50, 53, 129
Bush, George W.:
  anti-Americanism and, 67, 69, 70–73, 74, 78–79, 83, 89, 91–92, 121
  foreign policy of, 28, 39–41, 42, 47, 53, 55, 59, 60, 67, 69, 112, 129–30, 218, 230, 250*n*
  Iraq War strategy of, 46–51, 61
  religious convictions of, 80–81
Bush Doctrine, 55, 112, 230

Caligula, Emperor of Rome, 126
Cannes Film Festival (2004), 104
Canning, George, 137
capitalism, 21, 73, 79, 83–84, 89, 91, 95–97, 116–20, 145, 171, 178
capital punishment, 80
Caprivi, Leo von, 156
Carter, Jimmy, 25, 85, 222
Castlereagh, Robert Stewart, Viscount, 136–37, 156, 204
Ceausescu, Nicolae, 18
Central Intelligence Agency (CIA), 81
Charles V, King of Spain, 15, 53, 233
Cheney, Dick, 47, 50
China:
  alliances of, 54–55, 201–2
  Communist leadership of, 167, 198–202
  containment of, 143, 146–47, 210
  defense spending by, 165
  economy of, 165–66, 179, 198–99
  global influence of, 27, 51, 63, 120, 185, 198–202, 215–16, 219, 223–24, 227, 238
  gross domestic product (GDP) of, 165–66
  Imperial, 197
  Japanese relations with, 143, 144, 226–27
  nationalism in, 200–201
  nuclear weapons of, 163, 216
  as revisionist power, 215–16, 223
  Russian relations with, 143, 146, 226
  Tibet controlled by, 73–74
  U.S. relations with, 37, 45, 58, 63, 144, 145, 146–47, 163, 206, 215–16, 226, 235
Chinese embassy bombing (1999), 201
Chirac, Jacques, 56, 62, 63
Chomsky, Noam, 74
Churchill, Winston S., 132–33, 136, 183
Ciampi, Carlo, 80
"cittie upon a hill" concept, 108, 240–41, 261*n*
Civil War, U.S., 195, 196–97
Clausewitz, Carl von, 182
Clinton, Bill, 35, 36–42, 49, 53, 58, 62, 81, 83, 121, 170, 214, 222, 236
"coalitions of the willing," 135, 214, 238
Cold War:
  alliances in, 19, 21–22, 23–26, 62, 157, 236–37
  deterrence strategy for, 23, 27, 42, 47
  diplomacy in, 23, 32–33
  ending of, 34, 60–61
  European nations in, 21, 23, 24–25, 31–33, 168, 169, 224, 225, 227, 235
  Germany's role in, 16–17, 20, 62, 81, 98, 159, 230
  ideological struggle in, 21–22, 38–39, 62, 81, 158, 159

nuclear confrontation in, 22–23, 25, 27, 31–32, 42, 44, 62, 159
political stability and, 22–23, 31, 227, 236–37
Soviet containment in, 13–14, 21, 26, 38–39, 47, 53, 159–61
U.S.-Soviet rivalry in, 13–29, 31–33, 35, 38–39, 42, 44, 55, 62, 157–61, 179, 209, 215
colonialism, 154–55, 160, 177, 189, 193–94
communism, 18–19, 21–22, 37, 95–96, 116, 167, 176, 187, 191, 198–202
Communist Manifesto, The (Marx and Engels), 95–96
Comprehensive Nuclear Test Ban Treaty, 58, 59, 81, 89
Congress of Aix-la-Chapelle (1818), 137
Congress of Berlin (1878), 151, 152
Constitution, U.S., 109, 175, 183, 196
Crimean War, 186, 211–12
Crowe, Eyre, 156
Cuba, 22, 62, 159, 192–93, 197
Cuban Missile Crisis (1962), 22, 62, 159
Czechoslovakia, 26, 141–42
Czech Republic, 35–36

D'Annunzio, Gabriele, 119
Dar es Salaam embassy bombing (1998), 35
Dayton Peace Accord (1995), 34, 121, 235
Declaration of Independence, 109
Defense Planning Guidance for 1994–99 (1992), 33–34, 36–37, 43
de Gaulle, Charles, 25, 62, 96, 179
demonstration effect, 102, 111–12
Deng Xiaoping, 185, 198
Denmark, 141, 175
Derrida, Jacques, 118
dictatorships, 22, 38–39, 40, 183, 191, 192–93, 218, 230
Disraeli, Benjamin, 148, 203, 204, 237
Dual Alliance, 152

East Asia, 142–43, 222–24, 235
education, 84, 86, 101–2, 127, 196
Egypt, 31, 78, 149, 189, 190, 191, 220, 221, 229*n*, 246*n*
"18 October 1977" cycle (Richter), 106
Eisenhower, Dwight D., 85
Elizabeth I, Queen of England, 132–33, 140
Engels, Friedrich, 95–96
English language, 100–101, 108, 127, 253*n*
Enzensberger, Hans Magnus, 81
Eugenides, Jeffrey, 111
Europe:
alliances in, 52, 54–55, 127–61, 204, 224–25, 237
anti-Americanism in, 61–62, 67–68, 74, 80–94, 105–6, 108, 110, 112–26, 178–79, 249*n*, 254*n*
in Cold War, 21, 23, 24–25, 31–33, 168, 169, 224, 225, 227, 235
culture of, 85–87, 172–79
democracy in, 172, 173–75
Eastern, 17, 23, 24, 26, 35–36, 38–39, 52*n*, 102, 115, 146, 169, 178, 180–81, 183, 237*n*, 240
economy of, 59–60, 114–16, 168, 169, 170–72, 176, 198
as "empire by application," 120, 124, 173
gross domestic product (GDP) in, 114–15, 168, 176
integration of, 114–16, 173–81, 182
Iraq War II opposed by, 54, 56–57, 62, 92, 146, 184, 206, 208, 215, 227, 231
military power of, 168–70
Old, 169, 183
pacifism in, 61, 123–24
population of, 167, 170–71, 216
postnationalism in, 172–73, 176–77, 183
religious convictions in, 80–81
security of, 22–23, 31, 168–70, 173, 182–83, 214, 227, 235, 236–37
Soviet threat to, 21, 61, 81, 102, 146, 183, 197–98, 201, 224
as superpower, 168–79
terrorism threat to, 123–24, 184
U.S. relations with, 56–57, 121–26, 179–80, 183, 224–25, 227, 250*n*
welfare system of, 83, 115–16, 118, 176, 178, 183–84
Western, 23, 24–25, 61, 81, 102, 146, 183, 197–98, 201, 224–25
European Council, 173, 175–76
European Union (EU), 24, 27, 49, 105, 115–16, 120, 124, 137, 143, 146, 167, 168–81, 182, 183, 205, 214

fascism, 96, 183
Federal Reserve Bank, 158*n*–59*n*, 227
Feith, Douglas, 50
Ferguson, Niall, 135
feudalism, 95–96, 195
Fichte Johann Gottlieb, 119
Field of Dreams (film), 158, 234
First Naval Bill (1898), 196
Fischer, Joseph, 57
Forsyth, Frederick, 203
France:
African colonies of, 154–55
alliances of, 23, 24, 31, 36, 52, 54
anti-Americanism in, 80–83, 86–87, 91–93, 105–6, 108, 110, 118–19, 254*n*
British rivalry with, 135–36, 140, 141, 188
as EU member, 175, 178
global influence of, 27, 51, 57, 125, 201, 219
Iraq War opposed by, 54, 56, 206, 208, 215, 227
military power of, 168, 179
population of, 170–71
unemployment in, 169

France (*continued*)
U.S. relations with, 24, 31, 80–83, 86–87, 91–93, 105–6
Francis Ferdinand, Archduke, 220*n*
Franco-Prussian War, 141
Franklin, Benjamin, 93
Frederick II, King of Prussia, 52*n*, 131, 138, 140–41, 149
"free rider" problem, 212–14
French and Indian Wars, 27*n*, 135, 145, 188
French Revolution, 51–52, 93, 167, 191
Freud, Sigmund, 75, 83, 89–90, 107, 126
Fuentes, Carlos, 91–92

G-7 summit, 85
G-8 summit, 204
Gambetta, Leon, 149
General Motors (GM), 67–68, 69
genocide, 64, 74, 77–78, 79, 214
Gerasimov, Gennadi, 18
German Marshall Fund, 72–73
Germany:
African colonies of, 154–55, 160
alliances of, 24–25, 54, 98–101, 237
anti-Americanism in, 61–62, 67–68, 74, 86, 92, 93–94, 105–6, 112–14, 117, 118, 119–20, 122
bonding strategy of, 130, 131–32, 147–61, 162, 163, 179–80, 202, 203, 210, 225–28, 230, 232–33, 234
British rivalry with, 33, 140–42, 147, 149, 150–51, 154
Cold War role of, 16–17, 20, 62, 81, 98, 159, 230
defense spending by, 28, 32
as democracy, 208*n*, 230
domestic politics in, 61–62, 83, 113–14, 122, 247*n*
East, 17*n*, 18, 26, 52*n*
economy of, 67–68, 115, 117, 147, 169, 172*n*, 194–95
as EU member, 178
French relations with, 24, 54, 61, 62–63, 137, 146, 149, 150, 152, 157, 158, 160, 224–25, 227
Imperial, 16, 33, 130, 131–32, 136, 147–61, 194–95, 196, 197, 199, 200, 228*n*–29*n*, 237
industrialization of, 195
Iraq War opposed by, 54, 56–57, 62, 92, 206, 208, 215, 227
military power of, 28, 32, 168, 169–70, 179, 196
Nazi, 17, 20, 43, 52–53, 65, 69, 76, 81, 85, 91–92, 96, 121, 127, 136, 141–42, 176, 183, 209, 215, 248*n*–49*n*
population of, 170, 195
reunification of, 16–17, 31
Russian relations with, 153–54, 156–57
Soviet threat to, 16–17, 18, 24–25, 26, 39, 91, 98, 159
unemployment in, 67–68, 115, 117, 169
unification of, 52, 140–41, 147, 160, 195, 196
U.S. relations with, 24–25, 51, 98–101, 208*n*
Weimar, 141
West, 18, 24–25, 52*n*, 168
Gibbon, Edward, 16
globalization, 96–97, 114–15, 116
gold standard, 158*n*–59*n*
Gorbachev, Mikhail, 16–19, 31–33, 168
Great Britain:
alliances of, 23, 24, 27, 52, 54, 63*n*, 237
balancing strategy of, 130–47, 153, 162–63, 180, 202, 203, 210–12, 219–25, 226, 228, 230, 231, 232, 233, 234, 235
as EU member, 175, 176, 177, 183
French rivalry with, 135–36, 140, 141, 188
German rivalry with, 33, 140–42, 147, 149, 150–51, 154
military power of, 168, 179
naval power of, 131, 137–39, 148, 156, 160
unemployment in, 169
U.S. relations with, 24, 31, 43, 45, 46–47, 54, 129, 139, 142, 218, 230, 254*n*
see also British Empire
Grenada, 26–27, 35
Grenville, John A., 148
Grey, Edward, 156
gross domestic product (GDP), 19, 114–15, 165–67, 168, 172, 176, 188–89
Guantánamo Bay detention center, 73
Gulf War (First Iraq War), 30–33, 45, 47, 53, 61, 169, 189, 206, 207, 221, 229, 231, 235–36
Gulliver's Travels (Swift), 20*n*
Gulliver's Troubles (Hoffmann), 20*n*

Habermas, Jürgen, 93, 118
Habsburg dynasty, 15, 16, 27, 52*n*, 102, 127, 134, 135, 141, 152, 154, 187, 201
Hamilton, Alexander, 176
Händler und Helden (Sombart), 119–20
hard power, 103, 108, 173
Harvard University, 86, 101, 102, 107
Haymarket Riot (1886), 199
health insurance, 83, 116
Hegel, G. W. F., 93, 119, 182
Heidegger, Martin, 93
Heine, Heinrich, 68, 93
Henry IV, King of France, 134
Henry VIII, King of England, 132
Herder, Johann Gottfried von, 93, 119
High Noon, 212–13, 224
Hitler, Adolf, 17, 23, 27, 49, 52, 53, 69, 74, 91–92, 105, 127, 136, 139, 141–42, 153, 163, 233
Hobbes, Thomas, 183
Hoffmann, Stanley, 20*n*

Hollywood, 103, 104, 110
Holy Alliance, 137, 204
Hungary, 26, 35–36
Huntington, Samuel, 109
Hurricane Katrina, 84
Hussein, Saddam, 27, 30, 31, 32, 34, 41, 46–51, 53, 54, 60, 61, 74, 79, 122, 143, 189, 190, 192, 206–8, 229–32, 235–36
Hussein Ibn Talal, King of Jordan, 190
Hutten, Ulrich von, 101–2

India, 27, 120, 143, 202, 216, 219, 223
industrialization, 188, 189–91, 195–96, 197, 199
International Criminal Court (ICC), 41–42, 58, 60, 81, 89
international law, 41–42, 48–49, 51, 56, 58, 60, 73, 81, 85, 89, 205–6
International Monetary Fund (IMF), 91, 157–58, 205, 236, 237*n*
international public goods (IPGs), 234–39
international relations:
  alliances in, 19, 21–26, 27, 31–32, 35–36, 41, 52–55, 62, 63*n*, 98–101, 131–32, 135, 136–37, 147–63, 201–2, 209, 212–14, 217–18, 224–25, 231, 236–37, 238
  balance of power in, 14, 20–21, 26, 27–29, 48–66, 92, 125, 127–61, 196, 207–12
  bipolar approach to, 13, 14–15, 19–29, 31, 35, 38, 44, 61, 62, 122, 139
  Bismarck's bonding strategy for, 130, 131–32, 147–61, 162, 163, 179–80, 202, 203, 210, 225–28, 230, 232–33, 234
  British balancing strategy for, 130–47, 153, 162–63, 180, 202, 203, 210–12, 219–25, 226, 228, 230, 231, 232, 233, 234, 235
  building in, 210–11, 232–41
  coercion in (power politics), 207–9
  collective action in, 135, 212–14, 238
  containment in, 13–14, 21, 26, 38–39, 47, 52–53, 143, 146–47, 154–61, 210
  deterrence in, 23, 27, 42, 47, 139–40, 160–61, 164–65
  diplomacy in, 23, 32–33, 36–38, 44–45, 54–55, 56, 143–44, 160–61, 182–83, 207, 237, 239
  domestic politics and, 61–62, 83, 113–14, 122, 247*n*
  encirclement in, 152–53, 201, 234
  enlightened self-interest in, 239–41
  globalization and, 96–97, 114–15, 116
  grand strategies in, 126, 127–63, 202, 203–41
  hegemony in, 26–29, 33–44, 49–58, 62–63, 71, 121–28, 130, 131, 134, 150, 156–57, 162–68, 196–97, 201–41, 250*n*
  "hub and spokes" arrangement of, 153–55, 158–59, 179–80, 225–28, 232–33
  institutions for, 54, 57–61, 81, 122, 125, 157–58, 182–83, 204–5, 209, 235, 236–37, 240
  isolationism in, 52, 128–30, 137–40, 148–49, 163
  legitimacy in, 57, 204, 205–9, 222, 228, 231, 239–41
  multipolar (multilateralist) approach to, 14–15, 25, 56–57, 60–61, 121, 172, 182–83, 201–2, 205, 211–12, 227
  "playing field" for, 14–15, 142–43, 209, 210
  public goods in, 213–14, 218, 234–39
  realist school of, 51, 231
  regional balances in, 143–44, 235, 238; *see also* Berlin-Berkeley Belt; Baghdad-Beijing Belt
  renversement des alliances (reversal of alliances) in, 52, 54–55, 224–25
  revisionism in, 215–16, 223, 239
  stability of, 22–23, 31, 58, 144–47, 156–57, 168–69, 173, 211–14, 227, 234–36, 239–41
  supply-side approach to, 158, 210–11, 219, 234
  unilateralism in, 41–42, 55, 56–58, 121–26
  unipolar approach to, 13, 19–20, 26–29, 33–42, 56, 57
Iran, 27, 47, 62, 74, 128, 189, 190–91, 198, 208, 220, 221–22, 231–32, 239
Iran-Iraq War, 146, 221
Iraq, 232, 239
  army of, 31–33
  Kuwait invaded by, 30, 31, 191, 206, 221, 229*n*, 236; *see also* Gulf War (First Iraq War)
  oil resources of, 49, 50
  regime change in, 47–49, 161, 189, 206, 231
  Soviet support for, 31–33, 191–92
  weapons of mass destruction (WMDs) in, 35, 48, 128, 230
Iraq War II:
  anti-Americanism and, 70, 72, 78, 79, 81, 89, 92, 104, 121, 122
  European opposition to, 54, 56–57, 62, 92, 146, 184, 206, 208, 215, 227, 231
  legitimacy of, 206–8, 228, 229–32, 239
  Sunni insurgency in, 64, 66, 128, 185, 231, 232
  U.S. military forces in, 27, 28, 34, 46–51, 53, 54, 61, 62, 64, 221, 228
Iron Curtain, 17, 38–39, 115
Islamic fundamentalism, 41, 42, 64–66, 76–79, 120, 188–92, 208
Israel, 22, 32, 37, 50, 74, 76, 90–91, 118, 143, 149, 188–89, 190, 191, 198, 221, 222, 229*n*, 246*n*
Italy, 24, 25, 28, 35, 62, 141, 152–53, 167, 168, 170, 172*n*

Japan:
  automotive industry of, 107
  Chinese relations with, 143, 144, 226–27
  as democracy, 208*n*, 230

Japan (*continued*)
economy of, 115, 194–95, 198
global influence of, 27, 216–17, 219
Imperial, 43, 194–96, 200, 229*n*
industrialization of, 107, 195
Meiji restoration in, 195–96
military power of, 65, 91, 138, 142, 202, 216–17, 223, 224, 226–27
population of, 195, 216–17
postwar, 107, 115, 194–95, 198, 208*n*, 216, 230
U.S. relations with, 24, 32, 125, 143, 144, 157, 208*n*, 216, 226–27, 235
Jefferson, Thomas, 93, 217, 234
Jews, 50, 69, 74, 75, 76, 78, 79, 85, 87, 89, 90–91, 92, 94, 95, 96, 109, 119, 120
Joan of Arc, 80
Johnson, Lyndon B., 25, 85
Joint Chiefs of Staff, U.S., 30, 36, 50
Jordan, 190, 222
Jospin, Lionel, 91, 114

Kant, Immanuel, 40
Kaunitz, Wenzel Anton von, 149
Kayser, Paul, 155
Kennan, George F., 13–14, 17, 159–60
Kennedy, John F., 22, 62, 85, 176
Khamenei, Ayatollah Seyyid Ali, 74
Khomeini, Ayatollah Ruhollah, 191, 192, 221, 231
Khrushchev, Nikita, 17*n*, 19, 21, 22, 32
Kim Il Sung, 193
Kim Jong Il, 192, 193
Kissinger, Henry, 207
Kissinger *Diktat* (1877), 150, 152, 158
Kohl, Helmut, 16, 62, 247*n*
Korean War, 20, 22, 46, 145, 159
Kosovo, 35, 178, 185
Krauthammer, Charles, 55
Kuisel, Richard, 104, 254*n*
Kuwait, 30, 31, 221
Kyoto Climate Protocol (1997), 41, 58, 60, 72, 89

Land Mine Convention, 41, 58, 59, 81, 89
Lebanon, 143–44, 189, 190, 220–21, 229*n*
Lenin, V. I., 19, 186, 197
Libya, 35, 192–93
"Little Hans" case study, 89–90
Locarno Treaty (1925), 141
Locke, John, 102
London transit system attacks (2005), 184
Louis XIV, King of France, 53, 130, 132–33, 134, 135, 140, 201
Lusitania sinking (1915), 228*n*–29*n*

McDonald's, 107–8, 112–13
Macmillan, Harold, 183
Madrid railway attacks (2004), 184
Mahan, Alfred T., 197
Maistre, Joseph de, 93
Manifest Destiny, 197, 200
Mao Zedong, 185
Maria Theresa, Archduchess of Austria, 138, 141, 149
Marx, Karl, 95–96
Maurras, Charles, 119
May, Ernest, 197
Middle East:
Arab nationalism in, 188–92
industrialization of, 188, 189–91
oil resources of, 19, 30, 49, 50, 59–60, 73, 77, 79, 188, 221, 229*n*
Soviet influence in, 188–90, 221
U.S. influence in, 37, 49, 72, 143, 154, 188–89, 220–22, 230–31, 235–36
Middlesex (Eugenides), 111
Midway, Battle of (1942), 138
milieu goals, 129, 238
Milosevic, Slobodan, 56–57, 60, 121, 122, 187
Mohammad Reza Shah Pahlavi, 190–91, 221
Monroe Doctrine, 129, 197
Montherlant, Henry de, 67
Moore, Michael, 74
Mossadeq, Mohammed, 190*n*
Munich conference (1938), 141–42
Müntefering, Franz, 254*n*–55*n*
Museum of Modern Art (MoMA), 86, 88, 105–6, 107
"mutual assured destruction" doctrine, 23, 27, 42, 161, 164
Myanmar, 192–93

Nairobi embassy bombing (1998), 35
Napoleon I, Emperor of France, 27, 36, 52, 53, 119, 127, 133, 134, 136–37, 138, 139, 142, 163, 179, 201, 211, 233–34
Nasser, Gamal Abdel, 31, 190, 246*n*
nationalism, 186–202
bent-twig (wounded), 186–88
decline of, 123, 172–73, 176–77, 181, 186–202, 204
defensive, 201–2
failed-modernization, 188–92
failed-state, 193–94
fossil-state, 192–93, 197
post-, 172–73, 176–77, 183
religion and, 80–81, 183, 195–96
rising-state, 194–202, 204, 205
sovereignty and, 51, 56–57, 183–84
National Security Strategy (NSS), 43–44
Native Americans, 73, 77–78
Nelson, Horatio Nelson, Viscount, 138
Netherlands, 134, 140, 175
"nightmare of coalitions," 132, 150, 155, 163, 217, 240
Nijmegen, Peace of (1678–79), 134
Nixon, Richard M., 85, 158*n*–59*n*

North Atlantic Treaty Organization (NATO), 17, 23, 25*n*, 31, 35–36, 37, 45, 46, 52, 53, 57, 85, 122, 126, 146, 157, 185, 187, 188, 204, 208, 214, 225, 227, 235, 236, 237*n*, 240
North Korea, 27, 41, 47, 59*n*, 128, 144, 192–93, 198, 224, 227, 239
Nye, Joseph S., 102–3

Open Door policy, 129, 197
Operation Desert Fox, 35
Operation Desert Storm, 30–31
Ottoman Empire, 151, 187
"Our Renewal" (Habermas), 118

Paine, Thomas, 49
Pakistan, 198, 202, 216, 221, 224
Palestine Liberation Organization (PLO), 190, 191, 222, 229*n*
Palmerston, Henry John Temple, Viscount, 133, 135, 145, 156, 203, 207, 217, 237
Panama, 26–27
Paris, Peace of (1763), 135
Parrish, Carolyn, 69
patriotism, 125, 176, 177
Pearl Harbor attack (1941), 52, 91, 142, 196
Peloponnesian War, 20, 21, 22–23, 33
Perle, Richard, 50
Pew Research Center, 70–72, 254*n*
Philip II, King of Spain, 15, 132–34, 140, 163
Poland, 23, 26, 35–36, 52, 53, 123, 197–98
Pol Pot, 49
Portugal, 22, 230
postmodernism, 75, 124–25, 183, 184
Powell, Colin, 30, 79
Princip, Gavrilo, 220
Protocols of the Elders of Zion, 76
Pullman Strike (1894), 199
Putin, Vladimir, 74, 187

Rabin, Yitzhak, 37, 222
Reagan, Ronald, 19, 26, 35, 85
Reem al-Faisal, Princess, 77–78
regional public goods (RPGs), 235, 238
Reinsurance Treaty (1887), 153, 155
Rice, Condoleezza, 79
Richter, Gerhard, 106
Roger, Philippe, 93
Roman Empire, 14, 16, 24, 27, 28, 43, 102, 127, 128, 173
Roosevelt, Franklin D., 85, 129, 142
Roosevelt, Theodore, 197
Rousseau, Jean-Jacques, 183
Rumsfeld, Donald, 46, 90–91, 135
Russell, Bertrand, 87
Russell, Lord John, 133
Russia:
  anti-Americanism in, 54–55, 58, 70
  in Chechnyan conflict, 73, 74, 187
  Chinese relations with, 143, 146, 226
  democratic reform in, 18, 37, 185
  economy of, 167–68, 179
  as former Soviet Union, 15, 26, 27, 45, 51, 52
  German relations with, 153–54, 156–57
  global influence of, 183, 202, 219, 221, 223, 225, 227
  gross domestic product (GDP) of, 166–67
  Imperial (Czarist), 14–15, 140, 141, 150–51, 214–15
  Iraq War opposed by, 62–63, 206
  military power of, 165, 167, 179, 202
  nationalism in, 186–87
  nuclear weapons of, 163
  population of, 167–68
  as revisionist power, 214–15, 216
  U.S. relations with, 54–55, 58, 144, 163
  see also Soviet Union
Rwanda, 197, 214

Sadat, Anwar el-, 189
Salisbury, Robert Arthur Talbot Gascoyne-Cecil, Lord, 151
Saudi Arabia, 22, 30, 77–78, 192, 220, 236
Schabowski, Günter, 18
Schama, Simon, 94
Schmidt, Helmut, 19, 83, 247*n*
Schröder, Gerhard, 56–57, 61, 62, 63, 83, 113, 114
September 11th attacks (2001), 28, 39, 42–46, 48, 72, 76, 79, 81, 92, 139, 161, 164, 206, 236, 249*n*
Serbia, 34, 35, 53, 56–57, 81, 89, 121, 146, 177, 185, 208, 220*n*
Seven Years' War, 27, 52*n*, 135, 140–41, 145, 149, 188, 211
Shakespeare, William, 98, 192
Shalikashvili, John, 36
Sharon, Ariel, 74, 90–91
Shrek 2, 103–4
Shuvalov, Pyotr Andreyevich, Count, 151
Silesia, 138, 140–41
Silone, Ignazio, 98
Six-Day War (1967), 22, 143, 190, 246*n*
socialism, 18–19, 96
soft power, 102–4, 107, 112, 160–61, 173
Sombart, Werner, 119–20
Sontag, Susan, 74
"Sources of Soviet Conduct" (Kennan), 17
South America, 43, 129, 160
South Korea, 22, 24, 41, 46, 59*n*, 230
Soviet Union:
  Afghan invasion of, 19, 25
  alliances of, 19, 22, 23–24, 25, 31–33, 35–36
  collapse of, 13–20, 26, 27, 31–33, 45, 51, 52, 62–63, 127, 161, 218, 223
  Communist leadership of, 18–19, 21–22, 37, 191
  containment of, 13–14, 21, 26, 38–39, 47, 53, 159–61

Soviet Union (*continued*)
economy of, 18–19, 189–90, 197, 215
expansionism of, 13–14, 21–22, 25, 61, 81, 102, 146, 183, 188–90, 197–98, 201, 214–15, 221, 224, 237
Germany and threat from, 16–17, 18, 24–25, 26, 39, 91, 98, 159
gross domestic product (GDP) of, 19
industrialization of, 189–90, 197
Iraq supported by, 31–33, 191–92
nuclear weapons of, 22–23, 25, 27, 31–32, 42, 44, 159
as superpower, 13–29, 62–63, 160–61, 215, 223
U.S. rivalry with, 13–29, 31–33, 35, 38–39, 42, 44, 55, 62, 157–61, 179, 209, 215
see also Russia
Spain, 22, 50, 130, 132–34, 138, 139, 140, 159, 168, 197, 217*n*, 230
Spanish-American War, 159, 217*n*
Spanish Armada, 130, 132, 138, 139, 147
Sparta, 20, 21, 22–23, 33
Stalin, Joseph, 19, 21–22, 32, 49, 52, 53, 91–92, 186, 197, 201
Stanford University, 86, 101–2, 107
Stendhal, 93
Stern, 67–68
Stoiber, Edmund, 113–14
Strauss, Levi, 109
Sudan, 35, 74
Sudetenland, 141–42
Suez War (1956), 24, 31, 140, 143, 190, 246*n*
Syria, 143–44, 190, 191, 208, 220–21, 229*n*

Taiwan, 22, 24, 58, 147, 201, 202, 216, 223
Talbott, Strobe, 38, 40
Taliban, 27, 44–46, 48, 178, 192, 206
Talleyrand, Charles-Maurice de, 68, 93
Taylor, A. J. P., 154
Terror International (TI), 55, 64–66, 231, 236, 238
terrorism, 28, 35, 39, 41, 42–46, 48, 55, 63–66, 72, 73, 79, 81, 92, 123–24, 139, 161, 164, 184, 188, 206, 215, 221, 231, 236, 238, 249*n*
Theodorakis, Mikis, 69
Thirty Years' War, 51*n*, 134, 148, 211
Three Emperors' League, 152, 153
Thucydides, 20, 21
Tiananmen Square massacre (1989), 199
Tibet, 73–74, 199
Tito (Josip Broz), 187
Tocqueville, Alexis de, 14–15, 43, 164, 181–82, 251*n*
Todd, Emmanuel, 92–93
Toubon law, 105
Trafalgar, Battle of (1805), 138
Triple Alliance, 152–53
Triple Entente, 62–63, 155
Truman, Harry S., 85
tsunami disaster (2004), 177
Tucker, Robert W., 163
Turkey, 46, 61

Ukraine, 37, 195
United Nations, 27, 32, 38, 48, 49, 53, 54, 56–57, 60–61, 63, 85, 122, 157, 161, 185, 205, 206, 236, 237*n*
United States:
air power of, 30–31, 139, 177
alliances of, 22, 23–26, 41, 54–55, 135, 157–61, 209, 214, 217–18, 231, 238
citizenship for, 108–9
cultural influence of, 28, 70, 85–87, 88, 93–94, 98–107, 127, 249*n*, 254*n*
defense spending by, 28, 54, 161, 165, 179
democratic ideals of, 21, 22, 29, 38–40, 47–48, 49, 69, 128, 129–30, 159, 160, 181–82, 183, 196–97, 199, 208*n*, 218, 229, 230, 231, 234
diplomacy of, 32–33, 36–38, 44–45
economy of, 21, 24, 25, 27, 28, 38, 40, 59–60, 64, 68, 91, 93, 108, 113–20, 158, 165–66, 169, 171–72, 179, 194–97, 198, 238, 239, 240
energy consumption by, 30, 59–60, 73
foreign policy of, 13, 32–33, 36–41, 44–45, 47–48, 71–77, 128–30, 157–61, 196–97, 207–8, 218–19, 239–41, 250*n*
freedom promoted by, 55, 112, 230
global hegemony of, 26–29, 33–44, 49–58, 62–63, 71, 121–28, 130, 162–68, 202, 203–41, 250*n*
grand strategy for, 126, 127–61, 202, 203–41
as Great Organizer, 213–15, 224, 225, 236–37, 239
gross domestic product (GDP) of, 165–67
"Gulliver" image of, 20, 29, 38, 41, 46, 50–51, 60, 65, 179
immigration to, 84–85, 125, 171, 195
imperial ambitions of, 48–51, 81–83, 196–97, 217
as "indispensable nation," 36–42, 121, 211–17, 222, 236
industrialization of, 194–95, 199
isolationism in, 52, 128–30, 139–40
military power of, 7, 26–28, 30–51, 54, 58–59, 91, 108, 121, 139, 161, 164–65, 169, 179
moral standards of, 69, 76, 80–83
national security of, 58–59, 139, 163–65, 181–82, 230, 238–41
naval power of, 139, 197, 216, 223
nuclear weapons of, 22–23, 25, 27–28, 42, 44, 54, 58–59, 128, 159, 163–64
pollution by, 59–60
population of, 167, 171
potential rivals of, 33–34, 43–44, 183, 185, 198–202, 215–16, 219, 221, 223–24, 225, 227, 238

religious convictions in, 80–81, 93, 96, 109, 125, 183, 249*n*, 251*n*
Soviet rivalry with, 13–29, 31–33, 35, 38–39, 42, 44, 55, 62, 157–61, 179, 209, 215
as superpower, 13–20, 48–51, 55, 56–57, 72, 92, 123, 160–61, 215
as symbol of modernism, 95–97, 113–20, 178–79
technological superiority of, 31–32, 45–47, 139, 226
terrorist attacks against, 28, 35, 39, 41, 42–46, 48, 55, 63–66, 72, 79, 81, 92, 123–24, 139, 161, 164, 206, 215, 231, 236, 238, 249*n*
trade balance of, 147, 158*n*–59*n*, 210, 218, 226, 238
as überpower, 14, 28–29, 33–34, 42–51, 54, 60, 97, 121–26, 127, 162, 202, 203–41
unilateralism of, 55, 121–26
Utrecht, Treaty of (1713), 130

Védrine, Hubert, 28, 104, 105, 108, 118–19, 121, 162
Versailles Treaty, 200
Victoria, Queen of England, 15
Vidal, Gore, 74
Vietnam, 223, 227
Vietnam War, 20, 22, 44, 46, 104, 159, 208, 228
Villepin, Dominique de, 57

Waltz, Kenneth N., 51
War of 1812, 43, 129, 139, 142, 218, 230
War of Devolution, 134
War of the Spanish Succession, 135
wars:
asymmetric, 63–65, 128, 164, 231
balance of power and, 52, 53–56, 211–12
of choice, 228*n*–29*n*, 231
conventional, 59, 164
counterinsurgency, 65
defensive vs. offensive strategies in, 149
diplomacy and, 44–45, 54–55, 143–44, 182–83
force projection in, 139, 164, 215–16
of necessity, 228*n*–229*n*
network-centric, 45–46, 165, 230–31
nuclear, 22–23, 25, 27, 31–32, 42, 44, 58–59, 62, 128, 144, 159, 160–61, 163–64, 198, 220, 224, 239
preemptive or preventive, 43–44, 49, 55, 91, 128, 149, 206–7, 228, 230, 245*n*–46*n*
proxy, 31, 48
territorial conquest in, 138, 140–41, 145, 149, 160, 196–97
Warsaw Pact countries, 23, 35–36, 52*n*, 237*n*
Waterloo, Battle of (1815), 136
Westphalia, Peace of (1648), 51*n*
Wilhelm II, Emperor of Germany, 27, 133, 153, 155, 156, 196
Wilson, A. N., 83
Wilson, Woodrow, 49, 129, 159, 218
Winthrop, John, 108, 261*n*
Wolfers, Arnold, 129
Wolfowitz, Paul, 50, 64
World Bank, 91, 204, 236
World Economic Forum (2003), 90–91
World Trade Organization (WTO), 91, 158, 204, 236, 237*n*, 240
World War I, 16, 20, 52, 124, 136, 137, 142, 163, 211–12, 218, 220, 228*n*–29*n*
World War II, 14, 20, 23, 27, 46, 52, 85, 124, 136, 138, 141–42, 145, 157, 163, 197–98, 208*n*, 209, 211–12, 216, 218, 229*n*

Yeltsin, Boris, 187
Yom Kippur War (1973), 22, 31–32, 143, 221, 229*n*
Yugoslavia, 34–35, 187, 188, 214, 235

Zadek, Peter, 69, 248*n*–49*n*
Zawahiri, Ayman al-, 76–77
Zinnemann, Fred, 212

About the Author

Publisher-editor of *Die Zeit* since 2000, Josef Joffe was educated at Swarthmore and Harvard (PhD in government). A frequent contributor to *Foreign Affairs*, *Foreign Policy*, and the *National Interest*, he is Founding Board member of *The American Interest*, which started publication in 2005. He has taught international affairs and American foreign policy at Johns Hopkins, Harvard, and Stanford, where he is also a Fellow at the Hoover Institution and the Institute for International Studies.